TORTURE

TORTURE

Religious Ethics
and National Security

JOHN PERRY, S.J.

NOVALIS

ORBIS BOOKS
Maryknoll, New York 10545

© 2005 Novalis, Saint Paul University, Ottawa, Canada

Cover design: Christiane Lemire
Cover art: Nancy Strider
Layout: Caroline Galhidi

Business Office:
Novalis
10 Lower Spadina Ave., Suite 400
Toronto, Ontario, Canada
M5V 2Z2

Phone: 1-800-387-7164
Fax: 1-800-204-4140
E-mail: cservice@novalis-inc.com
www.novalis.ca

Library and Archives Canada Cataloguing in Publication
HV8593.P47 2005   261.8'73   C2005-904691-0
ISBN: 2-89507-604-9

First published in the United States by Orbis Books, Maryknoll, New York 10545-0308.
Phone: 1-800-258-5838
Fax: 1-914-941-7005
E-mail: orbisbooks@maryknoll.org
www.maryknoll.org

Library of Congress Cataloging-in-Publication Data
HV8593.P47 2005   341'.69--dc22   2005022016
ISBN: 1-57075-607-4 (pbk.)

Printed in Canada.

Excerpts from *The Railway Man: A POW's Searing Account of War, Brutality, and Forgiveness* by Eric Lomax. Copyright © 1995 by Eric Lomax. Used by permission of W. W. Norton & Company, Inc. and The Random House Group Ltd.

We acknowledge the financial support of the Government of Canada through the Book Publishing Industry Development Program (BPIDP) for our publishing activities.

5 4 3 2 1   09 08 07 06 05

Contents

Acknowledgements

In writing this book I have received generous assistance from a number of people. I would like to thank them for their contributions: Ron Mercier, SJ; Tom Donoghue; Nancy Strider; Dr. Francisco Madrid; Dr. John Stapleton; Ed O'Donnell, SJ; Dr. Richard Lebrun; Dr. Sean Byrne; Jack Costello, SJ; Jim and Kathy Martin; Fr. Carl Tarnopolski; Kay Yee; Archbishop James Weisgerber; Tika Ram Adhikari; and Dan Gardner. The editorial staff of Novalis in Ottawa and Orbis at Maryknoll, New York, have helped and encouraged me in this project. Ultimately the opinions I have expressed on torture, the tortured, and torturers are my own, and I take full responsibility for these.

John Perry, SJ
Arthur V. Mauro Center for Peace and Justice
St. Paul's College
University of Manitoba
Winnipeg, Canada

Foreword

Human beings are unpredictable; our behaviour, marked by light and shadow, values and anti-values, is certainly inconsistent. On the one hand, we build walls that divide and separate us from our neighbours, cutting them off from view, and thereby violating their fundamental human rights as individuals and communities. On the other hand, we are capable of creating the most beautiful things for the good of all.

Throughout human history, light and shadow have continually woven themselves into the fabric of our existence. The last century was catastrophic for the world: two world wars, thousands of conflicts, the starvation of entire nations, the holocaust of peoples – Jews, Gypsies, Africans. This new century is already heavy with armed conflicts and wars. Where is humanity headed? This is the question we must grapple with.

With the fall of the Berlin Wall and the end of the Cold War, optimism prevailed. Many felt that a new era of global co-operation was just around the corner, as was the development of ethical values to promote peace and understanding.

Alas, this was not to be. We were unable to demolish the walls within ourselves. Many existing conflicts went unresolved, more developed, and new walls blocking mutual understanding appeared.

Today there is but one superpower, but the planet is arguably less secure now than it was before, with vicious disputes and deadly battles a daily occurrence for many. It is sufficient to point to the situation in Africa: massacres in Rwanda, the Congo, Burundi and Zaire have claimed over seven million victims.

The terrorist attack of September 11, 2001, against the Twin Towers of the World Trade Center in New York City marked a turning point in world history; the long-term consequences are still unclear,

9

and frightening. Thus far it has served to unleash wars in Afghanistan and Iraq; to increase the use of torture in the prisons of those countries as well as in the U.S. military base at Guantánamo Bay, Cuba; and to ignite so-called wars of low intensity in various regions around the world.

A few years ago I stated that we needed to disarm our armed conscience. I reiterate this statement without hesitation. It remains humanity's great challenge. Analyzing group behaviour to understand how soldiers, doctors and civilians can turn themselves into torturers and assassins and how they can then justify the crimes they have committed is part of this quest.

When I was in jail during the Argentinean military dictatorship, I was tortured. At the time I was utterly dumbfounded that someone could actually torture, degrade and humiliate another human being, then take neither responsibility nor blame for this deliberate act of cruelty.

Experts in social psychology and collective behaviour tell us that torturers experience a "suspension of conscience." The torturer is part of a group with established ways of doing things and seeing the world. When this group is organized, widespread, persists over time, and participates in established patterns of behaviour, it is called an institution. The torturer internalizes its norms and values — or anti-values — and is nourished by them. The institution protects him and justifies his actions, by reference to such abstract notions as "the defense of Western and Christian civilization" or "the fight against international communism" or "the honour of the homeland"; these and other abstractions help legitimate behaviour that is utterly criminal in every way. Personal responsibility is diluted in the collective; together they pass together through the "purifying fire" and accept the "pact of blood and silence."

When an insider breaks this pact, the punishment is severe. I could cite many examples, but one stands out in particular. A former captain in the Argentinean navy, Adolfo Scilingo, claimed that throwing 30 prisoners – all former insiders – from airplanes into the sea was a noble deed that saved the country from the clutches of international communism. When Scilingo returned from this death flight, the military chaplain celebrating the Eucharist praised the captain and his men, saying: "What you have done is to give them a Christian death."

Throughout history, religion has played a key role in legitimating all sorts of behaviour. Just think of the Inquisition: the sword and the cross were inseparable, since "to torture the body is to save the soul."

Over time the Church changed, and the witness of her many martyrs who laid down their lives for the people gave rise to concepts and behaviours promoting the defense of life and the dignity of the person.

The political philosopher Hannah Arendt described the suffering that results from torture as a peculiar and incommunicable experience in which one is increasingly subject to control by extreme privation. The tortured person is reduced to a state of talking solely about raw need instead of liberty or conscience. It is pain that speaks, not the person. Torture, she argues, is the instrument of those who fear the personality, are afraid of responsibility, and want to convince themselves that the personality doesn't really exist, that liberty is weaker than physical necessity, that it is possible to destroy the will by inflicting physical or mental torment.

The Trappist monk Thomas Merton pointed out that this process is a Maloc that feeds on individuals. He eventually devours everyone. All should stop by the fire and leave "cured" – that is to say, destroyed: a non-person, a being with no identity. Oh merciful therapy! One need not be preoccupied by oneself – there is no one here!

Torturers are always looking for certainty. They act with an armed conscience, perpetrate heinous acts with impunity, and rely on institutional and group protection. This is true everywhere. Totalitarian regimes routinely torture people in their jails and police stations, but so, too, do "democratic countries." Just think about the international reaction to the news that female soldiers had participated in aberrant acts of torture in a Baghdad prison. They were following orders, but their behaviour clearly indicated a lack of ethical and spiritual values.

Torturers commit atrocities out of blind obedience. When the German war criminal Adolph Eichmann was being tried for crimes against humanity for his role in the Jewish Holocaust, he defended his behaviour with this explanation: "A soldier must obey his superiors; he has no business analysing whether the orders are just or not. The function of a soldier is to obey and to carry out orders without question."

When Oscar Romero, the archbishop of San Salvador, addressed his country's soldiers, he urged, "A soldier should in no way obey unjust orders. I ask you, I order you, in the name of God, cease this repression." The bishop was calling them to obedience in liberty, not to blind obedience; he was challenging them to take up the Gospel in the defense of life. The next day he was assassinated, while celebrating Mass.

Disarming the armed conscience requires education, values and awareness on the part of individuals and communities. Today we live in a culture of violence. Constructing new paradigms of life will require concerted, transformative action on the part of all.

More than ever we need information, analysis and reflections about human behaviour that will help us go beyond our personal and social limitations. John Perry's book *Torture* is a valuable contribution to this undertaking, one that will assist our search for new ways to promote respect for the human person and recognition that all human beings are our brothers and sisters and children of God.

Adolfo Pérez Esquivel
Buenos Aires
16 June 2005

Introduction

A Catholic Perspective on Torture

For the past several centuries we have learned that torture is always wrong, and those who organize or perpetrate it are usually, but not always, involved with moral evil as an institution or serious sin as individuals. These few words summarize the position on torture taken by this book, which is an exercise in human rights advocacy from a Roman Catholic perspective. Torture is immoral and sinful not only because it violates the dignity we owe to the human person but also because it directly or indirectly degrades any society that would tolerate it. Obviously this serious moral claim needs to be substantiated, and this will be done in due course.

While "immoral" and "sinful" would seem to be synonyms, this book will argue that they are not. Immoral refers to our objective assessment of the institution and practice of torture, while sinful describes the deteriorating relationship of perpetrators to God. An important argument of this book will be that the relatively recent prohibition on torture taken by the Catholic Church needs to become more clear and consistent through changes in its laws and practices. This insistence that torture is both immoral and sinful is necessary because the Catholic Church does not have a robust tradition against torture. Its inquisitions (Church courts) in the past made systematic use of this immoral interrogation technique to protect the unity of the Faith and to defend the truth of the Gospel. At the beginning of our present millennium, the late Bishop of Rome, Pope John Paul II, made a formal confession of the sin of torture "in the service of the truth" on behalf of the universal Church.[1] With the sincerity and humility of a reformed sinner, the Church has positioned itself today to be a strong advocate for human rights and to warn those involved in the state-sanctioned use of torture not to use this method even to protect citizens from terrorist threats.[2]

The contemporary situation

In a rare instance of moral unanimity towards the close of the last millennium, the human community represented at the United Nations agreed to support the condemnation of torture and its systematic practice through several international conventions and protocols. An articulation of this conviction occurred in 1978. The Red Brigade had kidnapped Aldo Moro, the former Prime Minister of Italy and personal friend of Pope Paul VI. A member of the security forces suggested to General Della Chiesa that he (Chiesa) use torture in the interrogation of a terrorist suspect who was thought to know where Mr. Moro was being held.

The general replied with these memorable words: "Italy can survive the loss of Aldo Moro. It would not survive the introduction of torture."[3] One would hope this position would continue into the new millennium. Organizations like Amnesty International and the Canadian Centre for the Victims of Torture are concerned that it will not. It has not survived the sad events of September 11, 2001, when terrorists hijacked four airliners in a successful attempt to destroy symbolic targets in the United States and kill thousands of civilians. With the global "war on terrorism" that followed the destruction of the World Trade Center in New York and part of the Pentagon in Washington, this consensus of post-Enlightenment Western society against using torture is under reconsideration.

The methodology used in this study of torture will borrow from the influential philosophical method of phenomenology. To provide an avenue to approach torture and to make a theological and moral evaluation of it, an important role will be played by carefully analyzed description of their torture experience by people who have lived to tell us about it.[4] Some readers may find this material disturbing and therefore might consider not reading longer quotations which contain accounts of actual torture, but restrict their reading of the book to the analysis and commentary of the author.

The method used in the book can be called moral phenomenology. Roman Catholic moral theology took a crucial phenomenological turn in the work of Adam Tanner, SJ (1572–1632), who no longer was content to apply certain theological principles to the use of judicial torture, but chose to describe what he observed actually happening to those accused of sorcery and witchcraft in southern Germany. Part of the phenomenon is our own gut reactions to what is taking place in front of us.

Asymmetrical threats

Serious discussions have recently taken place in the United States of America, Great Britain, Israel, Mexico, the Philippines, Indonesia, Singapore and other liberal and democratic countries about the ethics of using torture as the "lesser of evils" when faced with the prospect of the massive destruction of innocent human lives such as happened on 9/11 and since.

The phrase "asymmetrical threat" refers to the danger posed by the relatively weak power of a dedicated terrorist organization when it attacks the political, economic, or social fabric of a modern nation. When powerful nations feel threatened by an organization like al-Qaeda, Hamas, Hezbollah and the Taliban with their ideologically motivated combatants who are ready to commit suicide to accomplish their attacks, can the leaders of these countries avoid reconsidering a remedy formerly described by them in a different era as immoral? There is evidence that this reinstatement of the institution of torture is happening again today.

Definitions of torture

The world community has outlawed torture, carefully defined, in all circumstances, everywhere. No exceptions are made. On December 9, 1975, the General Assembly of the United Nations adopted a Convention against Torture and Other Cruel, Inhuman or Degrading Treatment or Punishment.[5] This title is instructive because it suggests that the international community recognizes a scale of suffering. There are not merely two categories of legal interrogation and torture, but a third one called "cruel, inhuman or degrading treatment or punishment," often simply called "ill treatment."[6] Just as the overall approach adopted by the United Nations Organization (UNO) in its declaration is instructive, so also is its definition of torture:

> …[T]orture means any act by which severe pain or suffering, whether physical or mental, is intentionally inflicted on a person for such purposes as obtaining from him or her or a third person information or a confession, punishing him for an act he or a third person has committed or is suspected of having committed, or intimidating or coercing him or a third person … when such pain or suffering is inflicted by or

at the instigation of or with the consent or acquiescence of a public official or other person acting in an official capacity...."[7]

The mention of "a third person" makes good sense when one realizes that during the Dirty War waged in Argentina by the military junta from 1976 to 1983 against left wing guerrillas and those thought to sympathize or support them, it was a common practice to torture a member of their family in front of the person from whom information was being sought or on whom punishment was being inflicted.[8] The hope of the interrogators and torturers would be that the subject of their depredations would provide them with information to save loved ones from torment. Key to understanding the meaning of torture that will be adopted in this book is the fact that a "public official or other person acting in an official capacity" performs or instigates torture as defined by the UNO.

The use of the word to describe the pain deliberately inflicted by one person on another in ordinary life, sad though it might be, is precluded here. Such brutality is not the topic of this book. What we are speaking about here is an egregious form of institutional violence undertaken by officially commissioned members of a political organization.

In common with genocide and slavery, international law has such a repugnance for torture that it considers it "to be criminal even in countries that have not signed international anti-torture conventions. Torture is also a crime of 'universal jurisdiction', so torture committed in one country can be tried and punished in any country."[9] In 1984, Canada, the United States and most other countries signed the UN Convention against Torture, which requires them to make torture a crime under their domestic law and specifies that "no exceptional circumstances whatsoever, whether a state of war or a threat of war, internal political instability or any other public emergency, may be invoked as a justification of torture."[10]

Global terrorism has tempted the leadership of America and other countries to revisit the admirable rules they agreed upon in the General Assembly 30 years ago, and to bend, or even break them.

Torture as an ancient institution

As an institution, torture is ancient. It was commonly practiced by ancient Greece and then by Rome both before and after the Christian era as a way for the judiciary to extract information and confessions from suspects accused of crimes, especially of treason widely defined. Slaves were routinely and legally tortured.[11] Roman citizens were not. Thus, while Pontius Pilate tortured Jesus, Felix, Festus and Agrippa did not torture Paul (Acts 22–26, esp. 22: 24-5) who, though a Jew like Jesus, was also a Roman citizen.

"What is truth?" (John 18.38) Before he ordered him tortured, Pontius Pilate expressed scepticism as to the possibility of his discovering what really lay behind and beneath the case against Jesus. But in his effort to establish the veracity of the allegations against Jesus of treason against the Roman Emperor, Pilate had him tortured by having him scourged with whips as part of the criminal procedure known in Latin as the *questio*.[12]

As Susan Neiman remarks in *Evil in Modern Thought*, the iconic status of Christ's crucifixion obscures for us the fact that it was a human rights atrocity. "To force a condemned prisoner to drag through a jeering crowd the instrument that will shortly be used to torture him to death is a refinement of cruelty that ought to take your breath away."[13]

However, both before and long after the era of Pilate's power in Judea, doubts persisted in Roman jurisprudence as to the reliability of evidence gleaned during torture. Ulpian, a third-century CE Roman jurist, pointed out in his *Treatise on the Duties of a Proconsul* that the Emperor Augustus had stated, "confidence should not unreservedly be put in torture." The reason for this, wrote Ulpian, was that the evidence produced by torture was "a delicate and dangerous business" (*res fragilis et periculosa*).[14] More often than not, such facts are exaggerated, false, or incomplete as the victim of torture is prepared to say anything necessary to end his or her pain and suffering. Humanitarian considerations played little or no part in the judicial caution displayed by ancient Romans. The central question was whether the evidence gained from torture was reliable.

The Germanic tribes who brought an end to the western part of the Roman Empire did not practise judicial torture, preferring instead the "ordeal" as a legal method to establish veracity. This ancient form of trial depended on divine assistance, which would enable the accused to handle red-hot iron or to put her hand into boiling water without injury, thereby proving innocence. The practice of torture practically disappeared in the West until the twelfth century and the rediscovery of the ancient Roman legal system. Sadly, at this point in history the legal minds of the Catholic Church accepted the practice despite the fact it was not used by ancient Israel and had been condemned as sinful by highly respected early Christian theologians and popes.[15]

Serious considerations of state and/or ecclesiastical security were/are, therefore, important reasons for using torture in ancient, medieval and modern times. In the twentieth century it became part of the state-controlled machinery to suppress dissent in many countries, and found its place as an integral factor in the security strategy of its military and/or dictatorial rulers.[16] The question today is this: If a terror suspect won't talk, should he be made to?[17] If wringing a confession by pain or suffering can prevent a devastating terrorist attack, should it be used?

The Gestapo asked similar questions and answered them in the affirmative. Consider the Belgian resistance fighter Jean Améry's account of being tortured by them:

> In the bunker there hung from the vaulted ceiling a chain that above ran into a roll. At its bottom end it bore a heavy, broadly curved iron hook. I was led to the instrument. The hook gripped into the shackle that held my hands together behind my back. Then I was raised with the chain until I hung about a metre above the floor. In such a position, or rather, when hanging this way, with your hands behind your back, for a short time you can hold at a half-oblique through muscular force. During these few minutes, when you are already expending your utmost strength, when sweat has already appeared on your forehead and lips, and you are breathing in gasps, you will not answer any questions. Accomplices? Addresses? Meeting places? You hardly hear it. All your life is gathered in a single, limited area of the body, the shoulder joints, and it does not react; for it exhausts itself completely in the expenditure of energy. But this cannot last long, even with people who have a strong physical constitution. As for me, I had to give up rather quickly. And now there was a cracking and splintering in my shoulders that my body has not forgotten to this hour. The balls sprang from their sockets. My own body weight caused luxation. I fell into a void and now hung by my dislocated arms which had been torn high from behind and were now twisted over my head. Torture, from Latin *torquere*, to twist. What a visual instruction in etymology![18]

Having written that "whoever was tortured stays tortured," Jean Améry eventually committed suicide.[19]

What is and what is not torture post 9/11?

What is torture? There are psychological tactics in interrogation of terrorist suspects referred to as "stress and duress" tactics which some would like to distinguish from torture. Sleep deprivation, and the use of bright light and loud sounds, have earned the name of "torture lite."[20] Another name used by the British military in Northern Ireland dealing with the IRA insurgency was the five techniques: hooding, food deprivation, sleep deprivation, bright lights and loud noise, and forced standing against a wall while leaning on one finger of each hand.

"In combination, they induced a state of psychosis, a temporary madness with long lasting after effects," says John Conroy.[21] As a young man in Russia, Menachem Begin, Prime Minister of Israel from 1977 to 1983, underwent torture lite. In his book *White Nights: The Story of a Prisoner in Russia*, he described how sleep deprivation broke the human will to resist the interrogators:

> In the head of the interrogated prisoner, a haze begins to form. His spirit is wearied to death, his legs are unsteady, and he has one sole desire: to sleep, to sleep just a little, not to get up, to lie, to rest, to forget.... Anyone who has experienced this desire knows that not even hunger or thirst is comparable with it. I came across prisoners who signed what they were ordered to sign, only to get what the interrogator promised them. He did not promise them their liberty; he did not promise them food to sate themselves. He promised them – if they signed – uninterrupted sleep! And they signed.... And having signed, there was nothing in the world that could move them to risk again such nights and such days. The main thing was – to sleep.[22]

Hard torture would be the "dragon's chair"[23] used in 1977 in Rio de Janeiro by the Brazilian military authorities. José Augusto Dias Pires, a 24-year-old journalist, described his experience in this way:

> The accused was obliged to sit in a chair, like one in a barber shop, to which he was tied with straps covered over with foam rubber, while other straps covered his body; they tied his fingers with electric wires, and his toes also, and began administering a series of electric shocks; at the same time, another torturer with an electric stick gave him shocks between the legs and on the penis....[24]

At a September 26, 2002, joint hearing of the United States House and Senate Intelligence Committees, Cofer Black, then head of the CIA Counter Terrorist Center, spoke about the agency's new forms of operational flexibility in dealing with suspected terrorists. "This is a very highly classified area, but I have to say that all you need to know: There was a before 9/11, and there was an after 9/11," Black said. "After 9/11 the gloves came off."[25] The dragon's chair might not be that to which Mr. Black was referring, but rather the grey area between aggressive, psychologically-based interrogation methods and physical torture.

The interrogation of John Walker Lindh, an American citizen who was captured with other Taliban and al-Qaeda prisoners trying to escape from the fortress at Mazar-i-Sharif in northern Afghanistan, was an instance of the gloves coming off after 9/11. Upon arrival at Camp Rhino, a US Marine base about sixty miles south of Kandahar,

> he was stripped of his clothes, blindfolded, and bound to a stretcher with heavy tape. He was then transferred to a metal shipping container. Already severely malnourished, suffering from untreated shrapnel wounds, and still naked and immobilized on the stretcher, he scarcely slept. He experienced continuous pain in his feet and legs, was given little food and was continually taunted by his captors. After three days of being held in this manner, he underwent the interrogation that yielded the telltale statements.[26]

As prisoners are moved into and within the facilities in Camp Delta at Guantánamo Bay in Cuba, where enemy combatants from Afghanistan are held, they are blindfolded and isolated from one another. Until a June 2004 US Supreme Court decision in their favour, they had not been told where they were, what charges they faced, when or whether they would have the opportunity to answer these charges and what judicial process, if any, they would undergo.[27]

In *Nunca Más*, the report of the Argentine national commission on the disappeared, a characteristic of the more than 340 secret detention centres in various places in the Argentine suggests comparisons to Camp Delta. In addition to formal torture sessions, deliberate attempts were made to break down the captive's identity by disrupting their spatial-temporal points of reference through the use of dark hoods they were always forced to wear for security reasons as well as to confuse and disorient the victim.[28]

Is the systematic use of psychological coercion by Western security forces, rather than the use of physical torture, merely a distinction without a difference? Would the use of an aggressive female interrogator with Muslim male suspects constitute torture? Bad though their situation is, the prisoners in Guantánamo Bay remain under the watchful eyes of the International Red Cross and the world's news media. However, most terrorist suspects are not imprisoned there. In 2003 about 3000 al-Qaeda and Taliban suspects were detained; some have since been freed. The largest known group is held in Guantánamo Bay.

But some senior al-Qaeda members such as Khalid Shaikh Moham-med, Abu Zubaydah, and Omar al-Faruq have not arrived in Cuba. It is reported that important captives in the war on terrorism have been sent for interrogation to countries allied with the coalition forces, countries such as Egypt, Morocco and Jordan where physical torture is routinely practiced.[29] Mr. Faruq, confidant of Osama bin Laden, and one of al-Qaeda's senior operatives in Southeast Asia, was captured in Indonesia.

"Agents familiar with the case said a black hood was dropped over his head and he was loaded onto a CIA aircraft. When he arrived at his destination several hours later, the hood was removed. On the wall in front of him were the seals of the New York City Police and Fire Departments."[30]

What followed was a mind game known as "false flag," which is intended to leave the suspect disorientated, isolated, and vulnerable. In his case, Mr. Faruq was in the CIA interrogation center in the Bagram air base outside of Kabul, Afghanistan, but he could have been in a country with a brutal reputation for torture during interrogations. What is known about the interrogation of Mr. Faruq is the following:

> ...the questioning was prolonged, extending day and night for weeks. It is likely, experts say, that the proceedings followed a pattern with Mr. Faruq left naked most of the time, his hands and feet bound. While international law requires prisoners to be allowed eight hours' sleep a day, interrogators do not necessarily let them sleep for eight consecutive hours.
>
> Mr. Faruq may also have been hooked up to sensors, then asked questions to which interrogators knew the answers, so they could gauge his truthfulness, officials say.
>
> The Western intelligence official described Mr. Faruq's interrogation as "not quite torture, but about as close as you can get...."[31]

Because of the complications involved with torture, international law defines it not in terms of techniques used, but in terms of its ef-fect on its victims. To do otherwise leads down the road of historical Catholic moral theology known as casuistry. "Not quite torture, but about as close to torture as you can get"[32] is casuistry.

Catholic positions today

The casuistry of torture has a long history. In the upcoming chapter in this book outlining the history of torture, the seventeenth- and eighteenth-century Catholic casuistry on the topic will receive special emphasis. The same chapter will focus upon the problematic use of judicial torture by the inquisitions of the Catholic Church over many centuries, for which the former Bishop of Rome, Pope John Paul II, has made his formal apology to God and to the world.[33]

The transformation in the official Church approach to torture and to other human rights issues in the twentieth century must come to grips with the relatively recent experience of state terrorism in many Catholic countries in Central and South America, as well as Burundi and Rwanda in Africa and the Philippines in Asia, where, at times, both the torturers and their victims were Catholic.

Argentina will provide the case study for how difficult it is for a fundamental conversion in the Church's position on human rights to take place and to be received throughout the world. In the 1970s, the Church in the Argentine was polarized between a minority of bishops who fully accepted the teaching of the Second Vatican Council and of recent popes on human rights, and a majority who selectively accepted this new approach only in so far as it was judged appropriate for the pastoral situation in their dioceses.

The figure of Argentine naval officer Alfredo Astiz, allegedly responsible for numerous and notorious human rights violations during the Dirty War, will provide the opportunity to study an important question in moral theology.[34] Could an institution such as torture be immoral without all the perpetrators of torture being necessarily involved with moral evil and serious sin?

The Argentine military believed they were fighting a war defending their Catholic and Christian civilization against atheistic communism in their country along with its various Peronist and secular sympathizers. So indoctrinated were Lieutenant Astiz and others in this ideology that a case could be made that his complicity in human rights abuses involved what in traditional moral theology theologians called "invincible ignorance" of the evil in which they were participating.

Some Argentine military officers claimed to have confessed the deep misgivings they harboured about their participation in the abduction and torture of journalists, psychiatrists, students, teachers and professors, social workers and others to various military chaplains and confessors. They were told by them that their deeds were rightful, a response not only to the legitimate orders of lawful military authorities, but also to natural law.

Displaying no significant character defects nor mental instability, meaningfully attached to his family and friends, sharing the ideology of the Argentine military junta but without fanaticism, Astiz would never have done what he did without orders, which he considered sacred, and he remains unrepentant for his part in the Dirty War.[35]

Related to this study of Astiz is the phenomenon known as "Massuisme...the argument that torturers may be responsible servants of the state in times of extreme crisis."[36] Twenty years after the revelation that the "civilized" country of France, home of the Enlightenment ideals that are the basis of modern human rights theory, had made systematic use of torture in its attempt to suppress the nationalist insurgency in Algeria, General Jacques Massu published his memoirs of the Algerian war, entitled *La Vraie Bataille d'Alger*. In his book and in subsequent media interviews, "Massu defended his use of torture on the grounds that the particular circumstances then obtaining demanded its use, and that military necessity dictated it."[37]

The present study will contest this defence of the systematic practice of torture. Not only do terrorists imperil us today, but the means we freely choose to fight them with do so as well. For instance, shortly after the capture in 2003 of Khalid Shaik Mohammed, the operations chief of al-Qaeda, the internet provider America On Line (AOL) provided its chat rooms with the following provocative question: "Making a Terrorist Talk: If Not Torture, What Is the Best Way to Break Him? Tell Us."

The respected lawyer Alan Dershowitz of the Harvard Law School supports the outright ban on torture, but argues that if the United States is going to make use of it, its Congress should regulate its use by law. He claims this argument belongs to those who would pry potentially life-saving information from suspected terrorists with the use of torture. But Dershowitz would add the caveat that he would involve the courts in this process. "In effect, the government would have to ask a judge for a torture warrant."[38] Based on the experience of Catholics, Jews, accused heretics, sorcerers and witches and others during the Inquisition, Dershowitz's solution will not prevent abuse.

What follows will be an argument supporting the conviction that the current Catholic teaching is correct: civilization is threatened by torture. The studies on obedience and authority by Stanley Milgram and the philosophical reflections of Hannah Arendt confirm that we can construct our society so that violence becomes normal if it has official sanction.[39] The torturer and the empowering state or organisation can always find justification for individual instances of its use. But as the practice grows, the warrant for its use weakens, and the common good becomes infected by the erroneous idea that the end justifies the means. Terrorists not only imperil us today, but also imperil the means we freely choose to fight terrorists. Faced with a terrorist threat as real as our own, the Argentine junta tortured on a grand scale, and in 2005 its latest president, Néstor Kirchner, was still attempting to bring a just resolution and closure to events that took place 25 years ago.[40]

The approach taken in the book will not dwell in the past, but will turn our attention to certain features of our present in order to imagine a future without the institution of torture. We live in a world that feels itself imperilled by terrorists just as those in seventeenth-century Germany did by witches and sorcerers. Despite this, we must not allow the dreadful institution of torture to return.

Why Torture Is Different from Other Warlike Actions

"What happens to you when you are torturing?"

"You may not realize it but it is very tiring.... It's true that we take it in turns, but the question is to know when to let the other chap have a go. Each one thinks he is going to get the information at any moment and takes care not to let the bird go to the next chap after he's softened him up nicely, when of course the other chap would get the honor and glory of it. So sometimes we let them go; and sometimes we don't." —Anonymous torturer[1]

The aim of this chapter is twofold. First, we will look at contemporary uses of torture and define the term "torture" as it will be used in this book. We will employ the definition supplied in the United Nations Convention on Torture because most nations in the world have signed this covenant and it is congruent with Catholic theology. Second, we will explain what makes torture uniquely immoral within the context of war and its general assault upon human values. To do this we will employ the relatively recent Catholic theology of the inviolability of human persons in order to show why state-sponsored torture is immoral and why Catholic thinking on it has made such a dramatic shift since the era of the Inquisition.

Lord Acton liked to cite Duc de Broglie (1718–1804): "We must beware of too much understanding lest we end by too much forgiving." In other words, to understand something is to justify it. In this study of state-sponsored or state-contracted torture, de Broglie might have a point. Could it be possible that too much understanding might lead us to forgive the unforgivable? This question could be addressed to Maher Arar.

The case of Maher Arar

One of the best-known cases of contemporary torture is that of Maher Arar. A Canadian citizen born in Syria, Arar came to Canada in 1987. He earned bachelor's and master's degrees in computer engineering, and worked in Ottawa as a telecommunications engineer. His wife, Monia Mazigh, has a Ph.D. in mathematics. They have two young children.[2]

On September 26, 2002, US Immigration and Naturalization officials at Kennedy Airport in New York detained Arar while he was returning alone from a family vacation in Tunisia after visiting his wife's family. Although he holds dual citizenship, he was carrying a Canadian passport. American officials alleged he had links to al-Qaeda, and transported him to New York City where, for the next 12 days, Immigration, New York City Police and FBI personnel interrogated him without informing Canadian officials.

During this time he was strip-searched, placed in shackles, denied food or sleep for 28 hours, injected with an unknown substance and bullied into signing documents he was not allowed to read. "They told me I had no right to a lawyer," said Arar later, "because I was not an American citizen."[3]

In the absence of his lawyer or Canadian consular representation, an immigration "hearing" was held at which Arar was informed that he was being deported to Syria. "They told me," recalled Arar later, "that based on classified information that they could not reveal to me, I would be deported to Syria. I said again that I would be tortured there. Then they read part of the document where it explained that the US Immigration and Naturalization Service was not the body that dealt with the Geneva Convention regarding torture."[4]

On October 7 or 8, 2002, US officials placed him in the hands of a special removal unit and flew him in a small jet to Amman, Jordan, only informing Canadian officials on October 10. Once in the custody of Jordanian security personnel, he was driven around Amman for half a day, during which time he was physically attacked. "Every time I talked they beat me."[5]

Finally he was delivered to the Syrian border, where he was immediately incarcerated in a military prison. The Canadian Foreign Affairs Minister at the time, Bill Graham, lodged an official complaint to the US government about the arrest and deportation of Arar and, on October 22, announced Arar was being held in a Syrian prison.

Canadian officials then issued a warning to all Canadians born in Iran, Iraq, Libya, Sudan or Syria to consider carefully whether they wanted to enter the United States. On November 19, 2002, Monia Mazig 1 met with Canadian Foreign Affairs officials.

Much later, on April 30, 2003, Syria told Canadian officials it would charge Arar with membership in the banned Muslim organization, the Muslim Brotherhood of Syria. Arar's case became, if possible, even more urgent when the London-based Syrian Human Rights Committee (SHRC) announced on August 6 that he was being tortured and beaten while in jail.

Ms. Mazigh was indefatigable in her efforts to gain Arar's release, demanding on August 7 that Canada recall its ambassador to Syria, saying her husband had been sent to Syria "like a parcel."[6] On September 25, appearing before the Foreign Affairs Committee of the Canadian Parliament, she asked Members of Parliament (MPs) to continue working on behalf of her husband. Royal Canadian Mounted Police Assistant Commissioner Richard Proulx refused to discuss the case with MPs.

Earlier, Foreign Affairs Minister Graham had said Canada would not recall its ambassador to Syria and reported that Syrian officials had assured him that Arar would be tried in a civil and not in a military court. On October 5, 2003, Syria suddenly and unexpectedly freed Arar after 375 days of detention. Graham notified Ms. Mazigh, crediting Canada's quiet diplomacy for the release.

Even though the then Canadian Solicitor General Wayne Easter had earlier refused calls for a public inquiry into the case of Maher Arar, on October 23, 2003, a commission handling complaints against the RCMP announced it wanted the force to answer questions about whether it had played a role in the deportation of Arar from the US to Syria.

On January 28, 2004, Federal Minister of Public Safety, Anne McLellan, announced that a public inquiry would be held into the role played by the RCMP and other Canadian government organizations in Arar's detention and deportation. Headed by Mr. Justice Dennis O'Connor, the inquiry would replace the work of the Complaints Commission.

Because of its similarities to the Arar case, Dan McTeague, Parliamentary Secretary to Foreign Affairs Minister Bill Graham, asked that the case of Muayyed Nureddin, a Canadian citizen of Iraqi origin and former principal of an Islamic school in Toronto, who also claims to have suffered torture in a Syrian jail in 2003, be added to the O'Connor inquiry.[7]

On November 4, 2003, Arar spoke for the first time publicly about his year in a Syrian jail. He said he had been mentally and physically tortured and forced to confess that he had spent time in Afghanistan. The next day Prime Minister Jean Chrétien told the House of Commons that the US government's deportation of a Canadian to Syria was unacceptable. He repeatedly insisted, however, that he would not allow an independent inquiry into the case. He added that his government had asked US Secretary of State Colin Powell for an explanation and that the Canadian government also wanted to find out whether its own intelligence officials had played a role in the affair.

"What I went through is just beyond imagination. I know that the only way I will be able to move on is if I can find out what happened to me," said Arar. He went on to deny he had ties to terrorism. "I am not a terrorist. I am not a member of al-Qaeda. I don't know anyone who belongs to this group."[8]

He said upon arrival in a Syrian prison, officials beat him with electric cables for several days. He endured the screams of fellow prisoners also undergoing torture. "At the end of the day they told me tomorrow would be worse."[9] He said in his November news conference that

> [i]nterrogators constantly threatened me with the metal chair, tire and electric shocks. The tire is used to restrain prisoners while they torture them with beating on the soles of their feet. I guess I was lucky, because they put me in the tire, but only as a threat.[10]

He was incarcerated alone in a small cell he called a grave. He described it as follows:

> It had no light. It was three feet wide. It was six feet deep. It was seven feet high…. There was a small opening in the ceiling … and from time to time, the cats peed through the opening into the cell.[11]

Arar went on to say that "[d]aily life in that place was hell … I had moments I wanted to kill myself."[12] Trying to make a connection between him and terrorists, Syrian officials forced him to falsely confess that he had been in Afghanistan. Threatened with torture by electric shock, Arar said, "I was ready to confess to anything if it would stop the torture."[13]

Torture by proxy, also known as extraordinary rendition, may have been what happened to Arar. This is the practice of security authorities turning over low-level suspected terrorists to foreign intelligence services, some of which are known to torture prisoners.

Officially US authorities deny they place persons in the hands of regimes that engage in torture. To do so would violate both international and US law. Since the tragic events in New York and Washington on September 11, 2001, there have been numerous rendition activities and they have been very productive, one unnamed US official told the *Washington Post*. Another anonymous official explained torture by proxy in graphic terms: "We don't kick the s___ out of them. We send them to other countries so they can kick the s___ out of them."[14]

We will argue that torture, in any circumstance, is immoral and illegal in those countries that have signed the UNO Convention and have implemented its protocols. In the case of Arar, the US had no real evidence linking him to any terrorist organization. His torture by Syrian military personnel might have been a US state security-commissioned fishing expedition,[15] the basis of which was Arar's guilt by association through his acquaintance with another Syrian Canadian, Abdullah Almalki, also imprisoned and tortured at the same time as Arar and a signatory to Arar's apartment lease agreement.

Almalki is believed to know a Kuwaiti-born Egyptian-Canadian, Ahmad Abou-El-Maati, whose older brother Amer was purportedly mentioned in an al-Qaeda document found in Kabul, and who named Arar and Almalki while undergoing torture in Syria.[16] US authorities could not hold Arar indefinitely at JFK Airport when they detained him since he had not been captured in Afghanistan and he was not in violation of US immigration rules.

That Arar was being held and tortured on behalf of Washington is suggested by the timing and suddenness of his release by Syria. He was allowed to return to Canada shortly after the US had publicly supported an Israeli bombing raid against Syria.[17] It is possible that Syria was angry with the US so it unilaterally stopped doing what its government officials thought of as the Americans' dirty work.

Torture as part of war

This bombing raid and extraordinary rendition are two aspects of the current war on terror. The battles fought against the Afghan and Iraqi governments by the coalition forces were classic actions of war. But President George W. Bush has made it clear the campaign against terrorism goes beyond such activities.

On September 29, 2001, he said, "Our war on terror will be much broader than the battlefields and beachheads of the past. The war will be fought wherever terrorists hide, or run, or plan."[18] For him this is no metaphor such as a "war on drugs," a rhetorical device to garner support for an important cause.

President Bush seems to think the war on terrorism is quite literally a classic war, a war that could be fought like the wars in Afghanistan and Iraq. This concept has problematic implications since the rules that bind governments to human rights are treated in a much looser manner during times of war than in times of peace.[19] In the metal containers stacked behind barbed wire at Bagram Air Base near Kabul in Afghanistan, there was evidence that beatings were routine; at least two men have died while under detention there,[20] and a third died in detention elsewhere in Afghanistan. In December 2002, US military doctors ruled the deaths of two Afghans in US custody there homicides caused by blunt-force injuries.[21] Similar concerns have been expressed about what is happening on the British island of Diego Garcia in the Indian Ocean. All of these incidents illustrate the abuse of human rights in the name of "war."

War is hell. Anyone who has fought in war, or suffered its consequences, knows this to be true. During war soldiers kill, maim and thereby overwhelm their enemies. Often the damage they do to their adversaries is impersonal. Bombs dropped from airplanes thousands of feet above the ground, land mines buried under the ground, torpedoes gliding through ocean waters do their killing and wounding without the pilot, soldier, or sailor actually seeing his or her victim face to face. While the death and destruction are fully intended, they are impersonal. The impact of the Pulitzer prize–winning photos during the Vietnam War in the 1960s and 1970s was precisely to personalize what was happening there every day by showing a little girl running naked down a road to avoid the horror of napalm[22] or a police officer captured in the very act of killing a Viet Cong suspect with his service revolver.[23]

Today we include among these high impact photographs the photo (made public in April 2004) taken in Baghdad's notorious Abu Ghraib jail of a hooded man standing on a box sprouting wires; he was reportedly told that he would be electrocuted if he fell off.[24] Equally appalling are the photos of Private Lynndie England humiliating Iraqi detainees.

Surely the war on terrorism is also hell. True, it is non-conventional in the sense that the two sides are vastly disproportionate in military capacity, and the tactics used by both sides are extraordinary. On one side, the Western democracies and their allies have sophisticated weapons and surveillance technology at their disposal. Despite this unprecedented capacity to know and to act they have seriously entertained the prospect of revisiting their earlier decision to renounce torture. On the other side, terrorists have the asymmetrical power of surprise, using weapons such as hijacked passenger airliners or shoe bombs, always depending on the self-sacrifice of those who choose to commit suicide for the cause.

But if one were to ask a soldier or police officer on duty guarding a potential target of a terrorist attack what he or she is doing and why they are doing it, the response would no doubt have something to do with their hope of making a contribution to winning the war on terrorism.

Every war is simultaneously the same as and different from every other war. As in every war, the war on terrorism has treated humanitarian rules more loosely than in times of peace. What makes this asymmetrical war different is the importance of accurate information needed to station the police officer or soldier on guard at the right target at the right time to prevent or defeat an enemy's attack.

Always important in any war, intelligence is especially crucial in a war that is understood to be fighting against terrorism. Because the battlefield seems to be everywhere in general and nowhere in particular, knowing what the enemy is about to do next is crucial to saving innocent lives in buildings, on airplanes, in the sea lanes, on subways and in commuter trains. Such is the rationale offered by those nations known as the "coalition of the willing" for the draconian effort to heighten intelligence capability and thus their security.

But how does one obtain this crucial forewarning and details of an impending attack? An important source of this information comes from the enemy. Suspected terrorists must be interrogated, a word derived from the Latin verb *rogo*, meaning "ask," and the preposition *inter*, meaning "between," to discover the future plans and present intentions of an organization like al-Qaeda.

How a government describes its means of obtaining information from enemy sources can be problematic. Thirteen times after the prison-abuse photos taken at Abu Ghraib Prison were first aired in

April 2004, President George Bush boasted of freeing Iraq of torture chambers![25] George Orwell pointed out most effectively that governments, or, one might add, religious authorities, control language as well as people. When the George W. Bush administration began dealing with the public relations disaster of the release of the photos taken at the Abu Ghraib Prison, the word "torture" was avoided. Government spokespersons originally admitted the prisoners had been objects of abuse, then of humiliation, but not "torture."

"My impression is that what has been charged thus far is abuse, which I believe technically is different from torture," said Secretary of Defense Donald Rumsfeld at a press conference. "And therefore I'm not going to address the 'torture' word."[26] While Secretary Rumsfeld's statement is technically true, the photos made the distinction into an avoidance of the truth. While a distinction can be made between abuse and torture, in this case it is a distinction without a difference.

Likewise, "sleep management," an apparently benign term used in medical circles in discussing insomnia, disguises a popular form of torture because it requires no special equipment and leaves no marks on the body. Widely employed in the Middle Ages and later used on suspected witches and heretics by inquisitors, it was called *tormentum insomniae* – torture by sleeplessness. Then and now "after being kept awake for a hundred hours or so, almost anybody will confess to almost anything."[27]

Some definitions of torture

What is torture? From Roman lawmakers of the second and third centuries CE to the diplomats and humanitarians responsible for the 1975 UN Declaration against Torture the definitions are similar. The third-century jurist Ulpian said the following:

> By *quaestio* [torture] we are to understand the torment and suffering of the body in order to elicit the truth. Neither interrogation by itself, nor lightly inspired fear correctly pertains to this edict. Since, therefore, *quaestio* is to be understood as force and torment, these are the things that determine its meaning.[28]

In the thirteenth century, the Roman lawyer Azo gave this succinct definition: "Torture is the inquiry after truth by means of torment."[29] The seventeenth-century civil lawyer Bocer said, "Torture is interrogation by torment of the body, concerning a crime known to have occurred, legitimately ordered by a judge for the purpose of eliciting the truth about the said crime."[30]

Article 1 of the 1975 Declaration against Torture adopted by the UN General Assembly states:

> For the Purpose of this Declaration, torture means any act by which severe pain or suffering, whether physical or mental, is intentionally inflicted by or at the instigation of a public official on a person for such purposes as obtaining from him or a third person information or confession, punishing him for an act he has committed, or intimidating him or other persons. It does not include pain or suffering arising only from, inherent in or incidental to, lawful sanctions to the extent consistent with the Standard Minimum Rules for the Treatment of Prisoners.[31]

Finally, the twentieth-century legal historian John Heath writes as follows:

> By *torture* I mean the infliction of physically founded suffering or the threat immediately to inflict it, where such infliction or threat is intended to elicit, or such infliction is incidental to means adopted to elicit, matter of intelligence or forensic proof and the motive is one of military, civil, or ecclesiastical interest.[32]

Contemporary theory of torture

If we agree that Maher Arar's allegations are true, then he suffered torture in Syria, but would what he went through in New York City constitute merely coercion? Would questioning a suspect for 28 hours straight under bright lights, without his lawyer or consular officials being present, without giving him food or allowing him to sit down or attend freely to his bodily functions amount to torture? Officially the answer would be yes in view of the fact that Article 1 of the United Nations' Universal Declaration of Human Rights states the following: "No one shall be subjected to torture or to cruel, inhuman or degrading treatment or punishment."[33]

Furthermore, Article 1 of its Convention Against Torture goes on to specify, "For the purposes of this Convention, torture means any act by which severe pain or suffering, whether physical or mental, is intentionally inflicted on a person."[34] But many otherwise morally upstanding and conscientious interrogators would describe what Arar went through at the hands of the American authorities as coercion, even though it was, in fact, torture.

Some, privately, might also say the same about the situation in which photos of Private Lynndie England sexually humiliating and degrading Iraqi detainees in Baghdad's Abu Ghraib were shown to men under interrogation by private contractors hired by the United States Department of Defence who were actively seeking information about the 2003-5 insurgency.[35]

"Extreme interrogation" is another euphemism used for torture. Since the late 1950s there has been a movement toward more scientific and touch-less techniques of torture.[36] The most famous compilation of these is found in the US Central Intelligence Agency's manual *KUBARK Counterintelligence Interrogation*, which first appeared in 1963. Particularly illustrative of this shift towards psychology is the chapter entitled "The Coercive Counterintelligence Interrogation of Resistant Sources" which includes the following comment:

> All coercive techniques are designed to induce regression…. The result of external pressures of sufficient intensity is the loss of those defenses most recently acquired by civilized man…. Relatively small degrees of homeostatic derangement, fatigue, pain, sleep loss, or anxiety may impair these functions.[37]

The purpose of such homeostatic derangement, according to the CIA manual, is to produce "the debility-dependence-dread state,"[38] causing the prisoner to feel the emotional and motivational reactions of intense fear and anxiety.

> …The circumstances of detention are arranged to enhance within the subject his feelings of being cut off from the known and the reassuring, and of being plunged into the strange…. Control of the source's environment permits the interrogator to determine his diet, sleep pattern and other fundamentals. Manipulating these into irregularities, so that the subject becomes disoriented, is very likely to create feelings of fear and helplessness.[39]

It is because of these now widely accepted theories that modern torture usually includes hooding of prisoners, sleep deprivation, irregular and insufficient meals and exposure to intense heat and cold. As a later version of this manual puts it, the interrogator

> is able to manipulate the subject's environment, to create unpleasant or intolerable situations, to disrupt patterns of time, space, and sensory perception…. Once this disruption is achieved, the subject's resistance is seriously impaired. He experiences a kind of psychological shock, which may only last briefly, but during which he is

far...likelier to comply.... Frequently the subject will experience a feeling of guilt. If the questioner can intensify these guilt feelings, it will increase the subject's anxiety and his urge to co-operate as a means of escape.[40]

"The basic purpose of all coercive techniques," says the *Human Resource Exploitation Training Manual* produced by the CIA for Honduras in 1983, an updated version of the KUBARK manual, "is to induce psychological regression.... Regression is basically a loss of autonomy."[41] As KUBARK put it, such regression has to be traumatically induced:

> There is an interval...of suspended animation, a kind of psychological shock or paralysis. It is caused by a traumatic or sub-traumatic experience which explodes, as it were, the world that is familiar to the subject as well as his image of himself within that world.... At this moment the source is far more open to suggestion, far likelier to comply.[42]

The problem of the definition of torture is similar to that of defining slavery. The image conjured up by the use of the word slavery "is of toiling blacks and whip-wielding whites, of Mississippi steamboats and bales of cotton – the world, in other words, of *Uncle Tom's Cabin* and *Gone with the Wind.*"[43] But this is misleading because it neither accounts for slavery in North America before the nineteenth century nor for the other forms of slavery that have existed in various parts of the world before or since. For instance, in 1943 Heinrich Himmler told the leaders of the Hitler Youth,

> Whether [Eastern] nations live in prosperity or starve to death interests me only insofar as we need them as slaves for our culture, otherwise it is of no interest to me. Whether ten thousand Russian females drop from exhaustion while digging an antitank ditch or not interests me only insofar as the antitank ditch for Germans is completed.[44]

Torture likewise means many things to many people. The meaning in this book is restricted to the Convention definition and focuses particularly on the physical and psychological abuse of prisoners, or of those suspected of being a social risk by officials belonging to and explicitly mandated by political authorities such as governments or those who believe they have a mandate or warrant to proceed in this manner.

But this still does not fully solve the problem of definition. A good example of a nation that has deliberated over a definition of torture is

Israel. Perhaps because the Hebrew Bible does not offer any warrant to engage in torture, the State of Israel has struggled long and hard to work out the difference between torture and aggressive interrogation and to create conditions for the possibility of practicing effective anti-terrorist investigations without resorting to torture.

A 1987 Commission led by Moshe Landau, the retired Israeli Supreme Court justice who was the presiding judge in the 1961 trial of Adolf Eichmann, produced a series of recommendations allowing members of their intelligence service to use "stress and duress techniques," such as moderate physical pressure and non-violent psychological pressure in interrogation of prisoners who may have information which could prevent impending terror attacks, the so-called ticking bomb scenario.[45]

Guidelines were formulated which detailed methods and defined when they could be used, and a high level committee was struck to monitor compliance. These guidelines with respect to the application of moderate physical pressure that could henceforth be used by the security services of Israel were and are secret. Despite all these safeguards, the use of these methods quickly went beyond the situation of the "ticking bomb" to become something close to routine practice. In 1999, the Israeli Supreme Court ruled that all stress and duress techniques were illegal, and their use has since declined.[46]

This ruling determined that shaking suspects and confining them in chairs tipped forward in painful positions for long periods were violations of Israel's national and international commitments against torture.[47] Yet the Israeli Supreme Court at the same time conceded that physical force used against suspects could sometimes ferret out information that saves lives in the circumstance of the ticking bomb. So the same decision allowed interrogators a justifying excuse to use physical force as a lesser of evils while it banned torture itself absolutely.

Why torture is different

The essential theological reason why torture is different from other aspects of war can be found in the "inter" of the word interrogation. Essentially interpersonal, torture is a uniquely cruel method of intimidation and domination by one person, or a group of persons, over another person. Torture morally degrades both its victim and its perpetrators. Its use is difficult to moderate or control, and as a result, any community that offers a licence to use it, or chooses not to attend to its use, thereby establishing it as an institution, creates a momentum which defies moral sensibility and discernment and destroys the capacity of the individual to distinguish between good and evil or, and this is perhaps worse, to act against a recognized wrong.[48] We need to distinguish people from their governments. While it can be argued that the governments of the United States could arrange for the torture of someone like Maher Arar and that the Canadian authorities could participate in this, the fact that a controversy arose over the case of Maher Arar in both Canada and the US is an example of differing moral perspectives on the practice. There still exists at the present time a sensitive public conscience in North America that is uncomfortable with and even denies the use of torture, despite its widespread practice by their own governments in the Middle East and elsewhere.

The return of nations to the selective use of torture is disturbing because the doctrine of human rights is a pre-eminent moral and cultural achievement of the last 250 years of Western world history. The absolute and universal prohibition of torture is central to it. Surely the most basic human right is neither the legal right to *habeas corpus* nor the moral right to humane interrogation methods, but the right to life.

But why is torture worse than, for example, shooting an enemy in a war? The morally warranted use of an M-16 rifle and morally unwarranted use of torture are surely both intended to protect innocent human life. In a May 2004 NBC television debate about the prisoners at Guantanamo Bay, one of the arguments used in ethico-legal justification of their ambiguous status was that, "They are those who were missed by the bombs."[49]

Because they were the targets of morally legitimate US bombing in Afghanistan and accidentally survived, no one, a participant in the debate argued, should complain about what happened to them afterwards as prisoners: whatever their situation, it is better than being dead.[50] There may be times when a soldier will shoot the wrong person, but if there can be a legitimate war, do the hellish aspects of it become the lesser of evils? Is torture less lethal than shooting someone? The torture might end when its victim divulges the sought-after information, and the torture victim might then be free. Physicians often attend the torture sessions to bring proceedings to a halt if there is a risk to the life of the person being deliberately injured by the torturers. By way of contrast, the effect of the "full metal jacket" of an M-16 round on its target is often fatal.

At his trial for ordering the January 1988 beating of two groups of Arab civilians near the villages of Beita and Hawara in Nablus on the occupied territories of the West Bank of Palestine, Israeli Defence Force Colonel Yehuda Meir testified it was harder for him to give the order to beat the men than to give his soldiers the order to open fire on them. Later asked to explain his remark he said, "It is something you do not learn in the army school. You don't know how to do it. I, myself, cannot see blood or see people suffer. It is very difficult for me. If you have to shoot somebody, it is far from you. You don't see him. And you are taught how to do it, to use the gun."[51]

The United Nations and Geneva Conventions and the earlier Declarations of the Hague refer to a set of norms agreed upon by the international community at the end of the nineteenth century. They continue to attempt to achieve universal agreements to prohibit certain weapons and practices thought to be inhumane and in violation of the laws and customs of war. For instance, the Hague Declaration (IV, 3) condemns the use of dumdum bullets because of the gruesome manner that the bullet exits from a victim's body.[52] Prisoners of war and civilians caught in the middle of war zones[53] have a right to protection of life and person. Precisely why certain practices were banned and others are not is hard to explain and seems to rest upon a collective moral intuition, which can be elucidated to some degree.

Catholic theology

The late German Catholic theologian Karl Rahner, SJ, surprised many when he wrote that anyone in the field of moral theology today realizes that the proofs we produce to justify a particular position often assume from the start the very conclusion they intend to prove. They convince only those who already accept the conclusion for other reasons.[54] Why? Rahner suggests one reason is that the argument proffered is an attempt to articulate a moral insight one already has and about which one is already convinced. Along this same line of reasoning, Catholic tradition speaks of a feel or instinct for the truth enjoyed by the faithful either individually, or as a group.[55]

Speaking about the contemporary situation of the moral evaluation of torture in the context of the Catholic community, one can argue our moral sense is that its use is a grave evil. This conclusion is not catholic in the sense that it is universally held within the Church. But it is catholic because Catholic and other moralists do condemn torture used for harvesting intelligence or, what is worse, as a means of social control, both as a practice and especially as an institution of intimidation and the deliberate stimulus of guilt.

This was not always so. In the recent past and the present, Catholics in Mexico, Central and South America, Spain, Portugal, the Caribbean Islands, Northern Ireland, Spain, Croatia, Rwanda and the Philippines,[56] to offer a partial list,[57] have engaged in widespread torture, much of it mandated by their governments. The use of torture within the context of the Inquisition elicited a formal act of repentance by Pope John Paul II on behalf of the Church at the beginning of the present millennium.[58] Even with these important caveats, it can still be said contemporary Catholic repudiation of torture in all its forms is a moral response to certain values regarding the dignity of the individual human person that have become more important today than other values, such as truth, that received emphasis in the past.

It should be acknowledged that we could consider the moral question as to whether or not torture is different from other warlike activities from other perspectives than the contemporary Catholic position. The history of Catholic thinking on the morality of torture is genetic, has changed over time and has shared in a variety of evaluations, including that of its permitted use by Inquisitors seeking to combat religious errors or heresy, witchcraft, or infidelity.[59] Following Vatican II and recent papal teaching, contemporary Catholic moral theologians have reversed the position taken by their confreres in preceding centuries and consider the condemnation of torture as a "virtually exceptionless norm."[60]

Acceptance of war itself, and of all of its methods and values, has never come easily for Christians in general, not to mention Catholic moralists. Early Christians were pacifists. Then, in the fourth century CE, they allied themselves with the Roman Empire, the foremost military power of that age, thus revising their theological thinking about official violence.

Catholic theologians deplored war and were filled with shame over the casualties of war on all sides, no matter how these occurred. They tried to draw up restrictions on when and how wars should be fought and what could and should happen within armed combat; these became known as the "just war" theory. The popes in the eleventh century moved on from this position. In 1095, Pope Urban II announced the First Crusade to recapture the Holy Land from Islam. It was now asserted that wars were exactly what God demanded, if they were directed against God's enemies.[61]

Vatican II, in its seminal declaration *Gaudium et Spes,* called for evaluating war with an entirely new attitude.[62] The official Catholic position on war is a "composite of non-violent and just war elements."[63] Archbishop Renato Martino, head of the Vatican's office known as *Justicia et Pax,* has compared the present official teaching on war to that on capital punishment. "In principle war, like capital punishment, is permissible, but in practice neither should receive support."[64]

The reason why the Catholic community has opted to reject the use of war in practice, if not in theory, is because war always represents loss, diminishment, and destruction of what should have been preserved and protected. Fundamental theological doctrines are foundational to Catholic moral thinking.[65] *Pace* Cardinal Martino's statement that war can theoretically be permitted, the theological category under which we would place war is sin, and under it we would include everything to do with combat including the deleterious effects of, for example, an M-16 rifle, or the sudden death and destruction caused by land mines, or the moral depravity induced in torturers by the deliberately ingenious cruelty of their methods, not to mention the often lifelong or life-ending effects on the victims.

The first response to the question of what, within the context of war, makes torture special would be to say that it is at least as sinful as all other aspects of armed and organized conflict in the 21st century, and this because it shares in war's darkness and sinfulness.

Philosopher Paul Ricoeur argues that sin is a religious reality before it is an ethical one.[66] Biblical Judaism and Christianity used concrete expressions for sin with metaphors such as missing the mark, straying, rebellion, deviation, turning away, going off to a far country. It is not first of all a transgression of an abstract principle or rule, but the violation of a personal relationship. Let us think about the widespread use of electricity as a tool of torture within the context of sin. It was widely used as a means of torture during the independence struggle in Algeria in the last century.

Henri Alleg, a Jew from Europe, was the Editor of the Communist daily newspaper *Alger Républicain* from 1950 to 1955. In September 1955, the French authorities banned the newspaper. In November 1956 Alleg went into hiding, but was arrested in June 1957 by members of a French paratrooper regiment, who kept him for a month in El-Biar outside of Algiers.

His account of his ordeal, *The Question*, represents a sadly powerful account of torture as it actually happened then and happens today; the book was banned by the French government two weeks after it appeared in print. As philosopher Jean-Paul Sartre stressed in his preface to *The Question*, the only information that Alleg's torturers sought was the name of the person who had offered him a hiding place.

> … Four Paras picked up the plank to which I was bound and carried me into the next room facing the kitchen, and put me down on the cement floor. The officers sat down around me on boxes brought in by their men. "Now!" said Ch____, still very sure of the final result, "I need some paper and a box, or something hard, to write on." He was given a piece of wood, which he put down beside him. Then, taking from Lo___ a magneto which the latter handed to him, he raised it to the level of my eyes, turning for my inspection the machine which had already been described to me a hundred times by its victims. You know what this is, don't you? You've often heard it spoken about. You've even written articles about it?"
>
> "You have no right to employ these methods."
>
> "You will see."
>
> "If you have any charge to bring against me, hand me over to the appropriate authorities. You have twenty-four hours in order to do it. And I would prefer not to be addressed as 'tu.'" There were bursts of laughter around me.
>
> I knew very well that my protestations were useless and that under the circumstances it was ridiculous to ask these brutes to respect the law, but I wanted to show them that they had not intimidated me.
>
> "Go ahead," said Cha____ .... Ja____, smiling all the time, dangled the clasps at the end of the electrodes before my eyes. These were little shining steel clips elongated and toothed, what telephone engineers call "crocodile" clips. He attached one of them to the lobe of my right ear and the other to a finger on the same side.
>
> Suddenly, I leapt in my bonds and shouted with all my might. Cha___ had just sent a first electric charge through my body. A flash of lightning exploded next to my ear and I felt my heart racing in my breast. I struggled, screaming and stiffened myself until the straps cut into my flesh. All the while the shocks controlled by Cha____, magneto in hand, followed each other without cease. To the same rhythm,

Cha___ repeated a single question, hammering out the syllables: "Where have you been hiding?"

Between two spasms, I turned my head toward him and said, "You are wrong to do this. You will regret it!" Furious, Cha___ turned the knob on the magneto to its fullest extent....[67]

This account inspired the artist Nancy Strider to create the cover of this book. Electricity used as a means of torture is sinful.

The Greek word used in the New Testament for "sin," *hamartia*, is associated with military usage and means to "miss the mark" in the sense of failing to make a bull's eye. Morally it connotes failing in one's purpose, to fail to live according to an accepted standard or ideal.[68] Electricity is responsible for making life today safe, productive, and enjoyable. When a torturer applies electricity to the genitals, ear lobe, tongue, or nipples of his or her victim, its use no longer shares in the humanized blessing of a great invention, but has become sinful; the torturer's use of it has missed its mark because of his motive, intent and use of electricity. Despite the ancient Catholic reflections on the theory of a just war based on the legitimacy of self-defence, no matter how justified it might be, war diminishes those involved, twists their moral perceptions and values, and leaves all involved spiritually less than they were before.

One response to what makes torture different is that it is different only in degree. An Afghan who survives after stepping on an anti-personnel land mine left in the ground near his home years before by occupying Russian soldiers is physically and perhaps psychologically handicapped for the rest of his or her life. An Afghan who is suspected of belonging to the Taliban and who might, or might not, know the whereabouts of the Taliban leader, Sheikh Mohammed Omar, is tortured at Bagram Airbase during interrogation and survives. He may carry not only physical injuries for the rest of his life, but also must live with the psychological and moral trauma of having been up close and personal with fellow human beings, possibly also Muslims and Afghans, who may have taken sadistic delight in causing him pain and terror. They may have also tortured his relatives, spouse, or friends in front of him to break his will, to destroy his loyalty to Sheikh Omar and to dishonour him in front of his fellow Taliban comrades should he ever emerge alive from his ordeal (since it would be assumed that co-operation was the price of his survival).

Torture is also personally destructive to the torturers because they intend to diminish or even destroy the personhood of their victims. It is this subjective, interpersonally destructive aspect of torture that makes it different and morally worse than many other destructive aspects of war.

The second response of Catholic theology to the question of what makes torture different is that torture destroys community and degrades the image of God in the human personhood of both the torturer and his or her victims. It is even worse than suffering or causing death in combat. The theological doctrine supporting this second point of view is that of creation.

The Book of Genesis in the first account of creation says that we are created "in the image and likeness of God (*imago dei*)." Jewish and Christian theologians have speculated about what permits men and women to share in the *imago dei*. One answer is hierarchical.

We humans are vice-regents of God on earth and have dominion over all other life forms. The cruelty of torture is special because no animal or other creature than a man or woman would inflict it in the same way upon someone else. While a cat might seem to torture a mouse, this is fundamentally different from what humans do to each other, which is intentionally cruel. Another answer to what constitutes the *imago dei* in us has to do with the way we think and act. What makes humans "like" God is their rationality and freedom. The fundamental purpose of torture is to overwhelm the victim's will and to leave the victim under the domination and control of someone else, to break him or her and to take freedom away.

As a result of the teaching of Vatican II that we humans are not fundamentally individuals, but rather persons,[69] many Catholic theologians today prefer a third answer to what the "image of God" is in man/woman. Basing themselves on the doctrine of the Trinity, they would say the human rights and dignity attached to our personhood and to the human talent of creating and sustaining various types of community-life are grounded in our similarity to the divine nature, the nature of God the Father, God the Son, and God the Holy Spirit, persons distinct only in their mutual relationships to each other in the unique community we call the Trinity. Thus, a torturer inflicting torments and suffering on a victim not only defaces another brother or sister, but implicitly attacks the face of God in the other, and destroys human community.

Similar to systematic rape,[70] finally recognized by the War Crimes Tribunals in the Hague and in Arusha, Tanzania, as a weapon of war in the Bosnian and Rwandan genocides, and just as egregious and replete with moral turpitude, state-sponsored torture drives a stake into the heart of human community through its violation of the human person. Any nation that tolerates the practice is diminished by it. With innocent lives at stake, and a war against terrorism going on, nations are greatly tempted to use torture as a weapon and a technique for questioning a suspect. This temptation must be resisted.

The Chilean poet Ariel Dorfman penned the following lines that summarize the spiritual harm done to all by systematic torture that makes it "special." The poem refers to the notorious torture and detention centre in Santiago, Chile, during the 1980s.[71]

Lord, you who are everywhere,
have you been
in
Villa Grimaldi
too?

2

Why Torture?

Decent people everywhere agree on this: torture is evil and indefensible. But is it always?—Mark Bowden[1]

The etymological root of "pain" is *poena* or punishment. This reminds us that an experience shared by many humans often leads to a judgment by them on the meaning of their own bodily experience. The meaning of their pain goes beyond their own body to the wider world, which shares in the responsibility for causing their suffering.[2]

Interrogation

Let us return to the experience of Maher Arar. Beaten with an electric cable, threatened with even more severe forms of torture, forced to endure the screams of fellow prisoners, Arar confessed to having been in Afghanistan. "They kept beating me so I had to falsely confess and told them I did go to Afghanistan. I was ready to confess to anything if it would stop the torture. They wanted me to say I went to a training camp. I was so scared I urinated on myself twice...."[3]

Unnamed sources in the Canadian intelligence community with access to secret files claim that they are "100 per cent sure" that Arar trained with al-Qaeda in Afghanistan. They allege that Arar travelled to Pakistan in the 1990s, and then entered Afghanistan to train at the Khaldun base camp run by al-Qaeda, the same camp where al-Qaeda terrorists had trained Ahmed Ressam. Ressam was later convicted of planning a terrorist attack after crossing into the United States with a car packed with explosives. Other graduates of the same camp have been convicted of bombing New York's World Trade Centre in 1993 and two embassies of the United States in East Africa in 1998.[4]

Torture can serve at least two purposes. It can be a tool for interrogation. It can also be an instrument of terror to persuade the victim and the community to which he or she belongs that the masters of torture will prevail over them and have ultimate power, power for its own sake, which is the definition we will use for the evil of this form of violence.[5] The supposed reason for Arar's ordeal was the former; as with much, if not all, torture, the result was the latter. Torture is reprehensible not only because it offends procedural justice, but also because it destroys social trust. The subject of this chapter will be interrogational torture, thought to be the ultimate shortcut for security and intelligence gathering, and in the past used widely for obtaining self-incriminating evidence by courts of law and the judiciary.

In practice, torture is a highly inaccurate method, and, of course, an immoral one. If someone undergoing torture willingly provides false information to interrogators, does the torture have anything to do with finding out the truth? Surely extracting a confession made under such duress is not merely illegal and unethical, but it is also creates a contradiction in the perpetrators who describe themselves as intelligence agents, even though the information they glean may be false. Our intention will be to argue that what the victim of torture will say may be what she thinks her torturers want her to say. I will use as evidence material that has emerged from the proceedings of the infamous Spanish Inquisition.

The Spanish Inquisition

At least three events made the year 1492 historically significant for Spain. On January 2, the armies of Catholic monarchs King Ferdinand and Queen Isabella, whose marriage had united the ancient kingdoms of Aragon and Castile creating a single powerful country, conquered the Muslim city-state of Granada. The Crusades against Islam in the Middle East may have failed, but with this victory Muslims lost control of Europe.[6] In 1499, Muslims in Spain would be given a Hobson's choice of conversion to Christianity or deportation.

The second event happened on March 31, when Ferdinand and Isabella signed the Edict of Expulsion, intended to rid Spain of its Jews, who were given the same choice of baptism or, again, deportation. Despite the fact that the Ottoman Sultan sent ships to take the Jews to Turkey, many were so attached to the world around Granada that they chose conversion and became known as "conversos," "marranos" or "New Christians."

WHY TORTURE?   47

The third event is the one many inhabitants of the Americas celebrate or regret: in August one of the people who had witnessed the
Christian occupation of Granada, Christopher Columbus, a protégé
of Ferdinand and Isabella, sailed from Spain ostensibly to find a new
trade route to India, but "discovered" the Americas instead.[7]

The status of the *conversos* was that of a group under threat. Never
fully trusted by Spanish Catholics, repudiated by fellow members of
the Jewish community, they found themselves generations later having to defend themselves and their actions from the accusation of the
Inquisitors that they were secret Jews still practising their old faith.
Perhaps a Muslim who innocently visited Afghanistan in the early
1990s to help the poor and to relieve suffering rather than to engage
in terrorism – and whose travels were duly recorded in data now available to Canadian or American security authorities – could appreciate
today the cloud of suspicion under which the *conversos* of Spain and
Portugal constantly lived.

A distinction should be made between the Roman Inquisition and
the Spanish Inquisition. At the end of the fifteenth century, under Ferdinand and Isabella, the Spanish Inquisition became independent from
Rome. The dilemma of *conversos* was that a Church official known as
an Inquisitor could begin to investigate anyone at any time. Normally
one did not know who had provided the evidence against him, nor
did he have the right to remain silent in the face of those investigating his case.

The accused had to testify against him/herself; both Church and
State demanded self-incrimination. It was acceptable for the Inquisitor
to take testimony from the victim's own family. The accused was given
a summary of the charges and had to take an oath to tell the truth.
Various means, including torture, were used to ensure the cooperation
of the accused.

The hard-won judicial presumption of innocence that we take
for granted today, did not exist in sixteenth-century Spain, nor in the
rest of Europe.[8] "There are two irreducible propositions to which legal
methods for obtaining evidence must conform. One is that the use of
force or fear is morally unacceptable. The other is that no intrinsically
unreliable evidence should ever be used to secure a conviction."[9] These
are relatively modern notions.

During the Inquisition, torture was not used for punishment, but as
a means of eliciting the truth. Inquisitors would not accept confessions

as valid if they were made during torture sessions, since they had been obtained under terrible pressure. Instead, the victim of torture had to ratify his or her confession the day after the ordeal. If she refused to do this, the Inquisition used a legal subterfuge. Since its rules prevented anyone from being tortured twice, the end of each torture session was treated as a hiatus or suspension. Refusal to confirm the confession meant that the torture would be resumed.[10]

Of the three methods of torture used by the Spanish Inquisition the most horrific was also the most common in the sixteenth century.[11] Called the *potro*, this method involved the victim being tied tightly on a rack by cords attached to the body and limbs; it was controlled by the torturer, who tightened the cords by turning the ends. With each turn, the cords bit into the body of the victim and travelled around the flesh. In all forms of torture used by the Inquisition, the victim was stripped except for minimally modest covering. It was standard practice in the Spain of the sixteenth century to record all proceedings of torture sessions. As a result, historians have inherited a large body of gruesome evidence of the pain and suffering of its victims; a secretary recorded every word and gesture.[12]

Consider the case of Elvira del Campos, who was tried at Toledo in 1567. Of *converso* descent, Elvira was married to Alonso de Moya, who seemed to have been an "Old Christian," as opposed to a "New Christian," like his wife. According to witnesses, "Elvira attended Mass, went to Confession and generally gave all indications that she was a good Christian, but she would not eat pork and when she cooked it for the household, she handled it with a rag so as not to touch it, which she explained by saying she had a throat-trouble which made it disagree with her, and that handling it made her hands smell."[13]

The chief witnesses against her were Pedro de Liano and Alonso Collados, her husband's employees, who lived in her house and observed the details of Elvira's housekeeping practices. Arrested in 1567, her first trial was conducted rapidly because she was pregnant. Despite the Inquisitors' efforts to handle the matter expeditiously, her confinement caused a three-month delay in the proceedings.

Because the evidence in the case against her was contradictory, she was tortured twice in 1568 in an effort to find out the truth of whether or not she secretly practiced Judaism. In addition to the accepted fact that she did not eat pork, the evidence against her included her practice of not working and of putting on clean linen on Saturdays.[14]

She was ordered to be placed on the *potro*. She said, "Señores, why will you not tell me what I have to say? Señor, put me on the ground – have I not said that I did it all?" She was told to talk. She said, "I don't remember – take me away – I did what the witnesses say." She was told to tell in detail what the witnesses said. She said, "Señor, as I have told you, I do not know for certain. I have said that I did all that the witnesses say. Señores, it does not help me to say that I did it and I have admitted that what I have done has brought me to this suffering – Señor, you know the truth – Señores, for God's sake have mercy on me. Oh Señor, take these things from my arms – Señor release me, they are killing me." She was tied on the *potro* with the cords, she was admonished to tell the truth and the *garrotes* were ordered to be tightened. She said, "Señor, do you not see how these people are killing me? I did it – for God's sake let me go."[15]

Eventually Elvira del Campos admitted that, when she was 11 years old, her mother had instructed her not to eat pork and to observe the Sabbath, and she also confessed to the Inquisitors that she knew this was against the Christian Law. The next day she ratified these statements, and added that her avoidance of pork and changing her chemise and observing the Sabbath were in deference to the Law of Moses as taught by her mother; she had never told this to anyone for fear of her life.[16]

The extraction of information from the victim has historically been the most important explicit purpose of torture.[17] Traditionally accepted as part and parcel of the judicial process, torture was intended to elicit a confession of guilt and to implicate other culpable parties. Resorting to torture was an acknowledgement by judicial authorities of presumptive guilt based on what they thought was solid, if not totally convincing, evidence. Interrogations using torture took place to corroborate and clarify alleged evidence by eliciting a confession, known as the "Queen of Proofs."[18] As opposed to torture, judicial penalties were meted out on those convicted by the Inquisition at the *auto-da-fé*, which followed.

Part of what makes the agony of the suspected crypto-Jewess Elvira del Campo so poignant is that what was done by the *señores* does not strike us as fair or just. In the opinion of many today, judicial interrogation using torture constitutes an assault against the defenceless. This was not the perspective at that time.

Is there a pure case of interrogational torture? Is there not a moral excuse for it inasmuch as it may represent protection against social or religious assaults against the community? Sixteenth-century Spanish Catholics feared the presence of secret Jews, and used torture to provide them with the information they wanted. Victims of torture needing an escape from the rack, or their *potro*, traded what they knew and also what they did not know for relief from their pain and suffering. They struck a Faustian bargain with their torturers that the torture would cease when the information was given.

Any implied agreement between a torturer and his victim, then or now, is plagued by uncertainty about when the fullest possible compliance has occurred. In the case of the torture of the wrong person, of course, nothing at all could be learned notwithstanding what they might say. The willing collaborator and the innocent bystander caught up in the torture system both depend upon the torturers being persuaded the victim has kept her part of the bargain by telling them all there is to tell and also upon the torturers choosing to keep their side of the bargain, even though agreements cannot be enforced upon them and they have nothing to lose by continuing the torture should they choose to do so.[19]

The Spanish Inquisition richly deserves its notoriety, although the anti-clerical animosity of many historians since the eighteenth century has led to their failure to notice the similarity of its methods to legal procedures prevailing in that age of absolutism. Furthermore, its *raison d'être* and public place within the Catholic Church, which had previously disallowed torture in ecclesiastical courts, is not unlike the situation today in Western democracies faced with the social threat of terrorism.

As many today fear and detest terrorism, so Catholics in the past feared and detested heresy, infidelity, witchcraft and sorcery. The moral ambiguity of the Spanish Inquisition, as viewed from our modern perspective, hides its potential role of teaching us today to stand fast in our opposition to judicial and other forms of torture. As well, it teaches us about socially constructed and promoted public fear.

The case for torture

If we were to conduct a thought experiment in our own day, could we make a case for torture? Is torture ever justified from a moral point of view? Consider the question of how coalition authorities should have proceeded in the interrogation of Khalid Shaikh Mohammed, who was captured in Pakistan early in 2003. At the time of his detention he was the operations chief and third ranking official in al-Qaeda.

He underwent "water-boarding" in an attempt to extract information. Investigators insisted this was not torture even though they had strapped him down and pushed him under water until he thought he would drown. In a similar case in 1995, the police in the Philippines after finding a bomb-making factory in the Manila apartment of Abdul Hakim Murad, broke his ribs, burned him with cigarettes, forced water down his throat and finally threatened to hand him over to the Israelis for real torture.

Eventually, the investigators got what they wanted: secrets of a terror plot to blow up eleven airliners, to crash another into the headquarters of the Central Intelligence Agency and to assassinate the Pope.[20] Asked by Wolf Blitzer on CNN television whether torture should be used on Khalid Shaikh Mohammed, the respected American criminal-defence lawyer Alan Dershowitz responded,

> I don't think so. This is not the ticking-bomb terrorist case, at least so far as we know. Of course, the difficult question is the chicken-egg question: We won't know if he is a ticking-bomb terrorist unless he provides us information, and he's not likely to provide information unless we use certain extreme measures.
>
> My basic point, though, is we should never under any circumstances allow low-level people to administer torture. If torture is going to be administered as a last resort in the ticking-bomb case, to save enormous numbers of lives, it ought to be done openly, with accountability, with approval by the President of the United States or by a Supreme Court justice. I don't think we're in that situation in this case.[21]

For the first time in public, a prominent American jurist had raised the possibility of judicial torture. Mr. Dershowitz referred to the ticking-bomb scenario and suggested it did not apply in this case. But suppose it did. Suppose you were certain that a planned suicide mission was in the offing that would endanger thousands of non-combatants. Let us say we have intelligence leading us to believe our prisoner, Khalid Shaikh Mohammed, knows the details of this conspiracy, including the names of those involved and the exact date and time when the attack will take place, and suppose we further believe torture might force him to divulge this information. Should he be tortured? Dershowitz would permit it, but with an important condition. "I'm not in favour of torture," he wrote, "but if you're going to have it, it should damn well have court approval."[22] Another commentator put the same point in a different way:

> We can't legalise torture; it's contrary to American values. But even as we continue to speak out against human-rights abuses around the world, we need to keep an open mind about certain measures to fight terrorism, like court-sanctioned psychological interrogation. And we'll have to think about transferring some suspects to our less squeamish allies, even if that's hypocritical. Nobody said this was going to be pretty.[23]

Especially after the events of 9/11, many would reluctantly agree with Dershowitz and answer "yes" to the question of whether or not to use torture in that case.[24] The reason for this positive response is the possibility of situations so desperate that torture may seem justified in the midst of moral uncertainty. In a crisis, respect for the rule of law and the niceties of legal procedure might seem irrelevant.[25]

Mr. Dershowitz points to another problem as well: the need for confirmation of what intelligence officials learn as a result of torture. When Mr. Murad's interrogators did not believe him and demanded that he prove his claims or else they would continue with the torture,

> He led them to a tailor who was making the robe that was going to be worn by the terrorist that had pockets in it for the explosives and showed them the equipment that was going to be used to blow up the plane. When that happens, you believe it.[26]

Alan Dershowitz takes his proposal in an even more disturbing direction when he proposes that torture in the ticking clock situation should not be directed at the prisoner's rights as an accused person, because the information obtained will not be used in the trial against him, and the torture itself should not formally count as punishment.[27] The underlying premise is that one should torture people, not as part of a deserved punishment, but simply because we think they know something. In this way, unwittingly, he was going beyond the bounds set earlier by the Spanish Inquisition!

Legal history of torture

Roman law constituted the greatest source of learned jurisprudence known to the Western tradition. Therefore, its doctrine of torture had a great influence on the two revivals of the practice in the thirteenth and the twentieth centuries. To summarize Roman law on torture, originally only slaves might be tortured and then only when they had been accused of a crime. A conviction could only be obtained with the evidence of two eyewitnesses, or a confession from the accused. Circumstantial evidence was important if there were only one eyewitness, but on its own was insufficient to convict.[28]

Later in ancient history, with some restrictions slaves could also be tortured as witnesses. Freemen, originally freed from torture, came under its yoke in cases of treason during the Roman Empire and then in a wide variety of cases by imperial decree. "The division of Roman society into the classes of *honestiores* and *humiliores* after the second century CE made the *humiliores* class liable to the means of interrogation and punishment once appropriate only for slaves. And even the *honestiores* could be tortured in cases of treason and other specified crimes, as defendants and witnesses."[29]

There was awareness in ancient Rome that the use of torture was a difficult and dangerous business (*res fragilis et periculosa*); this was not based on considerations of care or concern about its victims, but on the risk of judicial error. In Ulpian's *Digest* (48.18.1.23) we find the following important concern regarding torture:

> It was declared by the Imperial Constitutions that while confidence should not always be reposed in torture, it ought not to be rejected as absolutely unworthy of it, as the evidence obtained is weak and dangerous, and inimical to the truth; for most persons, either through their power of endurance, or through the severity of the torment, so despise suffering that the truth can in no way be extorted from them. Others are so little able to suffer that they prefer to lie rather than to endure the question, and hence it happens that they make confessions of different kinds, and they not only implicate themselves, but others as well.[30]

One searches in vain in all of ancient literature to find a single protest in principle against torture. In a number of passages Juvenal condemns the cruelty of torture, but presupposes it as an institution. There are a few legislative restraints to torture that appear in ancient Roman law, such as not applying it to children under the age of fourteen, not because of humanitarian concern, but because of awareness that youngsters may not tell the truth. Pregnant women are immune from the practice in order to protect the unborn foetus. Seneca blames the Emperor Caligula for having put Sextus Papinus under torture not because using the *quaestio* was immoral, but because Caligula used it in a capricious manner. Plato in a number of *Dialogues* praises the medical efforts of a surgeon who shed his patient's blood to cure him of his disease, and this seemed for some commentators to provide an analogy to torture.

If medical torture was not immoral, Plato asked, why is legal torture so construed? Aristotle established a distinction between the end and the means to attain it. Why, precisely, these ancient thinkers asked, does the end not justify the means?[31]

What did Catholics have to say about torture in ancient Rome, given they often suffered from it during the various persecutions? Tertullian, in his *Apology*, does not condemn torture in principle, but points out a contradiction. Torture was used on Christians in an effort to make them renounce their faith. As long as they continued to proclaim the truth that "I am a Christian and confess that Jesus is Lord," their torments continued. The moment a Christian would deny this truth, the torture ceased.[32] Tertullian's point was to say torture did not bring out the truth, but its opposite.

After the fourth century and the Germanic invasions, complex legal changes occurred leading to the gradual disappearance of judicial torture. Until the twelfth century and the rediscovery of the ancient Roman law codes, the criminal law of Europe was mainly private. Public officers did not seek out and investigate crimes. Those who had suffered injuries brought them to their attention, and it was the accusers who made certain legal officers act on their behalf.

> The accuser found the proper court (one that professed jurisdiction over both parties), made his accusation, swore an oath to its truth, and called the other party into court to answer. The accused, faced with the charge, needed in general only to take an oath that the charge was false.... In some cases, notably those against men whose reputation was bad, some charges, chiefly those of capital crimes, might entail the subjection of the accused to the ordeal, a process in which the judgement of God was invoked to determine an issue rendered insolvable by the limitations of human judicial procedure.[33]

In the twelfth century, a legal revolution occurred in Christian Europe that shaped jurisprudence until the end of the eighteenth century. This was the revival of Roman law and the consequent creation of a universal canon (Church) law. A complex religious and cultural change occurred which included the replacement of an immanent but unsystematic justice supported by the judgment of God with the value of effective human judicial competence and authority; and both clergy and laity had to concur in these changes. In his learned study on torture, Edward Peters writes:

> The older system of proofs gave way before two distinct but equally revolutionary procedures, those of the inquisitorial process and the jury; the ideal of a justice within reach of human determination came to be widely accepted, particularly with the creation of a legal profession and the spread of the new uniform procedures....[34]

This legal revolution required more than a century to take hold. Fear of error became significant because much more information, and many more witnesses, cases, and types of defendants emerged than had formerly been the case. To preclude miscarriages of justice, self-incrimination became allowable. Under the older procedures, confession was only one of several means of corroborating evidence. With the legal revolution, confession became the queen of proofs. Connected with this judicial trend, sacramental confession, an annual obligation for all Christians after the Fourth Lateran Council of 1215 CE, became one of the two most important arenas of canon law, the other being the canon law trial itself.

The earliest mention of torture in late eleventh- and early twelfth-century texts explicitly limits its use to known criminals and the "lowest of men." The first technical discussion of judicial torture appears in the Roman lawyer Azo's *Summa* (1210). Initially opposed to torture, the Catholic Church seemed to reintroduce torture reluctantly, because it was not congruent with the views of ecclesiastical scholars of the previous century, the greatest of these being Gratian.

Written around 1140, Gratian's *Decretum* became the basic textbook of Church law for the next 800 years and clearly states that "confession is not to be extorted by the instrumentality of torture" (C.15.q.6.d.1). Sadly, by the first half of the thirteenth century, canon lawyers had approved the use of the Roman law doctrine of torture for use in civil law procedures.[35] In 1252 Pope Innocent IV formally proclaimed heretics deserved torture and civil authorities had the responsibility to do the job.[36]

As the practice of torture gradually came back into medieval legal procedures, it had to take its place within the law of evidence and the place of confession. Both ecclesiastical and lay law insisted that no confession could be extorted. Hence torture was not considered to be a means of proof, but a means of obtaining evidence. It was not to be used as coercion for a guilty plea but to obtain specific details that none but the criminal could possibly know. This goal was considered achievable for several reasons.

> First, there had to be at least one eyewitness, or sufficient probable cause that the accused had committed the crime;... Second, when it was decided to apply torture, the court had to be reasonably certain that confessional evidence would be obtained. Third, the accused would be preached to and implored to make a confession, and to this end he was often shown the instruments of torture before the application itself.[37]

Gratian's remarks concerning torture represented a long ecclesiastical tradition of rejecting torture in Church affairs. He insisted clerics could not apply torture (*Decretum* D. 86, c.25). Some exceptions he recognized were that the accusers of a bishop could be tortured (C.5, q.5, c.4), that in some cases people in the lowest ranks of society might be tortured (C.4, qq. 2-3), and that slaves might also be tortured (C.12 q.2 c.59).

Despite the limitations imposed by Gratian, with the revival of the practice of torture in Europe subsequent to the revival of Roman law, canonists and moralists seemed to regard it as too integral a part of the judicial system to be abolished without endangering the whole legal structure. Long prohibited in ecclesiastical courts, judicial torture was unauthorized until 20 years after the ecclesiastical campaign against the Cathars in southern France had begun. It was this crusade that gave rise to the Inquisition. In 1252 Pope Innocent IV allowed the infliction of torture by the civil authorities upon heretics, and eventually torture itself found a recognized place in the procedure of the inquisitorial courts.

Catholic casuistry of torture

First permitted in the Church legally by Innocent IV in his Bull *"Ad exstirpanda"* of May 15, 1253, it was confirmed by Alexander IV on November 30, 1259, and by Clement IV on November 3, 1265. The limit placed upon torture was *"citra membri diminutionem et mortis periculum"*; it was not to cause the loss of life or limb or imperil life.

Catholics in the sixteenth and seventeenth centuries looked to the moral theologians known as "casuists"[38] for their detailed ethical guidance even more than to the Bishop of Rome. Once torture had received papal approval and was being used widely by the Roman and

Spanish Inquisitions, casuists in the Church turned their attention to how judicial torture should be ethically carried out. Antonio Diana (1585–1663), a Theatine cleric who was known as the "Prince of Casuists" and the "Atlas of the Casuistical World," included a treatise entitled *"De tortura"* in his massive *Omnium resolutionum moralium*.

He explains that "torture is necessary because heresy is occult and difficult to prove."[39] Even if there is no preceding evidence against the accused, if the inquisitors think there is reason to believe they are in the presence of a heretic, the inquisitors can show the accused the instruments of torture, and can interrogate the accused in a way that terrorizes him, since this is not, strictly speaking, torture.[40] When only *one* witness exists against the accused, which is not sufficient for conviction, or there are two witnesses with weak corroborating evidence, "elevate him," wrote Diana, and interrogate him while suspended.[41]

Children under 14 years, pregnant women, the elderly (over 70 years or even over 60), those suffering from malaria (*"laborantibus quartana"*), syphilis (*"morbo Gallico"*), hernias (*"patientes ruptionem venae"*), or breathing trouble could not be tortured.[42] Children could be frightened into giving evidence by being shown the instruments of torture and thus terrorized. They could be tied up and stripped naked as if they were about to be tortured.[43] The morality of threatening children with torture was much discussed in the moral manuals of the sixteenth and seventeenth centuries.[44] The Jesuit Juan de Lugo (1583–1660) argued that if we can frighten someone morally with death, then we can also do so with torture, for what is allowed in the more serious thing (death) is allowed for the less serious (torture).[45] Even though there is a risk that innocent people might be tortured, de Lugo wrote, this risk might be taken without committing a sin because of the social risk to the human community (i.e., heresy) unless this risk were taken.[46]

As casuistry entered the eighteenth century, it seemed to become more cautious. St. Alphonsus Liguori (1696–1787) would place certain limits on the use of torture. For example, a judge sins gravely if he does not try all other milder means of obtaining the truth before using torture, and Liguori also requires him to say the truth concerning everything which pertains to the case even before there is proof against the accused. Torture is not to be used if there is already full proof of the crime.[47]

No attack was made upon the theoretical basis of torture until the sixteenth century. Abuses in the use of torture under the penal law imposed by absolutist and authoritarian governments grew at this time and the extravagances of witch hunts and trials led thoughtful men and women to begin to question the practice. It was not until the eighteenth century that these protests bore fruit.[48] The doomed King Louis XVI solemnly abolished it in 1789 in France, where the Gestapo revived it in 1942.[49]

The long history of the use of judicial torture, the fact that kings and queens, philosophers, poets, judges, saints, popes, Theatines, Redemptorists and Jesuits had sanctioned it, suggests the contemporary judgment condemning it as immoral must be based on new considerations and insights arrived at in the last 200 years. It is to these that we now turn our attention in order to ask: Why should we not torture?

Why Torture Is Wrong

If one speaks about torture, one must take care not to exaggerate. What was inflicted on me in the unspeakable vault in Breendonk was by far not the worst form of torture. No red-hot needles were shoved under my fingernails, nor were any lit cigars extinguished on my bare chest. What did happen to me there ... was relatively harmless and it left no conspicuous scars on my body. And yet, twenty-two years after it occurred, on the basis of an experience that in no way probed the entire range of possibilities, I dare to assert that torture is the most horrible event a human being can retain within himself.—Jean Améry[1]

As we have defined it, to torture or not to torture is a political choice based upon a judgment regarding fundamental human rights. Often argued against philosophically within a utilitarian framework of a lesser evil permitted to forestall a grave harm, respect for human rights can also be considered non-negotiable or fundamentally valuable.

The decision of a society to respect human rights is something its citizens should never take for granted. A fragile blessing from God, it is vulnerable to social fear and outside interference. In its absence, politically sponsored torture can begin or continue to happen, and can quickly become widespread.

During the 1980s, when his country was immersed in civil war, a young Jesuit from El Salvador spending a semester studying English in Toronto visited the Canadian Parliament Buildings. Asked what had most impressed him about his visit to Ottawa, he surprised the other Jesuits in his community by answering, "The parking lot near the House of Commons." He went on to explain he had seen a parking place reserved for the "Leader of the Opposition"; in his country that person was in hiding lest he be apprehended, undergo torture, and then become one of the thousands of the disappeared.

In his autobiography, comedian Dave Broadfoot reflects on how precious it is to have the confidence that he can comment satirically on politics in Canada.

> In Myanmar, Thu Ra, a humorist who satirized the government was arrested and imprisoned. In the days of the Soviet Union, when a Russian humorist defined a string quartet as a Russian symphony that had just returned from a tour of the West, he was sentenced to two years' hard labour. Palestinian humorist, Naji Salim, drew a cartoon showing a dove pecking its way like a woodpecker through the upright pole of a gallows. For this impertinence, he was murdered. In Guatemala, Jose Rolando Pantaleon wrote a satire on Guatemalan labour problems. He disappeared. When he was found, his jaw had been broken, all the skin had been ripped from his back, and there were five bullets in his body. In Egypt, Faroud Fouda made fun of some Islamic fundamentalists. He was shot in the street in broad daylight. As he lay dying, his best friend arrived to tell him that he had discovered Faroud was number three on the Islamic jihad hit list. "I was too easy on them," he said, "I should have been number one." In Colombia, a Colombian comedian had made fun of the government. He also made fun of the rebels who were fighting the government. Later, while driving in Bogota, he was stopped at a traffic light. A car pulled alongside him, and he was shot dead. No one knows which side the killer was on, rebels or government.

"There are too many countries," Broadfoot concludes, "where the government tortures comedians. We can celebrate the fact that in our country, comedians torture the government."[2]

Withdrawal of impunity for torturers

In Western democracies with strong human rights safeguards, comedians torture their governments through their biting satire; in countries where governments and political regimes routinely and systematically employ torture, the victims of torture can now turn the tables on their former torturers who no longer enjoy unrestricted impunity. They do so not with humour, but by employing recently enacted international law.

The best-known example of this is the case of the former dictator of Chile, General Augusto Pinochet. The 1984 Convention on Torture made torture a matter of "universal jurisdiction" based on its use of the word "anywhere" found in its sixth article.[3] On October 16, 1998 this was the basis for Pinochet's house arrest in London and for the long judicial process against him that continues in Chile. From these historically significant events, we shall argue that human rights are fundamental values and not subject to utilitarian calculus.

In this chapter we will discuss various arguments about the immorality of state torture. The fact that victims of torture can now bring their tormentors to justice provides a framework that could and should (like the threat of hell in moral theology) suggest to heads of governments and those actively involved in torture that they respect human rights. After reviewing the casuistry on torture, we will study evidence in the Catholic tradition that the contemporary teaching respecting human rights and condemning torture has ancient roots and is grounded in pastoral wisdom.

Today we judge the position taken by Catholic casuists on judicial torture in the seventeenth century to be morally repugnant. If there were any moral activity judged totally and absolutely wrong by the modern person, it would be torture. But the early casuists disagreed. They wrote about it almost casually and placed it within the general framework of the rules and procedures of Catholic law. Torture might be used if there were quite, but not entirely, convincing evidence of guilt from other sources. "Torture might be inefficient and open to abuse, but it is not condemned as cruel and inhumane."[4]

Yet in the same seventeenth century when casuistry flourished, and for the next 200 years, a widespread consensus slowly emerged that judged the practice to be immoral. Cautious warnings about torture had been raised throughout Christian history, but it was with the Enlightenment that Europe constructed a legal and moral framework against it. In 1874, Victor Hugo could say, "Torture has once and for all ceased to exist."[5]

Catholic theological arguments against torture

How did European philosophers and jurists manage to make the political use of torture illegal? Notwithstanding the evidence of the period of the Inquisition and the casuistry that supported it, Catholic theology played a significant role in undermining the moral argument in favour of the use of torture.

The first published position on the morality of torture in the early literature of the West is in the Montanist works of Tertullian (active between 197 and 207 CE), who asks how, among so many other forms of wickedness, a Christian soldier could avoid administering torture. With biting satire, Tertullian questions how a servant of God belonging to the judicial profession could avoid causing torture.[6] Referring to torture suffered by Christians, Lactantius (active ca. 305–23) defines it in moral terms as contrary to human rights and every good.[7]

Augustine, the pre-eminent theologian of the ancient Latin Church, writing his *City of God* between 412 and 416 CE, does not take issue with the principle of the Roman institution of judicial torture, but makes a strong case against the morality of how it is applied. A man who is not yet known to be guilty suffers it, while a guilty person could undergo it without confessing. Reflecting on the double bind in which a Roman judge finds himself, Augustine wrote:

> What of those judgements pronounced by men on their fellow men, which are indispensable in cities however deep the peace that reigns in them? How sad, how lamentable we find them, since those who pronounce them cannot look into the consciences of those whom they judge. Therefore they are often compelled to seek the truth by torturing innocent witnesses though the case does not concern them. What shall I say of torture inflicted on the accused man himself? The question is whether he is guilty; yet he is tortured even if he is innocent, and for a doubtful crime he suffers a punishment that is not doubtful at all, not because it is discovered that he has committed it but because it is not known that he did not commit it. Thus the ignorance of the judge generally results in the calamity of the innocent. And what is still more intolerable, and still more to be deplored and, were it possible, purged by floods of tears, is that the judge, in the act of torturing the accused for the express purpose of avoiding the unwitting execution of an innocent man, through pitiable ignorance puts to death, both tortured and innocent, the very man whom he has tortured in order not to execute him if innocent.[8]

For Augustine, the dilemma of the conscientious judge, aware of his obligation to protect society from crime and treason, yet finding himself torturing to death an innocent man to avoid unjustly inflicting capital punishment on him, represents "our pitiable condition in that our acts are determined in spite of us."[9]

In other texts Augustine refers to this situation as "original sin," which is that prevenient moral evil inherited by all, thanks to the disobedience of Adam and Eve. "Here, then, is a clear proof of man's miserable lot.... But if by ignorance and by office he [the judge] is

constrained to torture and punish the innocent, is it not enough that
we acquit him of guilt? Must he be happy as well?"[10]

Augustine's reasoning concerns the fundamental injustice of torture,
not used for punishment of those convicted of criminal offences, but
used against possibly innocent people who are merely suspected by
a judge of having done something illegal. His position represented
a significant moment in the attack against the plausibility of judicial
torture. By pointing out that, in following Roman law and judicial
practice, a judge inevitably perpetrated injustice towards a possibly
innocent person, Augustine suggested that the institution of judicial
torture was wrong.

The papacy also raised concerns about torture; the year 866 is
significant for the development of the moral argument against the
practice. Torture had declined after the barbarian invasions, with trial
by ordeal becoming the preferred judicial modality. In that year, with
the conversion of the Bulgars, Pope St. Nicholas I wrote to them,
responding to a number of dogmatic and moral questions they had
raised about certain practices, including torture, they had used before
their conversion.[11] Pope Nicholas clearly and forcefully condemned
both the practice and the judicial institution of torture.

With the papal condemnation of torture by Nicholas, we find for
the first time in Western culture a clear formulation of the idea that
the institution of torture should be suppressed. The confession of the
accused, wrote Pope St. Nicholas I, should be spontaneous, and torture
is not permitted "either by divine or by human law."[12]

Echoing the problem raised by Augustine, the Pope pointed out that
through torture one obtains either nothing, or else something uncertain.
He recommended giving evidence under oath or by swearing on the
Bible instead. It is worth noting that Nicholas did not recommend trial
by ordeal either, which was the preferred method in the same period
of theologians such as Hincmar of Reims.[13]

Sadly, the correct position of St. Nicholas on torture did not
prevail in the later history of the Church. But voices continued to be
raised against judicial torture, despite the fact that it was so widely
practiced.

Other ecclesial voices addressed the morality of torture. In 1484, a
canon of the Church of St. Dorothy in Vienna, Stephen Lanzkranna,
published his *Die Himmelstrasse*. In this simple book written for devout
Catholics, he indicated the route to win a place in heaven includes the

use of the Sacrament of Penance. This offered him the opportunity to review the major sins. On the topic of the Fifth Commandment ("You shall not kill"), he discussed recent developments in moral theology on homicide and on judicial corporal punishment of which capital punishment, a licit form of homicide, was the most important. Simple priest that he was, he dared not raise his voice against the laws of his land, but it is clear that judicial torture horrified him.

He argued that it was cruelty in all its forms that is condemned by the Fifth Commandment, and that evil could only be overcome by charity and goodness. Whoever tortured an innocent person sinned against this commandment. Whoever tortured anyone excessively in a spirit of cruelty, vengeance, or cupidity, did so as well. His entire book is a hymn to kindness, pity, and forgiveness.[14]

The excesses involved in the Church's battle against witchcraft and sorcery, and the response to this injustice by priests of the Society of Jesus, also helped to discredit the use of torture. In 1489 the infamous *Malleus maleficarum* ("Hammer of the Sorcerers") was published in Cologne.[15] The doctrine of the devil found in this influential book and in other places represented a figment of the collective theological imagination of that age, and its mimetic power resulted in untold suffering and injustice, especially towards women.

Priests involved in pastoral activity experienced these deleterious effects first hand. Consider the witness of the German Jesuit, Frederick von Spee. Appointed by his Jesuit Superior to the pastoral care of convicted sorcerers condemned to be burned alive at the stake, he witnessed the horrific death of 158 victims in the year 1627 alone.

One day his student Peter Schoenborn asked him why his hair had turned completely white. Confidentially Father Von Spee replied he had suffered the cruellest of moral dilemmas in accompanying more than 200 convicted sorcerers to their deaths when not a single one was guilty. He stressed this was based on his theological understanding and not on anything he had heard from the condemned people in the Sacrament of Penance that was protected by the "seal of Confession." Knowing this, Peter Schoenborn managed to revise the trial process for sorcery in his constituency when he became the Elector of Mainz (1647–74).[16]

Pastoral experience leads to theological formulation, which in turn results in moral, legal and political judgments and moral change. For a key development in the history of Catholic moral reasoning against torture, one must await the seventeenth century and the work of two Jesuit theologians, Adam Tanner (1572–1632) and Paul Laymann (1575–1635).

Tanner condemned not only sorcerers and those involved in witchcraft, but, for the first time in published Roman Catholic theology, those who cruelly pursued sorcerers. Attacking the irresponsible persecution of witchcraft raging in southern Germany in his age, he excoriated the methods of torture, forced denunciation and wholesale execution.[17] Since the notion of human rights had not yet been articulated (a breakthrough that would only happen later in history), what von Spee, Tanner, and Laymann condemned was "procedural injustice." They presumed the Inquisition was a valuable and authentically Catholic institution. In his attack, Tanner took a considerable risk that he might be accused of collaboration with sorcerers. When von Spee wrote a book with the same criticism of the witchcraft trials, he did so anonymously, using the acronym *"PNSI theologien romain,"* "by an unknown Roman theologian," in its first edition.[18]

Just as he made use of theological propositions proposed by his predecessors, so, as an approved theologian in his own right, Tanner's opinions on the just and unjust use of torture would be used by the judges, notaries, censors and lawyers of the inquisitional system as probable, that is, reasonable and defensible positions to take with respect to their moral and conscientious decisions.

Tanner began his comments on torture, writing that sorcery, heresy and the poisoning of wells were cancers that could become widespread in society and might be perpetuated. For this reason they must be forcefully dealt with by competent judicial authorities, but only in a just manner.[19] He based his case on the probable opinion published by Bishop Peter Binsfeld (d.1598), who wrote that the obligation of the judicial investigator to discover all the associates of a person admitting to serious immorality should not include the interrogation of thieves, traitors, conspirators, sorcerers, witches or heretics about their collaborators, since the information they were likely to divulge would be deliberately false.[20] Tanner used this opinion of Binsfeld to argue that the false denunciations of innocent people for sorcery and of women for witchcraft was very common, and judges must be wary, for it was an intolerable error if a judge based a decision on something that was manifestly impossible, or condemned an innocent person.[21]

Can we put credence in the denunciations of tortured sorcerers? Tanner said we cannot, and based this opinion on the earlier view of Gregory of Valencia on the issue of tainted denunciations.[22] At that time in Germany, the great number of persons rounded up for interrogation, torture and execution based on the forced and illegitimate denunciations of sorcerers, placed the innocent in jeopardy. Many sightings of demons were, he thought, false and the result of what we would today describe as psychological causes such as hysteria.[23] He quoted Genesis 18 and the dialogue between Abraham and God concerning the possibility that there were ten innocent people in Sodom in order to argue forcefully against the wholesale executions happening in southern Germany. The situation there was terrible, and, Tanner wrote, "God does not permit this."[24]

In his *Theologie morale*, Laymann concurred with Tanner.[25] Laymann stressed that torture should not be used as a punishment such as exile, incarceration as a galley slave, or fines. Torture is to be used only to elicit a criminal confession. Two witnesses, as well as corroborating evidence, were needed concerning the guilt of someone before he or she could be tortured. A bad reputation alone should not suffice to permit torturing a suspect. Neither should a judge proceed to torture someone suspected of sorcery or heresy because of denunciations extorted from people already condemned to death. If a judge were to receive the denunciation of a single witch, or if the supporting evidence were strong for a large number of witches, the judge could investigate and use torture.

The number of denunciations was also important to assess their credibility, argued Laymann, as well as whether or not most of the people denounced were women. If six or more persons who had been denounced were of good reputation, a judge should not torture them, but could arrest and detain them lest they escape.

Certain people should not be tortured: imbeciles, minors (*impuberes*), frail old people (*senes decrepiti*), pregnant women (due to the danger of abortion), nobility, doctors, and royal counsellors. Among the convicted criminals exempted from torture were heretics, traitors, those involved with *lèse-majesté*, poisoners, sorcerers and witches – all of whose very crimes indicated that their evidence would not be trustworthy.[26]

In agreement with Tanner, Laymann deplored the fact that terrified suspects of sorcery would make a false confession in order to be put to death and thus avoid the torment of torture. Making a personal confession or naming accomplices could only justly be done after the torture had ended, and not during it, and this should be done in the correct manner in front of a notary.[27]

Laymann gave two reasons why denunciations by persons convicted of consorting with demons, or of sorcery, were invalid. First, the devil would profit from false denunciations of innocent people. Second, demons usually deceive us and are our enemies.[28]

Laymann did not take this argument one step further and say that a person suspected of sorcery either was or was not actually a sorcerer. If he or she were, then torture was imprudent since some or all of what emerged from the interrogation would be lies. If he or she were not a sorcerer and was innocent, then they should not be tortured at all. Hence torture should not be used at all in sorcery cases.

Both Tanner and Laymann struggled with the use of torture given the evidence of their own day that its use in the judicial process was unjust. But neither was able to free himself from the mindset created by the judicial system to which they and their Church were committed.

It took others to disconnect torture from the justice system of Europe. These eighteenth-century political and legal thinkers influenced legislation on torture by placing a moral framework around the way laws were formulated and states were governed. They measured every act of the law or the government according to the moral standards of the humanitarianism of the European Enlightenment. They associated torture with the moral evils of the royal government of the *ancien régime* before the French Revolution, and "shifted the grounds for the condemnation of torture from the specifically legal to the more generally moral. Torture was then condemned – by Voltaire, Beccaria and others – because it was incompatible with a new idea of human dignity."[29]

The Enlightenment shift from the law to the morality of torture

This shift from law to morality, while welcome, did lend itself to sentimentality, so that the notion of torture could refer to many different realities. V.S. Naipaul quoted a trade union leader in Argentina before the 1976 outbreak of the Dirty War; he said, "There are no internal enemies," but thought that torture would continue in Argentina. "A world without torture is an ideal world."[30] Also, there was a difference between one type of torture and another, depending on the type of person being tortured. *"Depende de quién sea torturado,"* said the trade unionist to Naipaul. It depends on who is tortured. "An evildoer, that's all right. But a man who's trying to save the country – that's something else. Torture isn't only the electric prod, you know. Poverty is torture, frustration is torture."[31]

In many Latin American countries in the past century, it was common for citizens like the trade union leader to distinguish between innocent victims of systematic terror – who had been mistakenly or unfairly tortured – and the violent activist "subversives" who presumably deserved what they had gotten.[32]

When Frederick II, King of Prussia and absolute monarch, prohibited torture in 1740, he made three exceptions, two of which would have been opposed by Tanner and Laymann: *lèse majesté*, murder, and treason.[33] The exceptions of King Frederick are illuminative for they direct our attention more than 200 years later to the modern setting of politics and the fear of a powerful state that it is vulnerable to an asymmetrical attack from within. The contemporary discussion of the use of judicial torture after 9/11 finds its plausibility in this same obsessive fear Frederick felt for his regime.

Two types of arguments against torture

Two types of arguments show why torture is wrong. Based on the distinction between acts that are evil and those that are simply very bad, one line of reasoning – deontological – is designated in Catholic moral theology as well as in other traditions and rests on non-negotiable principles.

Coming from the Greek word for rule, *deon*, this approach holds that a morally evil act remains evil quite apart from any consequences that emerge from it. From this stance, torture must always and everywhere be forbidden. "Let justice endure though the world should perish" is a deontological maxim from ancient Rome. This rule-based morality is well represented by the *Catechism of the Catholic Church*, which deals with torture in Article 5 under the "Fifth Commandment" in its sections on "Respect for the Dignity of Persons" and "Respect for Bodily Integrity."

Both the terror tactics of kidnapping and hostage-taking as well as torture, stand equally condemned by the *Catechism*. "Torture which uses physical or moral violence to extract confessions, punish the guilty, frighten opponents, or satisfy hatred is contrary to respect for the person and for human dignity" (*Catechism*, #2297). The various conventions and declarations of the United Nations against torture as a violation of human rights are also deontological in nature.

Deontological reasoning is deductive, not inductive. Catholic moral thinking is, however, both theoretical and practical. For this reason, another type of moral reasoning must be called on, one which is utilitarian or consequentialist in nature. This approach calculates the projected or hoped-for benefits of a moral option against its negative ramifications and asks the question "Overall, and taken as a whole, are there more and better reasons to do this than to refrain from doing this?"

This second approach argues that torture is counter-productive and leads to far worse results than the occasion that gave rise to it in the first place. As one commentator put it, "Torture is a beast with a rapacious appetite."[34] Because the results of torture are unpredictable, once a political system has sanctioned the systematic use of torture, it will have difficulty controlling the thoughts and actions of those who have suffered torture and survived.

One such victim of the beast was Dr. Ayman al-Zawahri. Accused of being a member of the Muslim Brotherhood in Egypt, Dr. al-Zawahri suffered torture and a long imprisonment following the murder of President Anwar Sadat in 1981. Many who knew Dr. al-Zawahri remain convinced that the torture radicalized him and his views. "After his release, Dr. al-Zawahri left for Afghanistan, where he met Osama bin Laden and ultimately became the No. 2 man in al-Qaeda."[35]

Potential prosecution represents a utilitarian reason for not engaging in human rights violations and torture. Basing their actions on arguments against the ethical legitimacy of torture, individuals and governments have begun to prosecute torturers. The cases being assembled against Hissène Habré and Miguel Angel Cavallo are examples of this movement. The fact that the world community is not prepared to extend impunity nor indefinite amnesties to those involved in torture, even in a remote setting such as the Kingdom of Bhutan, our third case study, ought at least to give perpetrators pause for thought.

The case of Hissène Habré

Souleymane Guengueng, a devout Catholic in a predominantly Muslim part of the world, was arrested in Chad on August 3, 1988, for reasons he still does not understand. When arrested, he was an official of the Lake Chad Basin Commission, a bureaucracy helping to improve the national supply of water. He spent two years in jail cells so small that he couldn't even stretch his legs. His family had given him up for dead.

He suffered severe torture and there were moments when he might have preferred death. During his ordeals he prayed under his breath, because if his torturers and guards had heard him they might have accused him of muttering oaths against the man who was responsible for his ordeal, the former dictator of Chad, Hissène Habré, who committed his immoral actions through his dreaded political police, the Documentation and Security Directorate (DDS) that reported directly to him.

Ironically, although he had worked hard to provide the people of Chad with potable water, Mr. Guengueng received just one bucket of water every day during his imprisonment. To relieve his thirst in the stifling heat of the prison, he would lick the perspiration off his body.

Mr. Habré fled the capital of N'Djaména on December 1, 1990, and went into exile in neighbouring Senegal. Mr. Guengueng was released from prison that same day.

When the Habré reign of terror ended, Mr. Guengueng and several other prisoners joined together in an organization called the Chadian Association of Victims of Political Oppression and Crime (AVCRP) to document the former dictator's crimes. They interviewed more than 1,000 people, including many victims of torture, and assembled 792 dossiers that presented in graphic detail what he had done. They presented their findings to a government-established Truth Commission set up to investigate what had taken place in Chad. The Truth Commission called for the "immediate prosecution" of those responsible for atrocities.

This inquiry declared that 40,000 people had lost their lives during the Habré era. Despite this finding, Habré loyalists threatened Mr. Guengueng and his confederates with death, prompting Guengueng to bury his precious dossiers for safekeeping.

In early 2000, these dossiers and personal testimony would become crucial in the case against Habré's use of torture. Sometimes it amuses Mr. Guengueng to imagine what the former president must have thought when he found out about the evidence Guengueng had secretly collected: "Who is this little bird who is singing songs about me? I killed so many, but I forgot to kill him."[36]

The prosecution of the retired dictator of Chile, General Augusto Pinochet, set a precedent for the case against Habré. When Pinochet arrived in Britain in 1998 to undergo back surgery, he assumed he would be protected from legal jeopardy by his diplomatic immunity as a former head of state. He had not counted on the crusading Spanish judge Baltasar Garzon, who became the General's worst nightmare.

Earlier that year, Spain's National Court had ruled that the 1984 Convention on Torture, ratified by 132 countries including both Spain and Britain, obliges states to prosecute – or to extradite for prosecution – persons on their territory accused of torture, no matter where the torture was committed. This meant Spain's courts had jurisdiction to try torture cases no matter where they had taken place. Garzon sought Pinochet's extradition from Britain for trial in Spain. The decision by the House of Lords that he could not claim sovereign immunity was a rude shock to Pinochet and to out-of-office despots everywhere.

Ultimately the prosecution of Pinochet in Britain and Spain shifted to Chile due to his old age and ill health. Human rights activists everywhere were encouraged by the precedent it had set and began scanning the moral and legal horizon for other suitable candidates. They settled on Mr. Habré partly because he had chosen law-abiding Senegal for his exile.

Two Harvard University graduate students specializing in human rights law and working for a non-governmental organization called Human Rights Watch secretly travelled to Chad to look for evidence against Habré. They stumbled upon Mr. Guengueng and his trove of dossiers. Despite the fact that the appeals court in Senegal eventually ruled that Senegal had no right to try someone for crimes not committed on its soil, these two human rights advocates continued in their pursuit of Habré in search of justice for Mr. Guengueng and his associates.

Belgium took up the case against Mr. Habré under its 1993 law, amended in 1999 and again in 2003, dealing with crimes against humanity. Belgium's law pushes the concept of universal jurisdiction to the limit because it allows victims to file cases against alleged torturers anywhere as long as the case had some link with Belgium. Such a link exists if the suspect is on Belgian soil, if the crime took place in Belgium, or if the victim is Belgian or has lived in Belgium for at least three years. The 2003 amendments were made because critics had called the 1999 Belgian law absurd. In a February 2002 editorial entitled "Less than Universal," the New York–based *Wall Street Journal* claimed the Belgian legal system had "run amok" and that Belgium was now posing as "the world's arbiter of good behaviour."[37]

Despite the amendments in 2003 to the Belgian law, in 2005 the case against Habré goes forward. The president of Senegal has agreed to hold Habré pending an extradition request from Belgium, and the government of Chad has told Belgium that it would waive any immunity that Habré might seek to assert.[38] Because it was begun before the 2003 amendments to its original law, the Belgian authorities have stated they will not seek to block this case.

When he had the opportunity to appear in N'Djaména before Daniel Fransen (an investigating judge of the Brussels district court, who was protected during his stay in Chad from February 26 to March 7, 2002, by five burly Belgian policemen), Mr. Guengueng said, "I have been waiting for 10 years to talk to a judge about what happened. Finally, I have emptied my baggage, and I feel lighter."[39]

A global battle against the impunity of torturers and those who order torture is under way. The establishment in 2002 of the International Criminal Court (ICC) is highly significant. With 66 countries using the ICC to enforce the 1987 Statutes of Rome, the enforcement protocol for the 1984 Convention Against Torture, torture victims in smaller countries or kingdoms who suffered after 2002 can approach Belgium or Spain and a number of other countries such as Australia, Germany, New Zealand and South Africa, who have amended their laws after joining the ICC.

The case of Miguel Angel Cavallo

The new international effort to reduce the impunity involved with torture does not include only former heads of state like Pinochet or Habré who authorize torture, but also the individuals who perform torture. On June 10, 2003, the Mexican Supreme Court decided to uphold the extradition of Ricardo Miguel Cavallo to Spain where he faces prosecution for atrocities committed against Spanish citizens during Argentina's military dictatorship of 1976–83.

This decision by the Mexican Supreme Court authorized Cavallo's extradition on charges of genocide and terrorism, but not on charges of torture, because a lower court had previously ruled Cavallo could not be extradited for torture on the grounds that, under Mexican law, the statute of limitations for a torture prosecution would have expired.

And tragically, in the case of Argentina, most people who underwent torture were also killed.

As a naval lieutenant known by the name of Miguel Angel Cavallo, and as a member of the notorious Working Group 3.3.2 based in the Navy Mechanics School (*Escuela de Mecánica de la Armada, ESMA*) in Buenos Aires, Cavallo may have involved himself in the kidnapping and torture of many persons perceived as leftists by the military. The indictment implicates Cavallo in the torture of Thelma Jara de Cabezas, and the killing of Mónica Jauregui and Elba Delia Aldaya.

The process of bringing those accused of human rights abuse to justice has encountered impediments. The Presidency of Raúl Alfonsín (1983–89) represented the end of the military regime. He came into office intending to restore respect for the rule of law and human rights in Argentina and, as a result of the findings of the Truth Commission, he insisted trials be held which convicted some former junta members. In its 1984 report of the Argentine Truth Commission entitled *Nunca Más* ("Never Again") the names of 8,961 who disappeared under the military dictatorship were listed along with the caveat that this figure was not exhaustive.

But facing serious pressure from the military and the possibility of another *coup d'état*, Alfonsín's administration passed a Partial Amnesty Law in 1986 and 1987 called the *Punto Final* or "Full Stop" law, which ended all proceedings against soldiers, sailors and air force members by setting a deadline of 60 days from December 26, 1986 for the lodging of any complaint against past violators of human rights. Alfonsín's successor, Carlos Menem, granted a universal pardon in 1989 to all officers convicted of human rights abuses in order to promote national reconciliation. A year later he issued a general amnesty to everyone involved in the repression. In 2001, two Argentine courts ruled the amnesty laws of 1986 and 1987 violated constitutional guarantees for human rights. On August 12, 2003, the Argentine Congress, perhaps in light of the Cavallo decision in Mexico and following the prompting of the newly installed President Néstor Kirchner, voted to rescind the Amnesty Laws.

These actions were taken because of public pressure to hold the perpetrators of crimes accountable and to bring justice to the victims of kidnapping, torture and "disappearances";[40] the new President of Argentina, Néstor Kirchner, has begun to revisit the Argentine amnesty laws.[41]

Meanwhile, in a maximum security prison in Spain, Cavallo was handed a 200-page indictment by Judge Baltasar Garzon. Garzon's successful extradition of Cavallo succeeded where his attempt to do the same with Chile's Pinochet failed. It represented the first time that one country had extradited a person to another country to stand trial for abuses that happened in a third. Cavallo is one of the first serving or former Latin American military officers to be prosecuted by a judge from a third country after being arrested in a country where he had no legal problems. At the time of his detention in Mexico, he was head of the private National Registry of Motor Vehicles and was one of Mexico's most powerful business persons.

The catalyst for his arrest was a news story by reporter Jose Vales published in the Mexican daily newspaper *Reforma* in 2000, which revealed the true identity of Ricardo Miguel Cavallo. When the story was published, Cavallo tried to flee to Argentina where he would be protected by the amnesty laws then in place, but he was arrested by Interpol during a stopover in Cancun.[42]

From all accounts, Cavallo represented the worst excesses of the moral nightmare Argentina endured for so many years. One quiet summer night in 1977, for instance, sixteen hooded soldiers burst into Malou Cerutti's home and beat her husband to a pulp while she and her children watched. Cerutti and the children, aged eight, nine and ten, were gagged with sheets, tied up and thrown to the ground. For the next eight hours, right before their eyes, their husband and father Omar Masera was struck with rifle butts, and finally dragged off. "He was covered in blood and wearing only underwear. From his groans I knew he was alive," Cerutti said.[43]

At the same time, in a house just 200 metres away, Cerutti's 73-year-old father, Victorio, who was a wealthy real estate developer and owner of vineyards near the western city of Mendoza, was also tortured in front of his wife, then abducted. Nearly three decades later the whereabouts of father and husband are still unknown. Cerutti says Miguel Cavallo was involved in what happened on that hellish night in 1977.

The men who attacked her family wore hoods, but she said that Cavallo's came loose at one point, giving her a glimpse of his face. And the main image that has haunted her all these years was Cavallo's eyes, peering through a slit.

"When I saw Cavallo's eyes in photos when he was detained in Mexico, I recognized him and I was shocked. He had the same icy, penetrating look of a perverse man," Cerutti said in an interview at her home in Madrid. "Cavallo now needs to tell us what he did with our disappeared. When did he kill them, where, if they are buried in mass graves or if they were thrown out of planes," she said.[44]

After long years of exile in Mexico and later in Spain, where she moved eight years ago, Cerutti tries to heal her psychological scars by turning nightmares into art. She paints with her fingertips. Most of her works have been displayed in Argentina and Spain. In shades of blue and black, her paintings depict prisoners being tossed to their deaths from airplanes; a self-portrait shows a person walking over graveyard crosses.[45]

In this chapter intended to discuss reasons why systematic torture should not be introduced into a kingdom, regime or state, and, if once present, why it should be stopped, moral and legal arguments have been raised. Former dictators, generals or rulers who allowed systematic torture are now vulnerable to prosecution under international law; those who acted as their torturers also are without impunity for their crimes against humanity.

The contagion of torture: The case of Bhutan

Two further consequentialist arguments can be made. First, like Souleymane Guengueng in Chad, surviving victims can become active opponents of the regime. Second, the logic justifying torturing one's fellow human beings in one particular situation can be used to justify torture in other similar situations, and the practice can become widespread and pervasive. This is the "contagion" problem.

To illustrate the way torture can transform an ordinary person into someone who is a major threat to his persecutors, one need only look at the current human rights cases of Tek Nath Rizal and Rongthong Kuenley Dorji, both citizens of the Kingdom of Bhutan and therefore subjects of its absolute monarch, King Jigme Singye Wangchuck.

A number of reasons suggest that it is controversial to choose Bhutan for discussing contemporary state-sponsored torture. Unlike the equally landlocked, obscure and economically deprived country of Chad[46] with its notorious former president Hissène Habré, Bhutan is not known for state-sponsored torture. Described as the "last Shangri-la,"[47] this picturesque Himalayan kingdom remains a favoured destination for the wealthy tourist able to afford the daily tariff charged for each foreign visitor.

In addition to its magnificent scenery, Bhutan is an unlikely setting for state-run torture chambers because the form of Buddhism practised by the majority of its population stresses compassion as a ruling virtue exemplified by the "bodhisattva" who chooses commitment to the relief of suffering of others in this world over nirvana in another world.[48]

In a legal sense, this communal compassion is reflected in the fact that capital punishment is in principle abolished in the Kingdom. Furthermore, the fact that Tek Nath Rizal and Rongthong Kuenley Dorji have survived torture and remain free men today is significant; this is not a typical outcome of torture. For instance, many of those who disappeared in Argentina during the Dirty War from 1976–83 were deliberately murdered after their torture sessions ended.[49] This goes on today in places like Kashmir in India where "many Kashmiris believe that killings in 'encounters' with the army or police ... are in fact deaths after torture in custody."[50]

A final reason for being nonplussed by a discussion of torture in Bhutan has to do with the scale of the problem. In 2003 China punished nearly 8,000 police officers for corruption, abusing suspects, extracting confessions through torture and illegal use of weapons.[51] The scale of the problem of Bhutan's state-sponsored torture is small in comparison to its neighbour to the south, India, and its neighbour to the north, China. Still, one case of state-sponsored torture is too many.

However, institutionalized judicial and political torture was and is part of Bhutan's reality.[52] Furthermore, evidence points to the increased use of torture in Bhutan for political purposes in the second half of the last century and in our present century as well.[53] Allegedly, torture was used in 1964, 1974, 1988 and 1997 during four political crises that threatened the modern monarchy. In the first two instances, it was used primarily to uncover the extent of the alleged treasonous plot against the father of the present king and against the designated heir to the throne to obtain the names of those involved.

The two more recent outbreaks of political torture represent a method of containing the popular and religious movements, first of the Nepali-speaking Hindus of southern Bhutan and, more recently, of Sharchop-speaking Buddhists of eastern Bhutan. Both groups are described by the Royal Government as anti-national movements, and it should be stressed that southern Bhutan suffered wide-spread destruction and death apparently perpetrated by both sides in the conflict.

At the same time, what concerns us today is the allegation by Amnesty International and other international human rights organizations that the Royal Government has attempted to contain the uprisings through intimidation and coercion, including the use of state-sponsored torture.[54]

In both the 1988 and 1997 outbreaks, state authorities had earlier submitted an individual to torture who then began and led an organization that became a political threat to the monarchy.

In April 1988, Tek Nath Rizal and B.P. Bhandari, two Royal Advisory Council members from southern Bhutan, received a number of written complaints about the manner in which a national census was being conducted. A number of prominent Nepali-speaking government civil servants composed a petition for the King, which Rizal presented to His Majesty.

"The petition primarily outlines the concerns of the general public, pinpointing the flaws and discriminatory aspects of the Marriage Act and the Citizenship Acts and the psychological impact of the methods adopted by the teams in the census enumeration. It concludes with an earnest appeal to the King."[55]

After assessing the situation, the King convened a cabinet meeting which Rizal, a cabinet minister, was not allowed to attend, depriving him of the opportunity to explain himself and to defend the petition he had submitted. Considering Rizal's action, but not that of Bhandari or of the others who assisted him in drawing up the petition, to be a case of lèse-majesté, the cabinet charged him with treason and ordered his arrest.

Those involved in drafting the petition were shocked by Rizal's arrest because the King had previously insisted that RAC members should be free to criticize government policy without fear of retribution. Rule 11 of the Rules and Regulations of the RAC provided that "the Royal Advisory Council will observe the activities of the Government officials, including that of His Majesty the King and report any activity which in its view seems to be in the disinterest of the Kingdom...."[56]

"Rizal was reportedly humiliated and tortured for three days under the personal supervision of Dago Tshering, at that time the Deputy Home Minister. Although pardoned by the King three days after his arrest, Rizal was at the same time coerced into signing a confession,"[57] and agreed not to meet with more than three persons at the same time.

Finding himself under continuous and close scrutiny in Bhutan, he left for exile in Nepal later in the year to found and lead the People's Forum for Human Rights (PFHR) to address the human rights situation in Bhutan. Rizal also began to contact other political leaders, notably Subash Ghising, the head of the Gorkha National Liberation Front in Darjeeling.

Subsequently, in November 1989, he was handed back to Bhutan through the official co-operation of the Kingdom of Nepal, but without any judicial process. He and five others were accused of organizing a campaign of violent civil disobedience and held in solitary confinement and in shackles for 20 months. The five others were later released, but Rizal remained in detention.

He was tried in 1993 on charges including treason and sowing communal discord between different communities. After a ten-month trial he was sentenced to life imprisonment. The King announced that Tek Nath Rizal would be pardoned once the problem of the people in the refugee camps was resolved.[58] As of September 2005, this resolution has not yet happened, but Tek Nath Rizal has been released.

A detailed discussion of the origins and development of the refugee crisis that developed as a result of the political unrest in southern Bhutan initiated by Rizal's PFHR is beyond the scope of this study. In the words of a recent Amnesty International Report, "More than 100,000 Bhutanese refugees, an estimated one-sixth of the population of Bhutan, have been living in camps in south-eastern Nepal since the early 1990s when they were arbitrarily stripped of their nationality and forcibly expelled from Bhutan in one of the largest ethnic expulsions in modern history."[59]

It can be argued that the initial humiliation and three-day episode of torture of Tek Nath Rizal has opened a Pandora's box of political violence and disruption in Bhutan and Nepal that continues to this day. Furthermore, the evidence of human rights judicial activity in Britain, Senegal, Chad, Chile, Spain, Mexico and Belgium suggests there are international legal implications for those involved in Bhutan.

The second point to be made has to do with the "contagion"[60] of torture. A common moral argument for a deontological norm is the so-called slippery slope or "wedge argument." Commonly misunderstood as an argument of prediction that A will lead to B, an analysis of the history of the slippery slope syndrome shows us that it is primarily an argument about the *logic* of justification.

Do the principles of justification now used to justify the use of torture already justify *in advance* further use of it in terms of political expediency?[61] If a community permits a prevailing norm to be broken in one case, this will lead to an ever more extensive moral impasse. For this reason, the rule must be absolute and allow for no exceptions.

The slippery slope argument is not a prognostication on the moral future, but rather the conviction that the logic of the original exception to the norm can be applied to any number of other situations that have a taxonomical similarity to the first one.

This seems to be the case in Bhutan where state-sponsored torture used in one political situation has been used later in another, similar case.

In 1997, a popular movement began in eastern Bhutan led by members of the Druk National Congress (DNC). The DNC, begun in 1994 by Rongthong Kuenley Dorji, has since campaigned for human rights in eastern Bhutan and demanded a democratic system of government. Amnesty International reports that the human rights violations include arbitrary arrest without charge or trial, incommunicado detention and the torture or ill treatment of ten people in August 1997. Among these are three farmers, three monks, a village religious co-ordinator (*gomchen*), a shopkeeper and two businessmen.[62] These arrests were apparently part of a wider crackdown on DNC sympathizers by the Royal Bhutan Police.

The founder of the DNC, and since 1997 the leader of the United Front for Democracy, a coalition of political parties in exile including those of the Nepali-speaking community, Rongthong Kuenley Dorji was tortured by members of the Royal Bhutan Bodyguards after his arrest on charges of treason in 1991. He claims he was subjected to the torture called *chepuwa*. He was submerged in a drum full of water until he nearly drowned. His body was also beaten with sticks and fists. He left Bhutan that year after being pardoned by the King and went to Nepal to seek political asylum. The UN High Commissioner for Refugees considers him a person of concern. In April 1998 he was detained in India while Bhutan attempted to extradite him.[63] Partly due to international pressure by Amnesty International and other human rights organizations, this effort has thus far proved unsuccessful.

The phenomenon of torture contagion appears in the history of many countries over the last 50 years. The discussion has focussed on Bhutan rather than Argentina, Uruguay, Chile, El Salvador, or Guatemala because it is not a place where one would expect to find evidence of an outbreak of the contagion. In addition to the risk of contagion, other reasons why torture is wrong include its injustice, its cruelty, and the fact that its victims can become transformed into political opponents of the regime that tortures.

Despite these and other reasons, torture continues throughout the world. Even in countries like Canada, the United States, and Britain that are officially opposed to it, torture under certain circumstances remains a constant temptation. The theological reason for this ongoing problem with torture would seem to be the one proposed by St. Augustine: the universal presence of original sin.

The late Bishop Sergio Mendez Arceo of Cuernavaca, Mexico, used to say in his homilies, "The desire for human power over others is demonic, the clearest manifestation of original sin." Given its long history and present reality, one can, with St. Augustine and Tertullian, ask moral questions about those who are responsible for torture and about those who perform it. Can even torturers, such as those working in the Argentine version of hell on earth, be saved?

4

Torturers

I hate violence ... I affirm that the terrible experience of having inflicted it on others gives me the right to hate torture. To accept torture, even to approve of it and to impose it is not ultimately difficult. It is sufficient to be convinced that the cause you espouse is just, that the action being undertaken is indispensable and that because of this the end justifies the means. One is not born a torturer.—Anonymous torturer[1]

Thanks to the term *homo sacer*, coined by the second-century CE Roman grammarian Sextus Pompeius Festus, we can understand better that the institution, practice and injustice of torture have a long history. Government-sponsored Central and South American torturers and their paramilitary collaborators kidnapped or caused to "disappear" those they wished to remove from the community in the 1970s and 1980s.[2] In the late 1960s, Greek military police selected and trained candidates to become torturers. This chapter will examine not only the harm done by torturers, but the harm that engaging in this practice does to the one who tortures.

The tortured one as *homo sacer*

The ancient Romans created a quasi-legal category called *homo sacer*, sacred man. In his 20-volume abridgment of the otherwise lost treatise by Marcus Verrius Flaccus, *De significatu verborum* ("On the Significance of Words"), Festus tells us that Roman law granted to the plebeians the right to pursue to the death (singly or collectively) someone whom they as a group had condemned.[3]

This irregular death was not precisely homicide, or punishment, or sacrifice, since, unlike capital punishment, it was to be carried out without benefit of the rituals of purification. Such a person for the ancient Romans was *sacer* in the sense of cast out, or utterly abandoned, a meaning more ancient than the connotation of "sacred," which emerged from the specific sending forth connected with sacrifice.[4]

Although exact numbers are still in dispute, about 30,000 persons in Argentina were relegated to the status of *homo sacer* during the Dirty War between 1976 and 1983. Suspected of subversion by the leaders of the military junta then ruling the country after their *coup d'état* in 1976, victims were kidnapped from the streets, from churches or from their homes, tortured in one of 340 secret concentration camps, and made to disappear, often by being thrown naked, drugged, but still alive, from airplanes into the Atlantic Ocean. These victims of torture came to be known as "the missing," or *desaparecidos*.

The British philosopher Ronald Dworkin describes *Nunca Más* ("Never Again"), the testimony of the Sábato Commission convened after the return of democracy to Argentina, as "a report from hell." In his introduction, Dworkin writes about *Nunca Más*,

> Its story has two themes: ultimate brutality and absolute caprice. People taken off the streets were driven to one of the many detention centers established by each of the military services, and sometimes transferred from one of these to another. Their houses were looted and their property stolen. Most of them lived the rest of their lives in the detention centers, hooded or blindfolded, forbidden to talk to one another, hungry, living in filth. The center of their lives – dominating the memories of those who survived – was torture.[5]

It is difficult to convey in words what went on in Argentina during those terrible times. Perhaps one of the most poignant accounts is found in File 2819, the testimony of a man imprisoned in the army's Campo de Mayo, describing a fellow detainee who represents in a dramatic way the abandonment of the *homo sacer*:

> We prisoners were made to sit on the floor with nothing to lean against from the moment we got up at six in the morning until eight in the evening when we went to bed. We spent fourteen hours a day in that position…. We couldn't utter a word, or even turn our heads. On one occasion, a companion ceased to be included on the interrogators' list and was forgotten. Six months went by, and they only realized what had happened because one of the guards thought it strange that the prisoner was never wanted for anything and was always in the same condition…. The guard told the interrogators, who decided to "transfer" [kill] the prisoner that week, as he was no longer of any

interest to them. This man had been sitting there, hooded without speaking or moving, for six months, awaiting death.[6]

Faced with such outrages, aware of grieving relatives who continued to hope years later that their loved one was still alive, moral theology must content itself with inarticulate, albeit sincere, expressions of condemnation. That said, there should be no room for moral equivocation on the institutionalized practice of torture.

Among the reasons why the use of torture as a technique of interrogation and state-terror must be condemned is that torture attempts to disintegrate and consequently annihilate the psychic and moral personality of the victim. This non-physical destruction of the person can have a lasting impact on those who survive.

Because of the absolute pre-eminence of human dignity, the rational freedom of the human person as created by God can never be sacrificed for the good of a social or religious system, or for any other perceived good. This dignity is autonomous in the face of any juridical institution or community imperative.[7] The theoretical purpose of any social movement, including the "Process for National Reorganization," the Argentinean junta's program to re-educate socialists and secular humanists during the latter part of the twentieth century, should be the welfare of all individuals in it. For the sake of argument, even if belonging to a left-wing political group were immoral or criminal, kidnapping, torture and extra-judicial homicide are not options open to those who disagree with socialists or communists.

The harm done by torture to the torturers

Part of the evil of the system of torture is what it does to the torturers. The torturer, too, undergoes a moral violation if he conceives of his victim as being without human dignity. This moral choice and his practicing of torture strip him of his own God-given nobility. In his introduction of the Catholic equivalent of Nunca Más for Brazil's period of state-sponsored counter-insurgency and state-sanctioned torture, Cardinal Arns of São Paulo quotes a Brazilian general's observation that "Whoever tortures once becomes changed as a result of the demoralization he has inflicted upon others. Whoever repeats torture four or more times becomes a beast."[8]

Despite this view, the intent of this chapter is to hold out hope for the possibility of salvation even for torturers. What this means is that, even though a person deliberately inflicts pain and horror upon another human, he might have made a fundamental commitment to God, thereby living a life of grace and forgiveness. This perspective on the fundamental possibility that even a torturer might make a basic option for God and his neighbour will raise certain questions about the black-and-white certitude of the Brazilian general about the individual status before God of those whose work is violence. This basic fundamental option for God and neighbour means a person is good in a sense that will be more fully explained later. The torturer is someone deeply involved in an evil system, someone who performs immoral actions within it. He himself may not be an evil person.

What follows should be read within the context of the whole book. The chapter is not meant to lull the reader into moral equivocation. However, the actual situations that prevailed in Latin America during the second half of the twentieth century give new meaning to the traditional categories of invincible ignorance and the obligation of following one's certain conscience, even when it is, objectively speaking, erroneous. Those involved in inflicting torture on behalf of their state's security may have pursued a defective good derived from their ideology and obedience to the orders they were given.

The moral obligation to follow one's conscience

For this reason it is important at this point to revisit some elements of the Catholic theological tradition. An example of this tradition would be the fact that Thomas Aquinas (1225–74) disagreed with the revered moralist of his age, Master Peter Lombard (1095–1160), on the question of whether or not one is always obliged to follow one's conscience.

"Here the Master is wrong" (*hic magister falsum dicit*), said the young Aquinas in a lecture that was eventually published.[9] "Lombard had argued that one is not always obliged to follow one's conscience; Thomas responded that one ought to die rather than go against one's conscience."[10]

Because this is accepted in Catholic theology, great importance is placed on the process of conscience formation. "Curiously, Thomas did not call the person 'good' who despite striving to know the right followed an erroneous conscience; rather, Thomas argued that such a person is 'excused' from blame."[11] This Thomistic position is the approach preferred with respect to certain torturers.

By and large, democratic governments in countries such as Argentina, Guatemala, Chile, and Peru that have undertaken a reconciliation process after the restoration of democracy and human rights following counter-insurgency oppression by military regimes have agreed with St. Thomas with respect to the actual torturers.

Perhaps this is because most of the Central and South American torturers, their supervisors and superiors as well as their victims, were Catholic. In the midst of what was perceived to be a widespread and continent-wide Communist insurgency, bishops and priests did not consistently engage in the formation of the consciences of the military or vigorously promote the official Catholic position on human rights as articulated at Vatican II and elsewhere by the teaching office of the Church. A subsequent chapter will argue in detail that the failure of some prelates and chaplains to inform the consciences of their subjects led to human rights abuses in Central and South America. This was a lost opportunity because the military dictators in Argentina and in other countries presented their project as defending the values of Catholic Christianity from atheism; they expected and, by and large, received both tacit and open support from other Catholics. As a result, torturers and kidnappers did not receive the moral guidance concerning human rights they both needed and deserved.

To this must be added the social complexities of the elite and secretive units to which they belonged in their military or paramilitary organizations, the methods of their recruitment, indoctrination, and the training and lifestyle of torturers. All of this suggests we can distinguish their wrong conduct from their ostensibly good motivation. Before discussing the role of the erroneous conscience in moral theology, we must ask a prior question about whether or not each of us is a potential torturer.

Biblical grounds for non-condemnation of torturers

There are both theological and psychological reasons for answering this question affirmatively. The theological basis is that each of us is a redeemed and forgiven sinner who, without the ongoing assistance of God's Holy Spirit, is capable, in theory at least, of committing any and all moral evil and sin.[12] The actual position at the moment of our moral superiority over torturers is an undeserved gift of divine grace.

As a religious thought experiment, let us substitute for the immoral activity described in the first chapters of Romans that of torturing others, and consider the teaching of St. Paul in this light. After leading us into a "rhetorical trap"[13] in his description of moral turpitude, St. Paul turns the tables on his readers by saying, "What then? Are we any better off? No, not at all; for we have already charged that all, both Jews and Greeks, are under the power of sin" (Romans 3:9). He goes on to say, "Since all have sinned and fall short of the glory of God, they are now justified by his grace as a gift, through the redemption that is in Christ Jesus, whom God put forward as a sacrifice of atonement by his blood, effective through faith" (Romans 3:21-25). The theological artistry of the Apostle leads us to condemn those involved in immoral practices; he then calls on his readers to examine their consciences with regard to the ways in which their own practices have contradicted the moral law. Similarly, it is easy to be self-righteous with respect to Argentinean torturers until one personally appropriates the saving truth of salvation in Jesus Christ.

Psychological grounds for non-condemnation

If texts such as these don't challenge our feelings of moral advantage over torturers and our need to join them in asking God for forgiveness, a thoughtful consideration of the implications of the 1961 Yale University obedience experiments by Stanley Milgram[14] as well as the 1973 experiments by Philip Zimbardo[15] and others should give us pause in our comfortable confidence that we could never do what the dirty warriors did in the Argentine. These experiments on American university students playing the role of prison guards demonstrate that people obey under pressure.

Psychological evidence suggests that most individuals who follow orders to inflict pain and suffering on others within accepted institutional settings are ordinary, and that such evil is "banal"[16] and understandable within the circumstances of the context in which it is committed. When individuals who are predisposed to obedience find themselves in situations where they are ordered to commit atrocious acts, and when the moral struggle involved in committing these acts is reduced through training or ideological convictions, the possibility exists that they will become inflictors of pain.

Milgram showed convincingly that people unlikely to be cruel in the ordinary conditions of life would administer pain if they were told to do so by someone in authority. "A substantial proportion of people," Milgram wrote, "do what they are told to do, irrespective of the content of the act and without limitations of conscience, so long as they perceive that the command comes from a legitimate authority."[17] In Milgram's study, white-coated authority figures directed adult Americans to inflict a series of electrical shocks on other people. Subjects were told that the purpose of the experiment was to study the effects of punishment on learning.

As a matter of fact, no real shock was administered, although the subjects did not know this. The victims were actors, but the people inflicting the apparent punishment did not know this. Of the subjects, 65 per cent obediently used what they believed were dangerously high shock levels when the experimenter told them to do so. The closer they were physically to their victims, the less likely they were to administer what they thought were high shock levels. However, 30 per cent continued to administer such dangerous shocks even when they were in physical contact with their victims.

Other researchers later confirmed Milgram's results and further reported subjects responded similarly regardless of age, political party, religion, gender, or nationality.[18] No study to date has explained the difference between the least obedient and most obedient individuals.

Haney, Banks and Zimbardo studied normal, healthy American Stanford University students, whom they subjected to daily simulations in which they played the role of prison guards. These students became ever more aggressive and abusive as their experience continued in the prison situation; they insulted and bullied students who simulated the roles of prisoners. All the subjects involved willingly took on the roles assigned to them.

In both Milgram's experiment and in the Haney, Banks and Zimbardo research, one of the subjects reported that they felt they had incurred an obligation when they accepted money, which helped to explain their commitment to the protocol of inflicting pain on others. Despite this, they experienced intense strain when they committed their actions in close contact with their victims.

These studies remain controversial within the discipline of social psychology; during these simulation studies, Milgram and Zimbardo themselves intentionally caused pain in their actual research subjects, who experienced immense discomfort later when they tried to make sense of what they had done. The researchers conducted their studies under institutional auspices for what they believed was a good reason: the desire to understand the conditions under which human beings could learn to behave in ways abhorrent even to themselves.[19] The ethical issue at stake was the obligation of all researchers to "do no harm."

The education of torturers in Greece

The apparently good end that seems to justify the unethical means was the ostensible justification for the training program developed for torturers in Greece during the military dictatorship between 1967 and 1973. This program was deliberately and skilfully designed to destroy any conscientious qualms of its students against the infliction of torture. While no external circumstances can offer someone impunity for violations perpetrated against others, still the formation program carefully designed for Greek torturers suggests they were willing victims as well as victimizers.

After the fall of the Greek military regime in 1974, two public trials of torturers took place in Greece, offering us a rare picture of the ways in which torturers were selected and trained in the Greek military police.[20] Until the "truth and reconciliation process" undertaken in various countries towards the end of the twentieth century, actual torturers, as opposed to those who gave them their orders, have enjoyed some measure of legal immunity. Mika Haritos-Fatouros followed the Greek trials closely and then interviewed a selection of sixteen willing subjects whose cases had emerged in the courtroom.

Drafted into the military at the age of eighteen, candidates for EAT-ESA (the chief military location for torture in Greece) from KESA (the training centre for military police cadets) were selected even before they entered the military training camp. In addition to physical strength, the main criterion for the selection of an EAT-ESA candidate was their own and their family's political beliefs and attitudes concerning the military regime and their anti-communist feelings and attitudes. From the very beginning, it was important they have a negative attitude toward their potential future victims of torture.

The former torturer Michaelis Petrou summarized the selection process as follows:

> The most important criterion was that you had to keep your mouth shut. Second, you had to show aggression. Third, you had to be intelligent and strong. Fourth, you had to be "their man," which meant that you would not report on the others serving with you,

that [the officers] could trust you and that you would follow their orders blindly.[21]

Systematic efforts were made to bind them to authority and to the subgroup of torturers. This began with an initiation rite upon arrival at the KESA training camp. After an initial beating in the vehicles taking the recruits to the camp and upon arrival

recruits were asked to swear allegiance to the totemic-like symbol of authority used by the junta, promising, on their knees, faith to their commander-in-chief and to the revolution. Thereafter, the binding ideas that they "belonged" to their commanding officers and that the junta officials were "gods" to be obeyed were continuously pressed upon them.[22]

Binding them to the group, the army military police corps, and later to the subgroup of torturers, happened in various ways. For instance, the members of the subgroup of torturers at EAT-ESA used a jargon of their own which helped give them their identity. Language played an important role. For security reasons, they used nicknames and they often gave nicknames to prisoners as well. They gave particular names to each of the different methods of torture. Most characteristic was the way they spoke of all people who were not part of their group as "the outside world."

Throughout the basic and advanced training of the recruits at KESA and EAT-ESA there was a systematic application of a particular learning model intended to inculcate behavioural change. Obedience without question to an order without logic was the way that recruits were prepared to carry out orders for acts of cruelty. Accordingly, the Greek servicemen were forced to perform degrading and illogical acts such as eating grass and making love to their kit-bags and screaming at the same time.

A reward and punishment method further diminished the recruits' uneasiness about torture. Among the rewards offered to willing torturers were relaxed military rules after the training was completed; torturers were often not punished for leaving camp, for instance, without permission. They were allowed to wear civilian clothes, to keep their hair long, and to use military cars for personal use. Torturers were frequently given a leave of absence after they forced a confession from a prisoner. Economic benefits included free bus rides and restaurant meals. Punishment consisted of constant harassment, threats and punishment for disobedience.[23]

The servicemen were gradually desensitized to the idea of torture in two ways. First, they had to endure torture as if it were an everyday, normal act. They had a daily routine of being forced to run to exhaustion, fully equipped, and to suffer beatings at the same time. "We had to learn to love pain," said one of Haritos-Fatouros' subjects.[24]

Second, an effort was made to desensitize them to the act of torture in order to eliminate the anxiety that might arise. Torturer candidates were closely observed and ten to fifteen out of the 100 servicemen at EAT-ESA were selected for the Persecution Section, which was solely responsible for providing torturers.[25]

Training in the Persecution Section included the following: the servicemen were first brought into contact with prisoners by carrying food to them and "occasionally" were ordered to "give the prisoner some blows."[26] The next step was to place them as guards in the detention rooms where they watched others torturing prisoners; they would occasionally take part in the "standing-ordeal" during which they had to beat the prisoner (on the legs mainly) every time he moved. The final step, the "chrism" of the chief torturer, i.e., the prison-warder, was announced suddenly to the servicemen by the commander-in-chief without leaving the prison warder any time for reflection.

Model learning was also used. Older servicemen flogged and degraded the freshmen, in preparation for the recruits' task of torturing that was soon to follow. Negative and positive reinforcement were used to maintain the behaviour of torturers once it had been learned. For instance, they trusted no one and spied on each other. Said one: "There were always two servicemen torturing a prisoner so that one would spy on the other and the officers spied on both, through the hole on the door of the cell."[27] During their trial, one of the accused torturers said, "With this training, they were aiming to turn us into blind agents of their paranoic intentions."[28]

The Greek example illustrates how the ability to torture can be taught. Similar techniques are found in military training all over the world when the intent is to teach soldiers to kill or perform other repellent acts. "They were never told why a particular person was tortured or what he had done; in some cases they even ignored his name."[29]

Christian moral theology has struggled long and hard to establish whether one could engage in such training and subsequent military service "in good conscience." A distinction must be made between routine military training and the training of torturers. A reluctant "yes" has been given down through the centuries to the former, moral condemnation to the latter.

The ordinary operation of torturers in Brazil

Mika Haritos-Fatouros and Philip Zimbardo established a research project on torturers in Brazil.[30] One of their subjects, Eduardo, took comfort in the fact he did not actually torture anyone. He was a police bureaucrat who learned how to keep parts of his various jobs separate. Steadfastly maintaining that his "job was just to look for information," Eduardo did not recognize that the information he collected and the arrests he and his team made led to his captives being tortured by others.[31]

This bureaucratic separation of repressive work is a significant way moral responsibility can seemingly be divorced from responsibility for any violent outcome.[32] Even when a civil servant like Eduardo assumed personal responsibility for his actions, he presented them as thought they were carried out by a separate and distinct professional self; in referring to the Nazi doctors in the Second World War death camps, Robert Jay Lifton called this "doubling" the self, the "Faustian bargain."[33] "One is always ethically responsible for Faustian bargains," wrote Lifton, "a responsibility in no way abrogated by the fact that much doubling takes place outside of awareness."[34]

Haritos-Fatouros and Zimbardo discovered that their subjects constructed certain stories or narratives about torture. At least five can be identified:

(1) diffusing responsibility into organizational, social, or cultural contexts: "In Brazil they are used to this kind of behaviour – like torture. The Catholic Church tortured people for years and years";
(2) portraying perpetrators as *uniquely* bad apples: "The police who are more identified with [torture are] very cold by nature...very aggressive";
(3) demonizing victims: "They were tortured because they were stupid," "thieves and assailants...deny things so cynically that if a policeman ... doesn't have a certain balance, he'll slap him around a little";
(4) advancing a just cause to explain their violence: "We worked as if at war. We were patriots...defending our country...We were a religious people, a Christian people"; and

(5) cloaking violence in professional and organizational mandates: "To kill [properly], you can't [just]react ... you have to act with reason."[35]

Decoding these stories and metaphorical narratives requires studying omissions, contradictions, characterizations of others, legitimations of violence, and how responsibility is assigned. In addition, one needs to distinguish between torturers, state murderers and assassins as different functional specialties with a division of labour. An interesting foundation for the moral calculus of the subjects of the study by Haritos-Fatouros and Zimbardo was that torture had to be kept operationally distinct from murder: torturers who did their jobs properly should not kill, and killers should not dirty themselves with torture.[36]

Torturers must develop a consciously manipulative emotional relationship with their victims, treating them as individuals without feeling empathy for them. And torturers need to master techniques for securing information quickly and skillfully without killing the victim. They must see each torture subject as part of an incomplete process in which the victim at best provides only some of the information needed to achieve the stated goal. Within an atrocity dynamic, the torturer's work is relatively slow and methodical, whereas the murderer's is often quick and spontaneous. A torturer's work is never done, but the killer's is provisionally accomplished each time someone is murdered. Killers must learn to see potential victims as aggregated, dangerous and faceless "others" to be eliminated reflexively – nothing personal, just business. Victims are seen as having nothing more to offer the social control system: killing them is the necessary terminus and appropriate outcome of the murderer's work.[37]

The Brazilian general's comment to Cardinal Arns about the serial atrocity perpetrator becoming a beast seems to be related to his socialization within a team or organization where he has worked out his proper emotional and operational role. It also has to do with his learning how to cope with the negative moral residue arising from committing or watching atrocity. The beast has settled into his proper role in the system.

The insular and secret world of the specialized atrocity organization or squad enables the functionaries to become morally separated from the consequences of their behaviour.[38] When a country like Brazil or Argentina considers itself to be in the middle of a national security emergency, members of its military and police forces believe they enjoy almost total impunity since they are engaged in waging their government's war.

In the words of a former São Paulo regional police commander, General Ustra: "We all lived in a race against time and against the unknown. Speed was vital...to discover and neutralize [terrorist] actions that could cause deaths and great material damage."[39] Two officials working for the Brazilian paramilitary police (DOPS), who perceived themselves as fighting for an ideology, described their deeds as good and themselves as heroic:

> We worked as if at war. We were patriots, we were defending our country, we were proud of that, so they were adversaries, the enemy. We were proud of what we did...working in DOPS ... [and] ridding the country of a threat, of a Communist regime .... [We were] people doing a patriotic job, a big job, an important job.... We were religious people, a Christian people. If I arrest someone who has kidnapped a little girl who might be killed in four hours, I'm not going to waste time by questioning him for two or three days just to wear him down. So...I'll hang that guy up [on the parrot's perch], work him over, and he'll tell me in five minutes.[40]

Ideology and motivation provide one set of moral entitlements to torture. Another set of explanations assigns blame for atrocities on other people or factors. For example, one participant asserted that "it was shocking...the first time to see someone hanging on the parrot's perch with a water hose in his mouth. I didn't agree with that, but I was inside the room and the [other] guys were [torturing him]."[41]

Another version of the diffusionist strategy is to place responsibility for violence on sociocultural conditions: "Living in an aggressive environment affects you, contaminates you little by little, without you feeling it," said one.[42] Another expressed the following opinion: "Brazil is a Catholic country. In Brazil they are used to this kind of behavior – like torture, for example, because Catholic churches tortured people for years and years, centuries and centuries."[43]

"Good" police torturers were reckoned morally by their peers to be rational and trained professionals who had a clear knowledge of their limits and were being directed by a rational superior officer. Under such circumstances and within the ethics of their guild, torture was legitimate for fighting a just cause and for professionally interrogating bad suspects. Within this paradigm, the good torturer's violence was justified by organizational or ideological necessity, or as guided by a rational mind. A torturer belonging to the elite arm of the French military combating the FLN insurgency in Algeria,[44] the CCI, said he was never interested in breaking people and took no pleasure in their suffering. Having seen the terrible experience people go through under torture, he hated torture itself.[45]

"Bad" police torturers, on the other hand, illegitimately used violence for pleasure. They were deliberately sadistic, habitually lacked self-control, or tortured under the influence of drugs, or alcohol, or for dishonest economic ends.[46]

The conventional morality of professionalism was the basis the police and military professionals in mid-twentieth century Algeria and Brazil used to decide the acceptability, accessibility, or unacceptability of gross human rights violations. The contemporary teaching of the Catholic Church seemed to play no part. The Church's past practices provided justification for using torture. It would seem the consciences of the police and military professionals were uninformed and they had erroneously established what the dictates of right reason or natural law told them to do.

Can we describe torturers religiously as good people?

Normally we describe people who perpetrate wrong actions as evil, and those who do right actions as good. We thereby combine two different evaluations of conduct into one. Over the past 30 years some Catholic moral theologians have distinguished between two different descriptions: an action is called wrong (as opposed to right), and a motivation is called good (as opposed to bad). An important question then is whether or not a wrong action can be good. Can erroneous conduct resulting from the dictates of conscience enable us to describe such persons as good rather than excusing them from blame as Thomas Aquinas expressed it? The Catholic moral tradition has discussed this question at length, albeit not in connection with torture, and has various opinions on what it calls the problem of the erroneous conscience.

The meaning of goodness in this context is the moral motivation of a person who acts out of love. Goodness describes moral motivation or moral effort. Normally a loving person tries to do what is right for another person, and so goodness is not inseparable from rightness, and our penchant to identify them can be explained by the fact that in this we are following our common sense.

A good person does not simply try to be good, but rather actually lives and acts in an ethical manner. There is a link between them, and this means that goodness requires that we make an effort to live and act not according to our own wishes, but according to the rational standards of our community.

The problem arises when these supposedly rational standards are found in the midst of a Communist insurgency, or in an age of heresy, or terrorism, and teach an individual that torture can and should be judiciously or professionally used despite the fact that this practice stands condemned as a violation of human rights, either at that time or later in history, by the wider human community.

A person striving for right in a particular historical epoch or social setting may not, therefore, actually attain it. Rightness describes whether a person's conduct attains the moral standards set by the wider world community. A number of Catholic moral theologians would maintain the distinction between goodness and rightness, and would also add that, to call a person good, it need not be the case that the person's conduct is objectively right. Striving out of love for the right describes a good person, but to call a person good, that person's conduct does not need to be right; "Yes, a wrong action can be called good when a person acts out of love but errs."[47]

Two descriptions can be made regarding the moral life that is captured by the distinction between goodness and rightness. Though distinctive, these descriptions are not completely separable.

A person can be right and bad, or wrong and good. Goodness describes someone who strives for rightness, but is separate from the question of whether one attains rightness.[48] That having been said, if goodness did not aim for rightness, then it would be nothing more than private and narcissistic justification. The person may be good, but act badly. Goodness does not lend itself to moral or legal observation, but is the thing that matters most of all.

The case of Alfredo Astiz in Argentina

In Argentina today, these theoretical considerations are being debated in a practical way as they apply to the case of the recently retired naval officer Alfredo Astiz. In her book *Children of Cain: Violence and the*

Violent in Latin America, Tina Rosenberg ironically entitles her chapter devoted to Astiz "The Good Sailor."

In May 1976, shortly after the military coup, Task Force 3.3.2 of the Argentine navy was born. Along with others, including Ricardo Miguel Cavallo, Astiz joined it at age 25. A recent graduate of the naval academy, he was stationed in Mar del Plata, a resort centre and naval base near Buenos Aires where he learned how to raid buildings, follow suspects and infiltrate suspicious groups, all in aid of prosecuting the war against subversion.

Working in the famous task force was the fulfillment of a dream. In January 1977, Astiz came to the navy's *Escuela Mecánica* (an Engineering Academy known as the ESMA) in Buenos Aires as a member of the operations department. He was good at his job.

During the Dirty War, squads of low-level officers like Astiz and Cavallo, with stable memberships of ten to fifteen, conducted the kidnapping, interrogation, torture, sustained detention, and murder of those whose files they received from their superiors. These files contained information about the person's guerrilla connections.

A settled division of labour developed. Each squad was associated with a detention centre – in the case of Astiz's unit, the ESMA – and directed its attention against a particular opponent. For the ESMA, this was the Montoneros, by far the largest of the guerrilla groups. Total membership in all the navy death squads was slightly over 300. Of these, roughly 50, not including Astiz, practiced torture on a regular basis. The task of torture fell to those in intelligence, but he frequently watched torture sessions in order to act quickly on new information such sessions might yield.[49] Those who participated in kidnapping generally looted their victims' homes. Again, Astiz did not do so.

Explaining the justification for torture, naval officer Jorge Acosta explained,

> You have to understand how the enemy worked. If by 9:30 p.m. one of the Montoneros did not arrive at his house, his partner [in the organization's cell structure] would take the arms, documents, and money and leave and burn what she could not carry. We'd get there the next day and there'd be nothing left.... We could have captured a guerrilla and not touched him.... But he'd just look at his watch, smile and say, "What time is it?" A few hours and we would have lost....Try combating *that* with the Geneva Convention.[50]

Astiz never seemed to concern himself with the Geneva Convention, or question his orders. "I have the soul of a soldier," said Astiz. "And the first thing they taught me was to obey my superiors."[51] He was deeply sympathetic to the ruling ideas of the Process for National Reorganization, the official creed of the military government. But he did not hold these beliefs with any kind of rabid intensity or fanaticism. He performed his duties imaginatively, enthusiastically, and cheerfully.

Astiz led several operations a day against those who potentially were armed guerrillas. When he was scheduled for a day off, he would ask if any shifts were left uncovered and if there was one, he volunteered to fill it. He quickly acquired autonomy and influence in 3.3.2.[52] He took pride in his technical proficiency. He enjoyed an apparently successful naval career, though his rise through the ranks was neither stellar nor meteoric. At the time of his retirement, forced upon him by public pressure, he held the rank of captain. In many ways Astiz was an ordinary man.

He has never claimed to have felt coerced by his superiors or by the threat of legal sanctions for disobedience to his orders. He has remained unrepentant to the present day, though he has expressed enduring respect for his adversaries.[53] He had personally taken as his own the government's goal of overcoming "subversion," a term understood to include not merely guerrilla violence but much liberal political activity and, in fact, virtually all secular thought.

"A soldier always follows orders," Astiz said, "but an official is a gentleman as well as a soldier, and if he always takes refuge in superiors' orders, he would be betraying the confidence the nation places in him when it entrusts him with its most precious things: the care of its land and the blood of its children."[54]

The depth of Astiz's commitment is apparent in his confession to a former childhood friend: "We have to kill all those who can't be recovered because if two or three stay alive, in a few years the whole dance will start again." Even some of his detainees, with whom Astiz spent much time explaining his views, were convinced of the sincerity of his commitment to the aims of the Dirty War: "He was a kind of 'worthy enemy' for us," one surviving Montonero remarked.[55]

Unlike many other officers, "He wasn't corrupt. He didn't rape. He was fighting subversion and communism, not trying to get rich. His vision was terribly Neanderthal, but he was convinced of what he was doing. He was there to 'save' his country."[56]

When one of his detainees, Sylvia Labayru, had a baby, Astiz personally took her from ESMA to register the infant, presenting himself as her husband. He then offered the child to its grandmother. He escorted another prisoner to visit her dying father and later to the wake. When this prisoner later testified against him at his trial, Astiz felt betrayed, according to his friends.[57]

To the present day Astiz has never disavowed and continues vigorously to affirm his principled commitment to the ideas that inspired the Dirty War. He made them his own; he did not recognize them as evil.

He was not narcissistic. The task of the torturer is especially gratifying to those with narcissistic tendencies. There is no activity other than torture that so effectively allows someone to make one's own whims and desires the absolute focus of the victim's attention. Certain members of squad 3.3.2 clearly displayed such narcissism, for prisoners who broke during torture and whose personalities dissolved under the humiliation of violence and confinement attracted them. Astiz was different. One surviving detainee reported the following about him:

> He had a better relationship with those prisoners who didn't break under torture. Acosta [another squad member] liked the ones who broke; he liked to see people on their knees. Astiz wasn't like that. He had a bad relationship with the collaborators on the Mini-Staff. I remember once Astiz went out to a meeting that was going to take place with a collaborator who was going to identify people. There was a problem and the meeting ended in a shoot-out. The collaborator later said to Astiz, "I was so worried, I thought something had happened to you." Astiz told me about it later. He said, "Four hours ago this man was a great Montonero soldier. Now he's worried about me and not his companeros. He makes my skin crawl."[58]

To the Mothers of the Plaza de Mayo, the well-known Argentine human rights campaigners, and to many others, Astiz is notoriously known as the "blond angel of death" because of the combination of his cherubic good looks and the terrible things for which he is held responsible. He successfully infiltrated this protest group, having convinced them that he was one of "theirs," the brother of a *deasparecido*. He was instrumental in kidnapping three of its founding members including Azucena Villaflor, its principal founder, and two French nuns, Alice Domon and Leonie Duquet, along with seven others after they left Santa Cruz Church in Buenos Aires on December 8, 1977, where they were meeting to collect financial contributions to publish the names of their missing loved ones. He identified the ones to be kidnapped, tortured and then murdered, allegedly by kissing them. A common gesture of greeting or farewell, Astiz's enemies interpret this as a biblical sign of a Judas-like betrayal of innocent persons.

In 1990 France convicted and sentenced Astiz in absentia for the murder of the nuns, claiming the nuns were interrogated "while being tormented" and were later transferred to death flights – planes from which some junta victims were thrown alive. In May 2004 Argentina frustrated attempts to have him extradited by indicting him for the murder of the two nuns. Astiz had been in jail since September 2003, facing possible extradition to France.[59]

There is a second reason why Astiz has international notoriety. Mistaking her for a Montonera guerrilla he was seeking to disappear, Astiz shot and wounded a teenager, Dagmar Hagelin, who was running away while attempting to escape. Paralyzed and confined to a wheel chair, she has since disappeared and is presumed dead. It is reported that Astiz went to see her to apologize for his mistake. Because Dagmar had Swedish citizenship, Sweden has announced it seeks to put him on trial for her murder. An international Interpol arrest warrant hangs over his head.

One might describe Astiz as a Catholic sailor who did hateful things during a crisis in his country's history, but who followed his conscience and sincerely directed his moral life towards what he perceived to be the good; such a description would be controversial for some, a sad truth for others. But if, in principle, this cannot be said about him, then the distinction discussed earlier between wrong actions and good motivations would need to be re-evaluated because it does not apply to torture as a practice or as an institution.

For those who have suffered torture and survived, the most significant and disturbing feature of these theological reflections may be their attempt to do precisely what the Duc de Broglie (1718–1804) warned us to avoid: "We must beware of too much understanding lest we end by too much forgiving."[60]

The Tortured

Sergeant Elpidio Rosario Tejeda, known as *El Tejano* ("Texan")...was....
a specialist He was a mythic figure at the concentration camp of La
Perla (Argentina), a ferocious torturer who delivered his blows with
an appalling micro-exactitude. Texas wore dark glasses and was rarely
seen without his stick. "He knew the limits of human resistance,"
testified Graciela Geuna. "Once after he had beaten me, I managed
to steal a razor blade from the desk. All I wanted was to kill myself,
it was the only way to escape the horror. Texas confiscated it, saying
"You're not going to be able to die, little girl, until we want you to.
We are God here."—Marguerite Feitlowitz[1]

Jean Améry and "losing trust in the world"

Jean Améry, a member of the Belgian Resistance movement who
suffered torture at the hands of the Gestapo, would probably disagree with any positive moral assessment of a torturer's assistant
like Alfredo Astiz. At the height of the Second World War, in June
1942, Heinrich Himmler issued an order authorizing the use of what
he called "the third degree" in interrogations, or torture. The third
degree[2] was to be used to extract confessions from prisoners when
preliminary investigation suggested the possession of useful information, particularly concerning the Resistance:

> The Third Degree in this case may be used only against communists,
> Marxists, Jehovah's Witnesses, saboteurs, terrorists, members of
> resistance movements, antisocial elements, refractory elements, or
> Polish or Soviet vagabonds. In all other cases, preliminary authoriza-
> tion is necessary.[3]

With this decree systemic, quasi-legal, state-sponsored torture
resumed in western Europe. As Améry pointed out, there was now a

fundamental difference between Nazi torture and torture conducted by the Inquisition. There was no longer a theological rationale for it.[4]

> Modern police torture is without theological complicity that, no doubt, in the Inquisition joined both sides; faith united them even in the delight of tormenting and in the pain of being tormented. The torturer believed he was exercising God's justice, since he was, after all, purifying the offender's soul; the tortured heretic or witch did not deny him this right. There was a horrible, perverted togetherness. In present-day torture not a bit of this remains. For the tortured, the torturer is simply the other....[5]

In discussing his own July 1943 experience of torture in Belgium at the hands of the Gestapo, Améry was careful to preface his description of his agony by pointing out that what he went through was by no means the worst experience of torture ever recorded. At the same time he was quite clear that the experience was devastating:[6]

> "Rien n'arrive ni comme on l'espère, ni comme on le craint," Proust writes somewhere. Nothing really happens as we hope it will, nor as we fear it will. But not because the occurrence, as one says, "goes beyond the imagination" (it is not a quantitative question), but because it is reality and not phantasy... Many things do indeed happen approximately the way they were anticipated in the imagination: Gestapo men in leather coats, pistol pointed at their victim – that is correct, all right. But then, almost amazingly, it dawns on one that the fellows not only have leather coats and pistols but also faces: not "Gestapo faces" with twisted nose, hypertrophied chins, pockmarks, and knife scars, as might appear in a book, but rather faces like anyone else's. Plain, ordinary faces. And the enormous perception at a later stage, one that destroys all abstractive imagination, makes clear to us how the plain, ordinary faces finally become Gestapo faces after all, and how evil overlays and exceeds banality. For there is no "banality of evil," and Hannah Arendt, who wrote about it in her Eichmann book, knew the enemy of mankind only from hearsay, saw him only through the glass cage. When an event places the most extreme demands on us, one ought not to speak of banality....[7]

"The first blow brings home to the prisoner," wrote Améry, "that he is *helpless*, and thus it already contains in the bud everything that is to come."[8] He went on to say that the person who is tortured loses his or her human dignity. With the very first blow by the torturer, the survivor of torture loses his or her trust in the world. By trust in the world, Améry includes all sorts of things: the irrational and logically unjustifiable belief in absolute causality perhaps, or the likewise blind belief in the validity of the inductive inference. But more important as an element of trust in the world, and in our context what is solely relevant, is the certainty that by reason of written or unwritten social contracts the other person will spare me – more precisely stated, that he will respect my physical, and with it also my metaphysical, being. The boundaries of my body are also the boundaries of my self. My skin surface shields me against the external world. If I am to have trust, I must feel on it only what I *want* to feel. At the first blow, however, this breaks down. The other person, *opposite* whom I exist physically in the world and *with* whom I can exist only as long as he does not touch my skin surface as border, forces his own corporeality on me with the first blow. He is on me and thereby destroys me. It is like a rape, a sexual act without the consent of one of the two partner.[9]

Torture as a violation of communion

Torture is a violation of our respect for others, a sin against communion. The central idea of Vatican II, communion, is related to trust in the world. The human person is essentially someone created by God for relationships in our world with others and with the Trinity. The theology of communion is grounded in Catholic tradition as well as in sacred scripture. There are also indications it is central to the way our world has evolved.

Charles Darwin mused, in *The Descent of Man*, "The first foundation or origin of the moral sense lies in the social instincts, including sympathy; and these instincts no doubt were primarily gained, as in the case of lower animals, through natural selection."[10] The emergence of our morality through our social instincts is also based on what we know about human psychology.

When a young child begins to crawl and then to walk intentionally toward some object of interest, a very important psychological task is being accomplished. The great Swiss pioneer of child psychology, Jean Piaget (1896–1980), called infant intelligence "sensorimotor" because it is embedded in the world of sensible reflexes.[11] The baby explores his or her world, feeling things, putting various items into her mouth in order to establish at some future point that the outside world and those who cohabit it with her are worthy of trust, that this world is benign and worth living in. Without thought, abstract concepts or language, this practical intelligence of infants makes real only what can be experienced by the senses. The supporting culture around the baby exercises control over him through the person who cares for him or her.

Other psychologists have noted the role of the experience of the senses in building confidence in one's environment. Sigmund Freud designated the first sexual phase as a sensual feeling of the kind of future that the child can expect in his or her world. Similarly, Erik Erikson described the psychodynamic apprenticeship in terms of a basic trust versus a basic mistrust of life. He argued that success in this apprenticeship lays the foundation for the incomparable virtue of hope.[12] "Babies get the feeling that the world is a good or bad place from the nurturing attitude of their immediate family," Erikson says. "Consequently, they feel at ease or anxious, secure or insecure in their world."[13] Perhaps the most invidious effect of torture is that it alters this personal and hard-won confidence in one's world.

Psychological trauma

Psychologists often describe the trauma experienced by survivors of torture as similar to post-traumatic stress disorder (PTSD) and/or major depressive disorder (MDD); there is also a third diagnosis of "enduring personality change after catastrophic experience" in the International Statistical Classification of Diseases and Related Health Problems, 10th Edition (ICD-10). This third paradigm is consistent with Jean Améry's own experience of losing his trust in the world.[14]

Post-traumatic stress disorders arise after natural disasters and as a result of man-made cruelties such as torture. Much PTSD arises as the unintended consequence of human conflict, but it can also be a deliberate and carefully nurtured product of the malicious skill of interrogators and torturers.

One study of PTSD from South Africa done by Paul Davis in 1986 should serve as an example. It involved the experience of 21 detainees whose detention lasted from two weeks to four years; four had been detained more than once. All alleged they had suffered mental and physical abuse, usually early in their detention, including beatings to body and head, using hands, fists, truncheons, sticks, planks and booted feet; electric shocks to ears, nipples, neck, and scrotum; abuse of sexual organs; and near-suffocation manually, with belts or wet canvas bags.

All detainees gave a history of being in solitary confinement for periods of thirteen days to four months; eighteen reported deliberate deprivation of sleep and food, and fourteen described major variation of routine and time disorientation. Periods of uninterrupted interrogation of up to ten hours were reported, often combined with the use of extremely uncomfortable positions such as prolonged standing, crouching, or being naked and shackled.

All suffered from PTSD. All had sleep disturbances such as insomnia, nightmares, night sweats, or early morning awakening; eighteen had significant disturbance of previously sound relationships with spouses, friends, parents and children; eighteen had sexual dysfunctions, including impotence, premature ejaculation and anorgasmia (inability to experience orgasm). Five showed moderate to severe depression after release.[15]

ICD-10 diagnosis is similar, but has more to do with the disruption, even the suicide-inducing destruction, of Third-Order premises. Watzlawick, Beavin, and Jackson have made a useful distinction between First-Order knowledge (direct sense experience), Second-Order knowledge (insights and judgments), and Third-Order knowledge, which is of a higher abstraction, dealing with the attribution of meaning to one's environment.[16] Torture induces the ICD-10 paradigm because it encourages what Barudy has called "repressive ecology" – "a state of generalized insecurity, terror, lack of confidence, and rupture of social relationships."[17] A moral theological study of torture needs to pay special attention to the damage done to Third-Order premises, based upon Third-Order knowledge, because deliberate damage to an individual's sense of meaning of the world is profoundly unethical.

The ICD-10 diagnosis "captures well some of the problems of isolation, emptiness and mistrust which may follow torture."[18] It may co-exist with PTSD in a torture survivor, and is characterized by permanent, usually irreversible, changes, including

- a hostile or mistrustful attitude towards the world;
- social withdrawal;
- feelings of emptiness or hopelessness;
- a chronic feeling of being "on edge," as if constantly threatened;
- estrangement.[19]

Religious trauma: Peter Moen's experience

In keeping with our methodology of recording the lived experience or phenomenon of torture, we will turn our attention to the problems described in ICD-10 as discussed in Peter Moen's diary. Moen came from a devoutly Protestant background. As an adult, he was agnostic with respect to Third-Order religious values. In peacetime Moen had been an actuary with the Idun Life Insurance Company, but he was a member of the Resistance at the time of his arrest on February 3, 1944, as part of a Gestapo "sweep" when the Germans succeeded in breaking up a large component of the clandestine press in Norway.

Moen's arrest took place shortly after the underground leaders had appointed him *pressesjef* – head of all the secret newspapers in the country. Before that he had been the editor of *London Nyatt*, one of the best and most widely circulated illegal papers.

On the day of his arrest he was driven straight to Gestapo head-quarters at Viktoria Terrasse, or "V.T." as he refers to it in his diary, for interrogation and torture. His cell was located in the prison on 19 Møllerg Street in Oslo.

The Gestapo interrogators quickly broke him with their torture, and he told them the names of two of his Resistance contacts. To deal with this trauma he kept a diary where he dutifully recorded his thoughts and feelings. What kept him sane was writing in his diary, his interest in mathematics, his religious explorations based on a re-evaluation of his previous agnosticism and above all, his loving relationship with his then deceased mother and his wife Bella, who was incarcerated at the same time but in a different place. This unique document represents an invaluable record of what it is like to undergo torture and solitary confinement.

From February to September 1944, while Moen was in prison in Oslo, he secretly wrote his diary on sheets of rough, greyish brown toilet paper handed out grudgingly by his guards every day. He used a pin from the cell's blackout curtain. One by one he pricked out letters into the paper until he had a word, then a sentence, then a page. Only in this way could he retain or re-evaluate his Third-Order premises, make some sense of his tortured condition and remain sane.

Finally, when he was of no further use to his interrogators, on September 6, 1944 he was sent with other prisoners to concentration camps in Germany aboard the *Westfalen* and perished when the ship was torpedoed and sunk by an allied submarine.

Moen and most of the prisoners on board drowned, but he had told a survivor the secret of his diary. After the war, it was retrieved from the air duct in his former cell where he had hidden it, and it was published.[20]

From my imprisonment

7th day at Mølergt. 19 (Thursday, February 10)

Have been questioned twice. Was whipped. Betrayed Vic... Am weak. Am worthy of contempt. Am terribly afraid of pain. But not afraid of dying.

I am thinking of Bella tonight. Wept because I have done so much harm to Bella. Bella and I must have a child if I survive.[21]

Among the factors that influence people who undergo coercive interrogation and torture are the fears these traumatic events engender. Menaces and threats are communicated in deed and word by their interrogators/torturers: threats of death and suffering, endless isolation, never getting home again, awful things happening to their family and confreres in the movement, betrayal, disgrace, indefinite continuation of isolation, interrogation, and incarceration. Thanks to Himmler's order, there seemed to be no controls to restrain Moen's Nazi captors. They made use of vague threats, and encouraged him to project his deepest fears into their menace. The effects were anxiety, dread, despair and a willingness to sacrifice long-term interests for relief from these fears.[22]

On the eighth evening, Moen recorded that he tried unsuccessfully to pray but was prevented by his fear and anxiety. Two days later he said he would pray "to my mother's God" if his interrogators resorted to serious ill treatment. He went on to express his guilt for having betrayed Victor and Erik. "I shall never forgive myself. Still I would do it over again under torture."[23]

On the eleventh evening, his birthday, he wrote, "I have prayed to God with tears for Victor and Erik – that they may not suffer and that they may live. I too should like to live. But it is now even more important for me to find a God. If he is to be found only in death ... then I must die. A kiss to you, Bella, on my forty third birthday. Good night, my beloved *belle amie.*"[24]

On the next evening he wrote, "I have knelt and prayed to Father's and Mother's God. I asked for my own and my comrades' lives. I wept.

I am not brave. I am no hero. I can't help it. I am infinitely unhappy. Good night, Bella, *You* will forgive me."[25]

Physical isolation, social isolation, separation from the sustaining presence of others and solitary confinement were alternated with periods of intense stimulation during interrogation sessions. Each amplified the other's impact.

Isolation forces a dependence on the interrogator, fosters concern with the self and one's immediate predicament, impairs coping and amplifies the other factors. Deterioration of complex Third-Order thinking and higher functions are observed and there is a drive for companionship and a desire to talk.

Many torture survivors report they experienced some of their worst anguish in the intervals between torture sessions. For the torturer, each session may last for only a few minutes. For the victim, there is often no break; his or her mental anguish fills up the void between torture sessions.[26]

Four days later, on February 16, Moen returned to his guilt. "I cannot bear my guilt. I should have been 10 times more watchful of the safety of others. Because of apathy and weakness many have to suffer and the free press in Norway is broken. Oh, comrades – I deserve your contempt. Life's fruit is bitter. By God, I cannot help it. I have to cry."[27]

As well, he records the horror going on in the interrogation rooms at Viktoria Terrasse. "It's V.T. that is the great terror. I was strangled – physically and morally for 30 hours over there. I tremble with fear of the next interrogations. They hit you to make you say *more than you know*! But – last night in a dream I received a sign. It said: Do not fear *too much*. You will be let off easier next time. Oh – could I but believe it. Did it come from you, Mother?"[28]

On Sunday, March the fifth, his 31st day in solitary confinement and still enduring torture he wrote, "Fear and anxiety fill my mind this early Sunday morning. Thinking is fatal to hope. I am pessimistic about the future...." Later he continued and mentioned another important survival technique, mental mathematics: "Feel very empty today. Neither fear nor longing has any special hold of me. I have not prayed to God all day. I have speculated on mathematical problems almost without interruption. Much has been cleared up...." The next night, March 6, he underwent a mystical experience:

This is a real experience:
On my cell I caught a glimpse
Of Christ's head – crowned with thorns –
His stilled pain had given way to deep peace
And he seemed to say mutely: all is atoned.
You, God and man, willed to die
And to suffer the bitter pain of innocence!
Did the blood flow less red
In your heart than it does now in mine?
Oh, no – but by the power of your sacrifice
You would stop the suffering of the world
And in your words: It is finished
Give sinners pass to heaven.
Oh, Christ – let me call you
My brother in need and pain!
Show me by your grace the way to salvation
From fear and sin and death!!

Møllegt. 19 Prisoner no. 5842
March sixth, 1944 Peter Moen[29]

Two days later, on March 8, he explained the background to this poem. He wrote that his experience was completely devoid of any exaltation, and had not been provoked by any previous thoughts he had had on Monday. From 7:00 a.m. until about 4:00 p.m. he had been busy with his mathematical problems. The vision itself came as a complete surprise to him, and lasted only one or two seconds. He saw a traditional crucifix of the Catholic Church.

I cannot say any more about this…but the wish and need to take hold of the divine in humanity is in my blood. All the same I cannot see the orthodox truth such as Father and Mother presented it. I pray for true information and experience. Often I just kneel by the bed. I'm dead inside, empty of thoughts and words and feeling. Nothing happens. I'm just alone – but it doesn't really matter. It is good to be alone!!

The only thing which lies like a frightening pressure just behind the emptiness – is Victoria Terrasse. It has changed me – so that I am positively unrecognizable. Perhaps Mother would recognize me. She has seen little Peter afraid before. Mother – pray for me![30]

One might ask whether the values for which Peter Moen lived in taking on the commitment to resist the Nazi tyranny continued to have meaning for him under torture. The answer would be yes. With the hope that his diary would eventually come to light and be read, on

March 15, the tyrant's day of death on the "Ides of March," he wrote
that the world continues to breed one tyrant after another.

"Does this fight pay?" Moen asked. "Yes and yes again. Without
this fight and the victims it exacts, all liberty would soon be strangled.
The fight of the Norwegian home front has brought the 300 of us here
to M. 19. I am not sorry for anything I have written or done; I only
regret what is left undone. There must be people in Nazi prisons. If I
didn't sit here you would – you who are still free."[31]

Moen's patriotism and principled opposition to the Nazis sustained
him in his sufferings and helped him face the prospect of his death in
detention with equanimity, if not with theological hope.

> Gollwitzer (1956) showed, as reflected in final messages and letters,
> that prisoners condemned by the Nazis for various political crimes
> varied in their responses. Those who were able to feel that their
> actions had served to help to defeat the evil regime, managed to
> face death with some calm and even serenity. The most desperate
> anguish was seen in those who had received the death sentence for
> such pathetic offenses as listening to an Allied radio broadcast or
> making some improper comment about Hitler.[32]

Moen's lofty sentiments alternated with expressions of deep
shame and confusion for what had gone on in the V.T. torture rooms.
In this mood he hoped that only his wife Bella would read the diary.
Shakespeare's character Hamlet inspired him with his gallantry and
final courage.

> I should like to be a brave man also. I am not one. I should have let
> the wild beasts at V.T. tear me limb from limb and kept silent – si-
> lent. I could not do it. Fear and pain broke me down. The secrets
> were plucked out of me during a succession of questionings. I am so
> ashamed of this that I have no desire to meet anyone after the war.
> I often think: a death sentence would be best. It would fulfill three
> wishes: my Hamlet wish would come true – I should atone for my
> cowardice and perhaps I should even receive the commemoration:
> He was a gallant man....

> Furthermore: the threat from V.T. hangs over me daily. They can
> come at any time to ask about things I won't tell, or others I don't
> know and then hell breaks loose with the torture that I dread so
> terribly....[33]

Six weeks after his capture, cold and half-starved in solitary confinement, he had finally been able to record in his secret diary what

had happened to him in the torture chamber of Viktoria Terrasse. He could well imagine his friends now describing him as "cracked":

Well, well, that's how it is. When one has stood a whole night in the ice-cold cellar at Viktoria Terrasse with the sweat of fear on one's brow – with one's back flogged by rubber whips and rope as thick as a clenched fist, with one's clothes and body filthy with blood and dirt from the floor and the kicks of heavy boots – then one becomes cracked. I have done it and become so weak in the knees that I bowed then and prayed, "Lord, save me – I perish." I was horribly near suicide then. A broken electric bulb and a cut over the wrist would have done it. I was alone ... no, I was not alone. Something invisible held back my hand.[34]

The thought that he was forgotten haunted him. On March 21, his forty-seventh day in solitary confinement, he wrote:

The fundamental mood is darker and darker. When I think of all the proud dreams of happiness and well being that are hatched here behind the prison walls – then I feel a searing pain somewhere in my soul. I know we will be forgotten – that we are forgotten.... Thousands of Norwegians are imprisoned in Germany. Many, many are dead – some died with sealed lips under torture. They must be remembered. But the suffering of the individual is merged into the total – the common sacrifice.[35]

Incessantly he returned to his performance under interrogation and his guilt for what he had revealed. On March 25, his fifty-first day and still in solitary confinement, he wrote,

My thoughts circle around the interrogation and the persons harmed by my disclosures. It is an intensely painful question – could this or that one have been kept out of it? Unfortunately I was frightened into talking too much the first day. They were "fiendish" in the true sense of the word – their cruelty and threats were enough to freeze a fellow's blood. Another factor was the large number of those rounded up. I was not the only one involved in the matters upon which we were questioned the first day. It was impossible to cover up either my part or that of others. Then terror tipped the scales. I writhe under these infamous questions. They are the moral equivalent of the old instrument of torture known as the "Spanish rack" by which a man was pulled out longer than his length. Then I'm lying there tortured and unable to free either my arms or legs....[36]

Despite his earlier mystical vision his prayer life is unsatisfactory on April 6, after 63 days in captivity.

> I tried sincerely to pray to God early this morning. After a few sentences I felt empty within – quite desolate. I had a definite impression of talking into a vacuum. Now let me put the question like this: What do you really expect from prayer? To that I'll say: As true as prayer is contact with the divine I expect it to give me an increase of spiritual strength and to impart it in a spiritually understandable or at least perceptible manner. When – after a long period of sincere prayer – *nothing* happens and the prayer seems like an insult to God – because I do not believe in him – what then?
>
> Should I continue to pray?
>
> That is the counsel of experience.[37]

The next day, Good Friday, Moen heard the screams of one of his fellow prisoners in mental agony:

> …a succession of screams rang through the stillness of the Good Friday afternoon. They came from below and still continue. They are obviously colored by a kind of explosive despair and hysteria. He screamed very loud and it took several minutes before he was calmed down. I hear the guard on my floor remarked: *"Der ist blöde"* ("He is stupid").
>
> It's someone who couldn't take it any longer. He went to pieces. The fear of ill-treatment at V.T. – despair over what *has* happened and what *was* said – the continuing fear of being forced to make new "denunciations" – the loneliness – the longing for home – wife – children and friends – the fear of death – pain – shame – grief – worry – impotent hate – all this while the Easter bells ring over a sunlit city … it *must* be screamed out of a tortured body and a tormented soul.
>
> Good Friday, 1944.[38]

On Friday, May 19, Peter Moen was released from solitary captivity to rejoin the general prison population.

> These 75 days will always stand out for me in a strange light. There were days filled with a mood of intense crisis… With a sad sigh I must state that the experiment gave a negative result. I found no anchor-ground for faith or conviction of anything divine speaking to me or in me. I found the wish for its existence is quite explicable from the point of self-preservation and egotism…No truth is found outside man. Everything originates with man himself and that includes all thoughts and feelings concerning "God."[39]

Elaine Scarry, in her classic study *The Body in Pain,* says, "there is ordinarily no language for pain."[40] Peter Moen's diary represents an exception to this. His Gestapo torturers misrepresented what happened to him as intelligence gathering. In fact it was a highly orchestrated, profoundly immoral instance of the violation of human dignity. At the same time, the justification for his interrogation, if not for the methods used, is the same used in situations of counter-insurgency by any regime, whether fascist, military dictatorship, or informed by democratic principles.

Diana Ortiz's experience of torture

Another poignant and articulate account in the same genre is by Sister Diana Ortiz, an American nun, who has written an important book describing her abduction in Guatemala in 1989, her own torture, as well as that of a man and a woman near her at the same place and time, and the subsequent attempt by various political authorities to cover up what had happened to her.[41]

Suffering severely from PTSD, Sister Ortiz made valiant efforts through various types of therapy described in *The Blindfold's Eyes* to regain some modicum of her former mental health, to reclaim the "Third-Order values" involved with her calling to the consecrated life and commitment to the poor in Central America, and to uncover the truth of what she had gone through on behalf of all the other victims of torture in Guatemala and beyond.

Possibly not knowing they were dealing with an American, her kidnappers and torturers made use of photographs taken of her associating with people considered hostile to the military junta then in power in Guatemala. Under the title of "The Rules of the Game," she described what she went through after she was kidnapped in Guatemala City, where had been participating in a religious course at a retreat house.

> They've taken my sweatshirt off and are explaining the rules. "We're going to ask you some questions. If you give an answer we like, we'll let you smoke. If we don't like the answer, we'll burn you."
>
> "The rules are unfair," I venture.
>
> They burn me.
>
> They ask me my name, age, and place of residence. The anticipation is worse than the burns – wondering if this answer is good enough. But for every answer I give, they burn me. Every time I am silent

they burn me. They ask me the same questions again and again. My throat becomes raw from screaming.

They remove my blindfold. Someone holds my head so I can't turn around. It takes my eyes a little while to adjust to the light. They show me some pictures. The first is of me in San Miguel during the festival two years earlier. The army was in town during the feast, I remember. A soldier asked me to dance and Mimi came to the rescue. "We're nuns," she said. "We don't dance."

"Do you know who this is in the picture?" they ask.

"It's me."

They burn me.

"And who's this?"

This one was taken in the village of Yalaj during Lent of 1988. I wasn't there often, but I remember that when I was there the army was also there. "Me."

They burn me.

The next picture is one of me at the teacher's demonstration in Guatemala City. Again they question me. I identify myself. They burn me. The one after that is of me with a group of people from the Bible course, visiting the ruins in Capuchina. It must have been taken just a couple of days before I was kidnapped. It's so useless to tell them it's me. Why don't I just stay silent? Either way I'll get burned. But still I answer. And am burned.

Then they show me a photo of an indigenous man holding a gun. "Who's this?" I don't know him and I tell them so.

They burn me.

They show me a photo of an indigenous woman holding a gun. "This is you," they insist. She bears no resemblance to me. She's an indigenous woman with long hair. "It isn't. It's not me."

They burn me.[42]

Scarry insists each person's pain under torture is immediately their own and incomparable with any other's: "The most crucial fact about pain is its presentness and the most crucial fact about torture is that it is happening."[43] One could justifiably accuse those tormenting Sister Ortiz as sadists, but this needs to be nuanced carefully.

Torture as sadism

Georges Bataille has studied the philosophy of sexual sadism articulated by the Marquis de Sade and concluded that it is a profound disorder quite different from the sadism described in psychology textbooks or Freudian analysis. For Georges Bataille, sadism must be understood, not in terms of sexual pathology, but existentially,

> as the radical negation of the other, as the denial of the social principle as well as the reality principle. A world in which torture, destruction, and death triumph obviously cannot exist. But the sadist does not care about the continued existence of the world. On the contrary: he wants to nullify this world, and by negating his fellow man, who also in an entirely specific sense is "hell" for him, he wants to realize his own total sovereignty.[44]

Bataille's insight into the sadist relates to religious reality. The sadist attempts to pre-empt God's dominion in his repudiation of the world and his fellow humans.

Catholic moral theologians would insist that torture represents the inversion of the social world and the common good. We can live in our world in a God-centred manner only if we grant life to our fellow man or woman, attempt to ease their suffering, and control our desire to expand our own ego. In the world of torture, a man (or woman) exists only by burning or otherwise ruining the other person who is standing or sitting before him. Sister Ortiz put it in this way:

> Every answer I gave to the torturers was wrong; they tortured me more. And I learned that my words – even the truth – can betray me.... I am but one of millions worldwide who has ascended from the torture chamber. In that place of unspeakable evil, again I was lucky. I found kindness and community. Another woman reached out to me. She told me to be strong.[45]

If an evil cabal inflicting torture on others can damage our trust in the world, so kindness and community such as Sister Ortiz experienced is where recovery, if it is possible, can take place.[46]

6

The Church and Torture in the Twentieth Century

Another sad chapter of history to which the sons and daughters of the Church must return with a spirit of repentance is that of the acquiescence given, especially in certain centuries, to intolerance and even the use of force in the service of truth.—Pope John Paul II, *Tertio millennio adveniente*, 35

Hiding a cleric accused of torture in South America

During the past decade Catholics in Canada, Ireland and the United States have suffered shame and confusion from Church authorities deliberately moving priests accused of sexual abuse of children and adolescents from one parish to another. In at least one instance the same seems to have happened in South America regarding a priest accused of involvement with torture.

The parishioners of St. John the Evangelist church in El Quisco, a coastal village in Chile, knew their pastor simply as the Rev. Christián González, but were aware he spoke Spanish with an Argentine accent. During the long dictatorship of General Augusto Pinochet in Chile, Cardinal Raúl Silva Henríquez of Santiago had played a pivotal role in defending human rights.[1] So the accusation that the church in Chile was complicit in harbouring a cleric allegedly deeply involved in torture came as a shock when the priest travelled back to Argentina in 2003 to face charges dating back to the military dictatorship of the 1970s. Under his real name, Christián von Wernich, he stands accused of 19 counts of murder and 33 of abduction and torture.

"I'm a Christian, and I cannot judge, because we are all sinners," said Isabel Beltrán de Avalos, one of his former parishioners in El Quisco before a Sunday morning Mass early in Lent. Learning of the charges against him "has caused a revulsion within me so great that I stayed

away from Mass for nearly a year and have only returned now at Lent,"
she said. Father von Wernich was "so charming and so charismatic that
it was hard to believe all the things they were saying about him," Mrs.
Avalos added. "I had neighbours and colleagues from work who were
taken away and never seen again when the military seized power [in
Chile], and I don't want that to happen ever again. We can't tolerate
a thing like that."[2]

Mrs. Avalos is repeating a refrain heard constantly throughout Latin
America: "Never Again." *Nunca Más*, the 1984 CONADEP (*Comisión
Nacional sobre Desaparición de Personas*) report commissioned by then
President Alfonsín to study "the system of licensed sadism the military
rulers of Argentina created in their country from 1976 to 1979, when
more than 12,000 citizens were 'sucked' off the streets, tortured for
months and then killed"[3] is an authoritative source for our study of
the relationship in one South American country between the Church
and torture. With respect to the official stance of the Catholic Church
on the human rights violations, the report is nuanced and careful. It
says,

> The bishops of the Argentinean Church repeatedly condemned the
> repression which this Commission investigated. Scarcely two months
> had passed since the coup on March 24, 1976 when the Episcopal
> Conference in a General Assembly described the methods used as
> "sinful." In May 1977, after making representations to members of the
> Military Junta, it published a strongly worded document on similar
> lines. Regrettably, some individual members of the clergy by their
> presence, their silence or even by direct involvement supported the
> very actions that had been condemned by the Church as a whole.[4]

Among the clergy whose names appear in *Nunca Más* is Christián
von Wernich. During the decade following the restoration of democracy in Argentina in 1983, he was the target of protest marches in
Argentina that forced the church hierarchy to move him from one
parish to another.

The case of Father Christián von Wernich

Former political prisoners such as Luis Velasco testified in chilling
detail to the commissioners about the priest's pastoral assistance to the
torturers of the military junta.

The prisoners recounted that after they had suffered days of
intense torture, Father von Wernich would appear offering them

spiritual consolation. But at the same time he would seek information and urge the prisoners to "get right with God" by acknowledging their political activities and identifying comrades still at large. "Once I heard Christián von Wernich reply to a prisoner who had pleaded with him not to die that 'the life of men depends on God and on your collaboration'," Luis Velasco testified at a court hearing. "I also heard him defend and justify torture, recognizing that at times he had been present. When he referred to an operation, he would say, 'When we did that operation'...."[5]

The most serious allegation against Father von Wernich relates to comes from the execution in 1977 of seven young people, all political prisoners, who were members of left-wing groups. The testimony concerning this tragic event in *Nunca Más* became even more problematic later because it is now claimed the killings were part of an attempt to extort money from the prisoners' parents, by suggesting that a bribe would free their children.

Thinking that a priest would naturally inspire trust, agents sent Father von Wernich to collect $1,500 US from the parents of each of the prisoners. As proof they were still alive, he produced letters written by the young people. Once the money was collected, the prisoners were allegedly taken from a clandestine detention centre and killed. One prisoner was pregnant.

In *Nunca Más* Julio Alberto Emmed, a former police officer, admitted his involvement in the incident and said he was coming forward as an act of penance. Mr. Emmed said the prisoners were put in a car and told they were being taken to the airport before being released. Instead, they were beaten unconscious, he said. Father von Wernich himself witnessed at least three of the killings.

"The priest was in the vehicle with me," he recalled in sworn testimony, adding that because one of the prisoners was whipped with a pistol, "various wounds resulted, with an abundant flow of blood over the priest, the driver, and the two of us at the prisoner's side."

"The three subversives were still alive, and their bodies were removed from the car and thrown onto the grass," Mr. Emmed testified. "The doctor injected each one twice, straight into the heart with a reddish liquid that was poisonous." When one of the victims showed signs of life, she was shot in the head, he said.

Afterward, those involved, including Father von Wernich, went to a celebratory barbecue "where we also changed our clothes because they were stained with blood," Mr. Emmed swore. Seeing Mr. Emmed was disturbed by what they had just done, Father von Wernich tried to console him. "What you have done was necessary for the good of the fatherland," the priest told him, according to Mr. Emmed's testimony at the hearings. "You have no reason to feel badly. You carried out a patriotic act, and God knows that what we are doing is for the benefit of the country."[6]

The official position of the contemporary Catholic Church against torture is clear, and so one could legitimately question why bishops in Argentina and Chile could allow Father von Wernich to continue in ministry in face of the notoriety surrounding scandals in his past.

Pope John Paul II on torture

Speaking on May 27, 2004, at an audience for seven new ambassadors to the Vatican, Pope John Paul II declared that anytime an individual is tortured and debased, all humanity suffers because all are created in God's image.

He then went on to say, "Because each person is our brother, or sister in humanity, we cannot be silent in the face of such intolerable treatment." Not restricting his remarks to the recent abuse of Iraqi prisoners at the hands of US soldiers, the Holy Father applied his teaching widely: "From every continent there continually comes disturbing information about human rights, revealing that men, women and children are tortured and their dignity deeply debased contrary to the Universal Declaration of Human Rights."[7]

All people of good will, from government leaders to ordinary citizens, have an obligation, the Pope said, to work to ensure that human rights are respected in their own countries and around the world. The Pope repeated this message after his June 27 Angelus, reminding pilgrims who had gathered in St. Peter's Square that June 26 marked the UN International Day in Support of Victims of Torture.

He asked that "the shared commitment by individuals and organizations banish completely this intolerable violation of human rights." Torture, he said, is "radically contrary to the dignity of men and women."[8]

The formation of conscience in human rights is a crucial and primary responsibility of the Catholic community, as well as of "all people of good will, from government leaders to ordinary citizens." Each citizen must be educated in the ways of peace and respect for others so that "the intolerable violence" present in so many parts of the world will cease. "We will not be able to live in peace and our hearts will not be able to remain in peace if all people are not treated with dignity," the Pope said.[9]

While the alleged collaboration of Father Christián von Wernich in torture and other human rights abuses is an offence, there was an attitude towards the enemies of Argentina's military rulers among both his fellow clergy and the wider Church community that created a social environment making his activities morally plausible in his own mind and in the minds of others.

The perceived national emergency faced by Argentina and other South American countries in the latter decades of the twentieth century that gave rise to the widespread use of torture offers us in the 21st century important object lessons in our own national security crisis, now called by some the war on terrorism.

In their role as vicar of Christ, head of the universal Church, and Bishop of Rome, Pope John Paul II and his predecessors Paul VI and Pius XII were outspoken advocates for human rights and have consistently condemned torture.[10] The College of Bishops, the worldwide community of bishops united with the Pope, also has clearly taught the same message.

Gaudium et spes and CELAM

Gaudium et Spes, the Declaration on "The Church in the Modern World" of Vatican II, along with the approach taken by and the specific teaching of the second plenary meeting of CELAM, the South American Bishops' Conference, in Medellín, Colombia, in 1968, and the third such meeting at Puebla, Mexico, in 1979[11] were key moments in articulating the fundamental Catholic option to be the voice of the voiceless (Medellín) victims of human rights violations and torture.

Chile

In the wake of the 1973 military coup by General Pinochet and his fellow officers, the Chilean hierarchy perhaps was painfully aware of the terrible suffering unleashed against the supporters of the lawfully constituted government of Salvador Allende. On October 7 of that year Pope Paul VI expressed his dismay to the Roman press over the bloody repression taking place in Chile. He was so moved that he wrote a letter to the Chilean episcopate expressing his concern for the violence and bloodshed, the circumstances of the many prisoners and the failure of safeguards for maintaining basic human rights. He emphasized the need to return to democratic institutions. The letter was to be made public; the consequences for the military Junta could have been great because they had described themselves as the restorers of western Christian civilization from the hands of a Marxist regime.

The letter reached the desk of the Papal Nuncio in Santiago, Sótero Sanz, who consulted Cardinal Silva. Two days after Paul VI's declaration to the media, four members of the Junta paid a visit to the Cardinal to complain about the Pope's words and attempted to elicit a promise of co-operation from the Cardinal. The Nuncio and the Cardinal feared that the letter, about which the Junta was unaware, would explode an already tense situation, give aid and comfort to armed guerrillas and harm the Church's ability to help those being persecuted by the regime.

Cardinal Silva was dispatched to Rome and on November 3, 1973, meeting alone with Pope Paul VI, he convinced the Pope to withdraw the letter. It was a mission Cardinal Silva came to regret deeply in the years ahead. Two years later he would ask the Pope to make the letter known. The Pope refused, saying the opportunity was long past.[12]

It appears that the commitment to defend human rights by Pope John Paul II during the last decades of the twentieth century was not accepted by each and every individual bishop, who is also the "vicar of Christ" in his particular diocese. At times and in certain situations some bishops have failed in their duty to form the consciences of those Catholics and others who look to them for moral guidance on the paramount importance of defending human rights.

This was true during the reign of the national security military dictatorships in South America and in Rwanda[13] and Burundi in Africa. Without absolving some of failing to do what they should have done to form the consciences of their faithful in human rights, it can also be said that the exercise of the teaching responsibility of bishops, always a challenge, is especially problematic (and important) in times of civil unrest, political upheaval, genocide and war.

Problems associated with Church teaching against torture

The rationale for episcopal silence in the face of torture is neither a normal nor genuine moral quandary, but would go something like this. Neither as simple nor as straightforward a matter as we might like, consistent condemnation of torture can appear to the supporters of a dictatorship to be unpatriotic and contradictory to the common good. During the time of the Inquisition, the Church permitted torture in its service of the truth. Today, individual bishops may remain silent even when they know about state-sponsored torture. Even in the face of this evil, their hope is that their silence will facilitate unity in the Church and, eventually, national reconciliation. While this may appear to their critics to be pusillanimous and disingenuous, they understand it to be the "lesser of two evils." The evils that these bishops might prevent by remaining silent about torture might include state persecution of the Church or the takeover of their government by even more vicious and irreligious guerrillas. Whether the justification is defence of the truth or the promotion of unity, the value of human rights is sacrificed to other apparently competing values.

Among the many challenges involved with public advocacy of human rights in the Church, one of the most important is to resolve the apparent contradiction between the Church's role of reconciliation and unification and its duty to condemn the use of torture and even to excommunicate torturers.

While recognizing they are primarily charged by Christ with the responsibility to bless and to pardon the faithful in their care and not to condemn them, bishops are also given the task "to bind and to loose" (Matthew 16:19). In December 1980, a group of seven bishops in Chile issued a decree of excommunication for those responsible for torture, not only for those who participated in the actual torture, but for those who had ordered it and for those who were in a position to stop it but did not do so.[14]

These bishops had seen with their own eyes the effects of torture on members of their own flock. They argued in their decree that when especially grave sins affect "the common good, the dignity of persons and the sense of unity that signifies communion," a bishop is charged with using excommunication to "avoid disturbing the order that God desires."[15]

Argentina

Publicly opposing the use of torture by security forces can be dangerous for all, even bishops, in a country like Argentina, most of whose citizens are Roman Catholic. "Sergio" was a political prisoner who survived his incarceration both before and after the 1976 coup in Argentina. In 1979, from his exile in Mexico, he wrote about the details of his experience in the Dirty War, for the Centre for Legal and Social Studies (CELS). Perhaps because he was held in a federal prison in Resistencia, the capital of Chaco, and not in one of the 340 secret detention centres set up after the coup, he survived to tell his story.

After the coup the food the prisoners received, always inadequate, "was now usually rotten and crawling with bugs.... We were literally starving."[16] The general behaviour of the jailers became more violent, and torture became routine. Guards uncomfortable with the new regime were shot.

The only human connection to the outside world was Bishop Bisoboa of Resistencia, who came to visit and hear the prisoners' confessions. The presence of the bishop was compelling. Even the guards posted outside the confessional obeyed his order to leave him alone with his penitents. A few days after Bishop Bisoboa delivered a public sermon on behalf of the prisoners who, he declared, were being tortured, it was reported in a local newspaper that he had been the victim of an accident "caused by an inexperienced driver."[17]

What had actually happened was that the driver of a large truck had aggressively cut off the prelate's jeep and forced it off the road. Then soldiers pulled the bishop from his vehicle and broke his arm and several ribs. He was, of course, forbidden to return to the jail, and the prisoners there had lost their last human link to the outside world.[18]

If Bishop Bisoboa's pastoral ministry with the prisoners in Resistancia and his public condemnation of torture were admirable, the same could not be said about that of many police and military chaplains such as Christián von Wernich. Zacarias Moutokias, an *ex-desaparecido* or disappeared one, survived the horrors of his incarceration in one of the secret detention sites during dark years of Argentine history. Speaking from his adopted country of France on Argentine radio on April 15, 1995, he said,

> One needs to be careful about mentioning the names of kidnappers and torturers, and maybe I should not, but...the person who, even

after all these years, still holds the most horror for me, is a priest. Just before releasing us [from the concentration camp], they let us wash, and the priest was standing behind us talking to the guard. Th priest suggested they give us "the machine" one more time, so we wouldn't forget that we had been there. I recognized him later as Father Von Wernich.[19]

Mr. Moutokias' revelation shocked Catholics in Argentina in part because it was made during Holy Week of 1995. If clerical responsibility in torture had been restricted to Father von Wernich that would have been bad enough. Another bombshell was dropped later in the week on Good Friday from the Archbishop of Viedma, Miguel Hesayne, when he said in a homily, "We lament that repentance has not yet come to those who should be sorry, including [many bishops]."

Counting himself as one of the sinners in his Church, Hesayne went on to speak in the first person plural. "Official meals were taken with those we were denouncing as torturers…. And yet [in 1977 at the Plenary Assembly of the Annual Conference of Bishops] we refused to receive the Mothers of *desaparecidos* who waited outside all day in torrential rain."[20]

That, he declared, was "a tragic day," not only for the Mothers but also for the Church. Even as the Mothers waited, the bishops ate lunch with the commanders. In those dark hours of the observance of the torture and crucifixion of Jesus, with the crosses and statues covered with purple cloth in his cathedral, Archbishop Hesayne dramatically declared in his homily that he still shudders to think of Christ's reaction.

Of the scores of bishops present at this meeting, only a small group led by Hesayne – Jaime de Nevares (from Neuquén), Jorge Novak (Quilmes), Alberto Devoto (Goya), Vicente Zaspe (Santa Fe) – argued to admit the Mothers, who had been branded as communists by others. After an impassioned debate, these men were voted down, and the assembly issued its May 1977 declaration upholding human rights praised by *Nunca Más*.

In a separate statement Archbishop Hesayne expressed his gratitude to Mr. Moutokias for his candor and indicated he would raise the matter of his testimony against an Argentine priest still in good standing at the Conference of Bishops in early May 1995. "It has always worried me that certain men of the Church have not understood that torture is never humane or Christian. This is a subject we need to discuss at the upcoming conference."[21] If Moutokias's testimony could be proved or substantiated, then Hesayne said that the penalty would be clear: any cleric who tortures must be removed from his office.[22]

He went on to say, as several other bishops had said, it would be well and timely to revisit the subject of excommunication since the threat was used in the past to silence priests who objected to a theology of terror.[24] Archbishop Hesayne continued,

> Reconciliation does not mean covering [history] with a blanket of oblivion. Reconciliation means truth, justice and love. Justice without love can degenerate into vengeance. We need to know the truth for medicinal reasons, so that what happened during the Process will never happen again.[24]

Hesayne, Novak, Justo Laguna, and several other bishops urged their brothers in the Church to come forward if they had information "that could help relieve the anguish of the families of *desaparecidos*."[25]

What led to the painful recollections of Moutokias and Hesayne was the public revelation on March 2, 1995 by retired navy Captain Adolfo Scilingo that he had participated in two death-flights that we know now, thanks to his confession, to be a hallmark of Argentina's Dirty War. Not only did Scilingo admit to the murders of the tortured and disappeared inside the airplanes, but he also declared that the death-flight duty was rotated to almost every naval officer.

Until recently the *Punto Final* amnesty as well as the "Due Obedience" laws of Argentina permitted those involved in human rights atrocities to come forward publicly, without fear of judicial sanction, to admit what they had done and had observed.[26] Following Scilingo, a half-dozen other military men directly involved with kidnapping, torture, and murder in the secret camps also appeared and, being willing to speak publicly, were featured, day after day, on radio and television, in newspapers and magazines.[27]

The media drama included the appearance in a May 1, 1995 television interview of an infamous and still unapologetic torturer, Julio Simón, known by those who survived his depredations as "Julián the Turk."

The Scilingo Affair

In 1976, Scilingo was an officer in his late twenties with ambitions for an elite career in the Argentine navy. In some ways he was similar to Alfredo Astiz and Miguel Angel Cavallo, not only because of his commitment to the junta's ideology, but also because he requested at around the same time as Astiz, that his superiors send him to the ESMA in Buenos Aires "to serve with the saviors of the Nation."[28]

At the time, "[he] believed what [they] repeated every day, that the only good guerrilla was a dead guerrilla."[29] Before receiving his chosen assignment, Scilingo was stationed at the Puerto Belgrano base in Bahia Blanca. As he tells it,

> Vice Admiral Luis María Mendía [then Chief of Naval Operations] got us together in the cinema at the base and explained that, given the circumstances, certain instruments to be used against the enemy would be out of the ordinary. Since colonial times, he said, armies had distinguished themselves by their uniforms, but that had changed. Now we too would go without uniforms, so as to mask our presence among civilians. With regard to the subversives who had been condemned to death, Mendía told us they "would fly," and that the ecclesiastic authorities had assured him that this was a Christian, basically non-violent form of death.[30]

If anyone had a problem with this he could be assigned elsewhere, said the Chief of Naval Operations.[31] At the time, Scilingo had no problem with this. The prospect of dressing as a civilian didn't feel right to him, but he rationalized this was an unprecedented struggle for national survival and for the preservation of Catholic values against the leftist insurgency.

A few days after arriving at the ESMA, where he was in charge of the auto shop, Scilingo went upstairs to repair a ventilator and accidentally ended up in a *capucha*, an area forbidden to unauthorized persons.

> I opened a door and out came a woman in an advanced state of pregnancy, dressed in a nightgown, slippers, and robe. She stopped in front of me, looked at me with sad eyes, then continued on to the bathroom. There were other pregnant women in that room.... It was unnerving to see future mothers in these circumstances, in spite of the hatred I felt for subversives....This was the war I had asked to fight, but did it have to be like this.... It was a scene out of the Middle Ages.... There were prisoners of various ages.... Most of them were pestilent .... Trembling. You could hear moaning. Some of them were praying.... The air was suffocating...You could feel their terror, as they tried to adjust their leg irons, so they wouldn't rub against the open wounds on their ankles.[32]

Scilingo calculated that during his two years at the ESMA (1976-7), on"a hundred Wednesdays between 1,500 and 2,000 people" were thrown into the ocean in varying numbers on each occasion.[33]

Scilingo took part twice in these flights, which were considered "a form of communion," "a supreme act we did for the country," in April and June of 1977.[34] He recalled that the prisoners selected "to fly" were called by their numbers, ordered to form a line and march in leg irons to the basement where the officers said they were being flown to a recuperation camp in the south and would now receive vaccinations. A physician then administered the first dose of a tranquilizer (sodium pentothal), dubbed by Scilingo and his fellow officers as Pen-Naval. "It made them drowsy," Scilingo said, "and we had to help them to the plane. Once on board, a physician administered a second shot to knock the prisoners out; then they were returned to their seats. The doctors moved back to the cabin so as not to violate their Hippocratic oath."[35]

Scilingo added this gloss without any apparent irony. "Once the prisoners were asleep – this is very morbid," he commented, "we undressed them, and two of us would drag one prisoner down the aisle and then push him out into the sky...."[36] Scilingo did this to 30 individuals: 13 on the first flight, 17 on the second. Among them were a 65-year-old man, a 16-year-old boy, and two pregnant women in their early twenties.

On his first flight, Scilingo slipped and nearly fell out of the plane with a prisoner who was struggling and would not let go. He survived only because a comrade grabbed him and pulled him back. "It's a recurring nightmare, one I'll have for the rest of my life."[37]

He is still tormented by "the heavy scrape and jangle of [the prisoners'] chains and shackles ... the clothing left strewn on the floor of the plane after the 'cargo' was dropped."[38] On the return flight no one said a word; back at the ESMA Scilingo drank himself into a long, deep sleep and then went to confession, where he was immediately absolved by the chaplain.[39]

Scilingo first shared these personal recollections with journalist Horacio Verbitsky in early 1995. He stressed with Verbitsky how disturbed he was after completing his first murderous flight, and said that after he had received the sacrament of reconciliation he and other officers involved talked things over with the chaplains, who approved of what they had done.

After my first flight ... it was very hard for me to accept it on a personal level. After returning, although I might coldly have thought everything was fine, that was not the reality inside me. I believe all human beings have this problem; if I had had to shoot someone, I would have felt the same way. I don't think any human being takes pleasure in killing another. The next day I didn't feel very good and I was talking with the chaplain of the school, who found a Christian explanation for it. I don't know if it comforted me, but at least it made me feel better.... He was telling me that it was a Christian death, because they didn't suffer, because it wasn't traumatic, that they had to be eliminated, that war was war and even the Bible provided for eliminating the weeds from the wheat field. He gave me some support.[40]

Unlike the earlier case of Alfredo Astiz, Scilingo gives every indication of the beginning of religious repentance for his part in these atrocities. At the time, he had sought assistance from certain Catholic priests ordained not only to absolve sinners in the Sacrament of Penance but also to form the consciences of the faithful according to the authentic teaching of the Church concerning what the tradition calls "natural law."

As Scilingo put it: "I don't think any human being takes pleasure in killing another."[41] After taking part in the first flight, Scilingo was moving towards the truth that all persons deserve our respect and have an intrinsic dignity and the right to life and protection from harm, including protection from torture.

Expecting to find his guilt-troubled conscience confirmed by the judgment of his confessor and the other chaplains he and the others consulted, he found the opposite.

If we were to use the traditional moral category of "invincible ignorance," it would not apply to Scilingo. Scilingo's conscience was not ignorant. The ones who may have suffered from invincible ignorance were his chaplains. His account of the misuse, in fact abuse, of the Sacrament of Penance and of pastoral counselling by the chaplains at the ESMA is as serious as the various allegations made against Father von Wernich. This is because some Catholics believe that God's presence can be found both in the human person, allegedly violated by von Wernich, and in the sacramental encounter, violated by the unnamed chaplain(s) at the ESMA.

Earlier testimony from CONADEP indicated that Scilingo's account of the negative approach taken by chaplains at the ESMA to the human rights of prisoners in their custody was not an isolated situation. Trade unionist Plutarco Antonio Schaller said that Chaplain Felipe Perlanda López had justified and agreed with his torture during the pastoral counselling he received from him:

[T]he chaplain Perlanda López visited me briefly on Sundays, chatting for a short while in the cells. He would justify torture. On one occasion one of the detainees told him, "Father, they are torturing me terribly during interrogations and I beg you to intercede to stop them from torturing me any more." Perlanda López replied, "Well, my son, but what do you expect if you don't co-operate with the authorities interrogating you?" On another occasion I told the chaplain that they could not possibly continue to torture me as they were doing, to which Perlanda López replied, "You have no right to complain about the torture…."[42]

One could ask whether any Argentine bishops had first-hand knowledge about the human rights abuses taking place in the secret detention centres and whether they had taken similar pastoral approaches to them as the chaplains. The Bishop of Jujuy, José Miguel Medina, was replaced on March 29, 1982 in his diocese to order to work full-time as head of the military vicariate. In CONADEP testimony, we learn that, as Bishop of Jujuy, he was convinced of the military ideology before he took charge of the armed services chaplains:

I remember that during my stay at the penitentiary [Villa Gorriti-Jujuy Prison] the Bishop of Jujuy, Monsignor Medina, conducted a service, and in the sermon he said that he knew what was going on, but all that was happening was for the good of the Fatherland, that the military were doing the right thing and that we should tell all we knew and that he was available to take confession (Testimony of Enesto Reynaldo Saman, file No. 4841.)[43]

I found him [Pedro Eduardo Torres] in the early days of June 1976 in the prison [Villa Gorriti-Jujuy Prison] where I was able to speak with him; he said to me that he had been told they were going to kill him…. Monsignor Medina, who frequently visited the prison, spoke to me about this "transfer" (Testimony of Maria Heriberto Rubén López, file No. 4866.)[44]

[W]hen I entered Villa Gorriti Prison I was alone in a cell, in solitary confinement. Monsignor Medina came to see me and he told me

I had to tell him everything I knew. I replied that I did not know what it was I had to tell him, and that all I wanted to know was the whereabouts of my children. Medina answered that they must have been up to something for me not to know where they were. He insisted that I should speak and tell everything and then I would find out where my children were. (Testimony of Eulogia Cordero de Garnica, file No. 4859.)[45]

Eleven years separated the first set of revelations of the Dirty War horrors published in CONADEP from the confessions by Scilingo and other perpetrators that helped to explain how the victims of torture met their final end. One might ask how the government and Church reacted to the details of the deaths of so many of the Disappeared.

The first reaction in 1995 to Scilingo's revelations came from Carlos Menem, then President of Argentina. It was dismissive: "Scilingo is a crook. He is rubbing salt on old wounds."[46] To prove his first point, Menem had Scilingo arrested for having written a number of bad cheques in 1991. To an incredulous Mike Wallace on CBS television's 60 Minutes, Menem repeated his position: "Now I ask: What is the reason to go back to a past that leads nowhere?"[47]

Archbishop Hesayne disagreed with Menem's point of view on Scilingo's public confession of his sins. "The position of the president that enforcers like Scilingo should simply 'confess to their priests' is wrong," said the always candid Bishop of Viedma. "It is not Christian; it is not part of the doctrine of this Church. In order to properly repent, he who has sinned against the public must make public reparation."[48]

He went on to explain that because they had not yet done so, the ex-commanders were forbidden to receive communion in his diocese. "To violate a person is to violate God," Hesayne stressed. "For those men to receive the Holy Host would be a public sacrilege."[49]

The Conference of Bishops of Argentina announced that on May 17, 1995 it would release an official document responding to the content, character, and ramifications of the testimonies of Scilingo. But as the date approached, the bishops were divided and the May deadline was cancelled. Announcing this delay was the Archbishop of Buenos Aires at that time, Antonio Quarracino. He declined to say when the response from his institution would be forthcoming. Rather, he insisted that "in order to examine its conscience, the Church would need time and serenity."[50]

Canada: The case of Father Mark Sargent

Awaiting this "time and serenity," one matter that would need to be examined by the Church would be the role of chaplains.[51] Lest anyone in North America think this is a question germane only to the Church in Argentina, they should recall the sadness and outrage felt by Canadians over the torture perpetrated on teenagers by Canadian soldiers in Somalia. This incident came to light with the publication in 1993 of photographs showing the teenagers' humiliation and the particularly gruesome photograph taken just moments before the death by torture at the hands of the Canadian military of 16-year-old Shidane Abukar Arone.

Some of the anger arose because of the attempted cover-up of these human rights abuses, including torture and murder. This led the Canadian government at the time to disband the Canadian Airborne Regiment, which had been stationed in Somalia in 1993, and whose members were accused of perpetrating the atrocities.

Military investigators discovered that the abuse was widespread and the subsequent cover-up suggested it was systemic. The Regiment was disbanded in January 1995, an almost unprecedented move for a Western democracy.

The government then called for a judicial review of the whole tragedy, the "Somalia Inquiry," in an attempt to discover what had happened, why it had happened, and who was ultimately responsible. This inquiry was deliberately shut down in July 1997 before it could determine at what level in the chain of command the cover-up happened. An election was called, and the federal Liberal party was re-elected.

In the preface to her book *Dark Threats and White Knights: The Somalia Affair, Peacekeeping and the New Imperialism,* Sherene H. Razack explains that she did not choose for the cover image the trophy photo of the bound and bloodied Shidane Aroun just before his death. Rather, she used one of five young Somali captives, bound and blindfolded, three of whom wore signs reading "I am a thief."

She did this because one of the Canadian soldiers who appeared in the picture was a Catholic priest serving as a chaplain in the Airborne Regiment, Captain Mark L. Sargent. "This photo, perhaps even more than the ones of a tortured Arone," Dr. Razack writes, "seemed to leave no room for doubt that something had gone terribly wrong in Somalia, something more widespread than a single incident of brutality."[52]

Father Sargent has declined to comment publicly about his role in the 1993 abuse of the children in Somalia. In 1999 he was appointed as an investigator for the military ombudsman in Canada amidst considerable controversy. The ombudsman and others claimed the chaplain had been merely attempting to make certain the children were not further harmed.

Others said that he had simply participated in the common practice of having trophy photos taken whenever there were detainees. Military police investigations at the time discovered several soldiers had posed for such pictures, and some sent them home as souvenirs. One had even been posted on the refrigerator door in the unit's tent in Belet-Huen, Somalia, where the Regiment was based.[53] Nevertheless, Father Sargent was summoned to testify *in camera* at the Somalia Inquiry.

Later, at the time he received his position in the office of the ombudsman, he was quoted as saying: "The chain of command did their investigation, and I was cleared [of wrongdoing]."[54] With respect to his proclamation of Gospel values and his defence of human rights according to the teaching of the Church, it is puzzling that Father Sargent does not explain why he posed in that terrible photo, nor what, if anything, he had done to defend the children involved. There are no extant photos of Argentinean chaplains similarly compromised by finding themselves in the centre of torture.

Chaplains and the law of the Church

The late Dr. Emilio Mignone was a lawyer, former president of a Catholic university, co-founder of CELS, and grieving father of Mónica Mignone, who had been abducted from the family home on May 14, 1976 at the age of 24 and subsequently Disappeared. In his highly critical study of the role of the Argentine Church during the Dirty War, he raised serious questions about the publication on April 21, 1986 by Pope John Paul II of the apostolic decree *Spiritualis Militum Curae*.[55]

In this Vatican promulgation, 29 military vicariates around the world, including that of Canada, the United States and Argentina, were raised to the status of dioceses to be governed by a prelate as an "ordinary"[56] enjoying the same rights and privileges as any other bishop except that his jurisdiction is not defined by territory but by a specific type of person.[57] This arrangement falls under the heading in church law of the "personal prelature."[58]

Thus the jurisdiction of a military diocese would cover all the Catholic faithful who serve in the military, their families, as well as civilian employees working for the armed forces and members of their families – spouses and children living in the same house. Such an arrangement, Mignone pointed out, could create potential conflicts with diocesan prelates who have jurisdiction over the territory where one finds these military people.[59]

More serious in regard to the implementation of the Church's teaching against the use of torture, even during a national emergency, is that "No one can serve two masters" (Luke 16:13). A double hierarchy has been set up for bishops and chaplains, military and ecclesiastical. Mignone argues the following:

> Ordained to serve God, they end up obeying Mars. That will inevitably happen when priests are subordinated to military regulations that bestow on them rank, salary, promotions, and privileges, and impose on them corresponding obligations. In Argentina they betrayed the gospel by justifying and supporting state terrorism.[60]

A third problem is that military dioceses are now permitted to establish their own seminaries to train priests. This has not yet happened and at the present time priests are trained in ordinary diocesan seminaries and from there join the military diocese, or are seconded by another diocesan bishop. But should such seminaries be established, Mignone fears "moral, spiritual, and intellectual deformation of candidates" would take place as they pursue their priestly vocation in a school similar in ideology to that set up to train other junior officer candidates.[61]

The late Dr. Mignone's concerns indicate that *Spiritualis Militum Curae* should be revisited and possibly revised. But more fundamental change needs to happen. The official teaching of the Catholic Church has used essentially moral arguments against state-sponsored torture. In addition to this approach, legal sanctions against Catholics involved would strengthen this position, and the clearest place to begin is with the Catholic clergy. The bishops and priests of the Catholic Church as a group need to hear, accept and put this official teaching of the papal magisterium into practice. To ensure that this is done, at the next revision of the official law of the Church, the Code of Canon Law, care should be taken to enact explicit legislation against clerical involvement in torture[62] and in favour of church approval for suspects having to submit themselves to the full justice of the state when their actions have clearly violated human rights requirements.

In an article published in the prestigious British medical journal *The Lancet*, Steven H. Miles strongly disapproves of the part played by medical professionals in the abuse of prisoners in the Abu Ghraib Prison near Baghdad. He writes,

> The role of military medicine in these abuses merits special attention because of the moral obligations of medical professionals with regard to torture and because of horror at health professionals who are silently or actively complicit with torture."[63]

In its service of global human rights, the International Committee of the Red Cross maintains strict neutrality in order to obtain the co-operation of governments and combatants. All of this is thought to assist the imprisoned and the vulnerable. Given this long-standing approach, it is striking that with respect to the US detention facility in Guantánamo Bay, officials in the ICRC have privately revealed that doctors there were informing interrogators about prisoners' weaknesses in what they described as "a flagrant violation of medical ethics."[64]

Physicians in Chile, Egypt, Turkey and other nations have taken personal risks to bring to light state-sponsored torture and have created organizations such as Physicians for Human Rights to advocate their position against the use of torture.

Should not similar obligations apply to military chaplains, especially Catholics, in view of their official mandate to defend human rights? Given that in the last century some of the worst human rights abuses took place in Catholic countries, surely their combined voices speaking against torture in union with that of their bishops would carry even greater weight with torturers and their superiors than that of physicians.[65]

Canon law

At the very least, the central administration at the Vatican should plan to put in place a legal framework to prohibit clerical involvement in torture. Such laws would serve to educate the Catholic laity on this question as well. Following a judicial process, the penalty of excommunication can be imposed at the present time on any cleric found to have participated in mutilation, abduction and/or homicide. Should this not be extended to torture?

Given that Pope John Paul II taught us the need to educate the consciences of the faithful about the grievous immorality of torture, there is no better way than to impose a canonical excommunication for it. An excommunication means, among other things, that, when someone has seriously offended God's law, the person not only must undergo repentance through God's forgiving grace in Christ leading to forgiveness of sins in the Sacrament of Reconciliation, but also is not allowed to receive Holy Communion until formally permitted by his or her bishop.

The penalty of *ferendae sententiae* excommunication is used by the Church to highlight for the clergy and faithful a grievously serious offence against God's commandments. Because this ecclesiastical sanction involves a public process within a diocese, with evidence taken from witnesses testifying under oath and a publicly announced verdict by the church court, this sanction would greatly assist in the process of conscience formation as well as give public witness.

Like abortion, which also carries the same sanction of excommunication under a different procedure, torture is an offence that directly attacks the common good as well as the sanctity and dignity of the human person. While the world community as a whole does not accept the Church's teaching on abortion, it has achieved a consensus against torture.

Because even the world community considers torture to be of such gravity that its prosecution enjoys universal jurisdiction, the Church should also similarly give it a universal legal and moral condemnation.

7

Justice and Forgiveness

Blessing...has a close family resemblance to the concept of ubuntu, which guided many of us through the taxing days of the Truth and Reconciliation Commission. Ubuntu speaks of the essence of being human. It includes qualities of generosity, hospitality, friendliness, caring and compassion. It expresses the fact that humanity is shared and that through our human connectedness we find our identities. People with ubuntu feel good about the well-being success of others.—Archbishop Desmond Tutu[1]

The torture and murder of a teenager by Canadian soldiers in Somalia is reprehensible. The unexplained presence of a Catholic priest-chaplain during the abuse is disturbing. Is justice possible? What does one do with torturers and those who give them aid and comfort, whether spiritual or political? Should they be court-martialed? Their regiment disbanded? After they have fully disclosed what they have done and to whom, should we offer them amnesty on condition they not engage in torture again? Create conditions for the possibility of a world without torture? All of these choices have been tried; none has fully achieved justice.

Many victims of torture do not survive their ordeal, but some do. How do they proceed with their lives after their suffering is over? The danger is that their inner pain will never end. What should they do? Personally forgive their persecutors so the damaging effects of hatred and the desire for revenge do not destroy their lives? If true justice is impossible, can someone who has suffered torture, inflicted it, or been a willing accessory to it forgive or be forgiven? In many cases the survivors of torture experience guilt for their part in what they went through. Can they forgive themselves and be forgiven? How would this happen?

Peter Moen, suffering in his solitary confinement in Oslo, was tormented by guilt over having given to his Gestapo torturers the names of his collaborators in the Norwegian Resistance. What sustained him were his faith, his love for his wife and mother and their love for him, and his hope that his contribution and that of others in the Resistance would lead to a better future for his country and the rest of the world.

These questions relate mainly to the surviving victims of torture. What about the perpetrators and their willing and aware accomplices? If they are repentant, can they forgive themselves and be forgiven? How would this take place?

The majority report and minority report on forgiveness

Within this concluding chapter no compelling answers can be offered to these questions. Following our phenomenological method, we will study the recovery process of two torture survivors and a person who actively participated in the suffering of one. The contributions of scripture and early Christian tradition will also be examined for possible routes out of the self-hatred in which so many survivors of torture find themselves.

The first distinction: between forgiveness and justice

The discussion here will be guided by several distinctions. The first is the relationship between forgiveness and justice. Within the religious context of the Judaeo-Christian tradition, there is a majority report on forgiveness as well as a minority report.

The majority report insists that, between suffering a grievous individual or communal injury and forgiveness, there must be a middle term of either repentance by the guilty party or just retribution in acknowledgement of their guilty involvement in what has happened. In other words, the majority report insists justice is a *sine qua non* for forgiveness.

The minority report is rooted in the paschal mystery – the suffering, death and resurrection – of Jesus Christ and models itself on his teaching and practice so that the middle term is not demanded before forgiveness is offered. For the minority report, justice is desirable, but not required, before forgiveness is given.

The second distinction: between internal and external forgiveness

The second distinction is between two kinds of forgiveness. One, internal and highly personal, relates to the victim's feelings and attitudes toward the perpetrators; the other is interpersonal and relates to "something the victim does or says to the perpetrator, directly or indirectly."[2] The interpersonal type of forgiveness represents an effort to begin to achieve post-torture justice. The first kind of forgiveness is important for the torture survivor's inner healing; the second constructs a world without torture.

The contemporary theory of how to make the best use of torture as an interrogation tool has as important goals generating guilt and causing moral disintegration in the person being tortured. Modern torturers not only inflict physical pain and hardship on their victims, but also try to fundamentally alter their ways of thinking about themselves, how they act in the world, and how they relate to God.

It is this intention that makes modern torture so grievously unjust and immoral. Interrogators do this not only to get the information they seek, but also to insure that, should their victims survive, they will no longer pose a problem for the regime sponsoring the torturers. The imperative becomes "Don't even think of disobeying us in the future."

During interrogation under torture, the victim is often asked for the names of his or her collaborators and like-minded colleagues in their project. If they should give some names – and the pain of torture can elicit these almost involuntarily, as happened to Peter Moen – then others might face the same horror. Also, the reason for their torture is drummed into them; the victim is told repeatedly he has only himself to blame for what is happening.

Revictimization: the case of Diana Ortiz

If a torture victim survives, revictimization becomes an issue. Upon release from captivity, some in their community might think they have survived only because they have become collaborators with the regime, and thus betrayed the cause. Even if this is not the case, the moral choices made during and after the ordeal continue to haunt the survivor of torture.

Abducted and tortured in November 1989 while working as a missionary in Guatemala, Sister Diana Ortiz heard a policeman in her torture chamber say to her: "If you live to tell about this, if you somehow manage to survive, no one will believe you."[3]

Among the moral residue she carries, Sister Ortiz, after she had been gang-raped in detention and had conceived, underwent an abortion, for which she suffered tremendous guilt. She also felt survivor's guilt for still being alive and for having stopped the torture after four days, when the mysterious Alejandro visited her place of detention after the first day:[4] she felt guilty because she had mentioned an aquaintance named Miguel Os and some well-known facts about him, and he subsequently disappeared;[5] she felt guilty she had not told Miguel's wife Rosa about this; and finally she felt guilty because, during her incarceration, her torturers had forced her to participate in the torture of another woman.[6]

The memory of a man and a woman who had undergone torture at the same time as she continued to haunt her. The shame and the rage, the feelings of being dirty and crazy, almost overwhelmed her so that she remained convinced that "surviving torture is worse than the torture."[7]

Her lifelong consecration as an American Ursuline nun meant she was supposed to have reacted differently than she did. One day during her process of recovery, Diana said to her best friend in the Ursuline community, Sister Mimi, that she felt she had to leave the religious life:

"I'm thinking of leaving the community."

"Diana, why?" She put her cup down and searched my face.

I dropped my eyes. "I don't feel worthy to be an Ursuline."

"You're worthy. Of course you're worthy."

Her answer baffled me. She knew about the things I had done. What I had done with the pregnancy – the Church considered that murder. And I couldn't look down at my hands without thinking of them splattered with blood. I was living in a state of mortal sin. What that meant was that whatever torture I might get from here on out – even for all eternity – I deserved.

There was the sacrament of confession, but I didn't believe in it. Whenever I went to Mass, I dreaded the Lord's Prayer – "Forgive us our trespasses as we forgive those who trespass against us." I wanted desperately to be forgiven, but I couldn't forgive my torturers. I didn't understand how I could forgive them without condoning what they had done to me and to other people. So what right did I have to forgiveness?

After a few minutes of silence, broken by nothing but the shrieks of a blue jay, Mimi suggested a leave of absence. She explained that I would still be an Ursuline, but the leave would be a way of claiming an exemption from some of the expectations and traditions. I would only be bound by the vows.[8]

Like Maher Arar later in Canada, Sister Ortiz attempted to find out the full truth of what led to the injustice she had suffered and, particularly, the part played by her own government in her ordeal. She and others took on a political crusade to have the US government officially inquire into what had happened and to admit that one of her torturers, the cologne-wearing man she knew as Alejandro, actually worked for the CIA or at least had connections with the American embassy in Guatemala City. One tactic she used was a hunger strike in Lafayette Park in front of the White House in Washington. Sister Ortiz recalled,

> People who visited the vigil site sometimes wrote messages in my notebook. One woman who wrote was teaching religion in an inner-city school. Many of her students came from broken homes, with one or both parents serving time for minor or serious crimes. A lot of the children carried anger inside, and they resented how their lives were turning out. Her class discussed the issue of forgiveness and decided that forgiveness wasn't possible. "You, as a Catholic nun," she insisted, "have the responsibility to set a good example by forgiving your torturers. If my students knew that you were able to forgive the people who hurt you, maybe they would learn from you."
>
> She waited while I read her message.
>
> I didn't respond. I just covered my anger and guilt with a noncommittal little smile.
>
> I respect and appreciate her and all the people who took the time and energy to visit with me and share their ideas. Having had time now to ponder the question, I would answer her by explaining that I don't hate my torturers. I only despise their actions. While I'm not forgetting the torture, I am getting on with my life. I'm not doing what I was trained to do – I'm not working with children – but I suppose I am working for children, trying to ensure that they have a future that doesn't involve torture. Holocaust survivor Elie Wiesel said, "To forget would be an absolute injustice. To forget would be the enemy's triumph. The enemy kills, tortures, and disappears twice, the second time in trying to obliterate the traces of his crime." By

refusing to forget, I hope I am keeping the memory of the dead alive. As to forgiveness, I would say this: get my government to tell me who my torturers were and who Alejandro is. Bring them to Washington, D.C. Get my government to bring to the table those who formulated the policies that resulted in my torture and those in the U.S. government who for years covered it up. And then we will all sit down and discuss the question of forgiveness together.[9]

This type of full disclosure leading to reconciliation and forgiveness never happened in Sister Ortiz's case, nor does it happen in the case of most other survivors of torture. Because of its inherent injustice, forgiveness for torture is a counterintuitive concept. Yet the possibility of forgiveness speaks to human freedom and to the fact we are not condemned to replay endlessly and for all eternity the evil actions involved with torture.

Transformation of memory: The case of Eric Lomax

If it is memory, or the distortion of memory, that is the great enemy of forgiveness, then it is also the transformation of memory that enables us to alter what has happened in the past, enabling us to progress into the future.

There is no forgiveness in nature. Forgiveness is a religious virtue. The laws of nature, as in the case of electricity being applied to erogenous zones of men and animals, make no room for forgiveness. Electricity as such is not guilty of anything, nor are the lighted cigarettes that Diana Ortiz's victimizers ground into her body. But within nature we find the human person who enters into communion with the world and with other humans. Forgiveness has to do with human relationships and with the relationship between persons and God.

The prophets of the Hebrew Bible are credited with the introduction of the concept of monotheism. Despite the significance of this breakthrough, it pales in comparison with their other central idea, that God is personal, that there is someone at the heart of all reality who affirms and responds to our existence as persons. "We are here because God wants us to be here."[10] Despite the experience of a torture survivor who has lost his or her trust in the world, we can affirm the world and know it is not hostile to our existence.

At the heart of the concept of forgiveness is love – not abstract or theoretical love, but concrete attachment of one person for another. Love distinguishes between a person and his or her action. An act may be evil in the sense of lacking some crucial aspect of goodness, but because a person is free, he or she is not irrevocably committed to that evil.

Wrongdoing such as torture corrupts the structure of our world by creating injustice. It damages relationships. But these things are not beyond repair, because wrongs can be righted and wounds healed. When the wrongdoer expresses remorse and undertakes not to repeat the wrong, he or she testifies they are no longer identified with what they have done. "Forgiveness is, and can only be, a relationship between free persons: between the forgiven, who has shown that they can change, and the forgiver who has faith that the other person will change."[11]

This process, especially with respect to torture, can take a lifetime. We find this in the example of Eric Lomax, a British soldier captured by the Japanese in the Second World War. For the next 50 years, Lomax carried resentment against Japan and the Japanese, for his torturers and, especially, for the translator/interpreter, Nagase Takashi, who had passed on to him in English the questions of his interrogators. In his autobiography, *The Railwayman*, Lomax wrote about his torture in Thailand in 1943 and the emotions he experienced in the years after the war:

> In the cold light of day my anger was more often turned to the Japanese who had beaten, interrogated and tortured me. I wanted to do violence to them, thinking quite specifically of how I would like to revenge myself on ... the hateful little interrogator ... with his dreadful English pronunciation, his mechanical questions and his way of being in the room yet seeming to be detached from it. I wished to drown him, cage him and beat him and see how he liked it. I still thought of his voice, his slurred elocution: "Lomax, you will be killed shortly"; "Lomax, you will tell us"; you remember phrases from encounters that have hurt you, and my meetings with him were cast in a harsh light.[12]

Although Lomax resumed a normal life, his emotional and psychological scars ran deep. "There is," he wrote, "no statute of limitations on the effects of torture."[13] For almost 50 years Lomax lived with his obsession to find out more about the Japanese who had tortured him and other prisoners of war.

> Physical revenge seemed the only adequate recompense for the anger I carried. I thought often about the young interpreter.... There was no

single dominant figure…on whom I could focus my general hatred, but because of his command of my language, the interpreter was the link; he was the centre-stage in my memories; he was my private obsession. His slurred and struggling English; his endless questions; his repetitiveness; the way he gave voice to the big torturing NCO; he represented all of them; he stood in for all the worst horrors.[14]

In January 1985, Lomax wrote a story for a newsletter published by ex-prisoners of war asking for information about what had happened to him and others in Burma and Thailand in 1943. He hoped to identify his torturers and their interpreter. The stakes were high for him to begin some resolution of this issue, because the repressed memories of torture and his anger associated with it, had contributed to the failure of his first, unhappy, marriage and were causing him problems in his second, happy marriage.

In response to his letter, Lomax received a copy of an article from the *Japanese Times* of August 15, 1989 about a certain Mr. Nagase Takashi, a 71-year-old Japanese veteran of World War II.

After the war, Nagase had assisted a team from the Allied armed forces by translating for them as they tried to find unmarked graves of prisoners of war buried alongside the railway line they had been building in Burma. Until this experience, Nagase said he had not been aware of the final fate of the trainloads of POWs whom he had seen shipped from Singapore to Thailand to work on the railway. As a result, he committed himself to dedicating the rest of his life to memorializing these unknown victims of the Japanese military. The article included a picture of Nagase. Lomax recognized him as the man who had served as the interpreter for the torturers. "The face was unsmiling, thin and familiar with pain, the face of an ailing 71-year-old man…."[15]

Nagase had suffered from cardiac illness for many years. The article quoted him as saying that with each attack he had "flashbacks of Japanese military police…torturing a POW who was accused of possessing a map of the railway. One of their methods was to pour large amounts of water down his throat…. As a former member of the Japanese Army, I thought the agony was what I have to pay for our treatment of POWs."[16]

The article described how Nagase had visited an Allied cemetery in Thailand many times to atone for his guilt by laying wreaths there, and added he had established a foundation for surviving Asian forced labourers, vast numbers of whom also died working on building the railroad.

Lomax "experienced a strange, icy joy of the weirdest kind."[17] He wrote:

> ...I knew that this was the man I wanted. His face was recognizably the face of the interrogator, his sunken cheekbones and eyes and mouth an older edition of that serious young man's features. He was speaking about me, and guardedly admitting that he had been there during my torture. I felt triumphant that I had found him, and that I knew his identity while he was unaware of my continued existence. I had apparently found one of the men I was looking for.... The years of feeling powerless whenever I thought of him and his colleagues were erased. Even now, given the information about what he had done since the war.... The old feelings came to the surface and I wanted to damage him for his part in ruining my life.[18]

Lomax pursued an investigation of Nagase and learned that he was a dedicated opponent of resurgent Japanese militarism, but,

> what I could not tell was whether his expressions of remorse were genuine or not. I needed to see that for myself. The thought was entering my head, distantly at first, that perhaps I should try to meet this man, to make up my mind with that face in front of me again .... I wanted to see Nagase's sorrow so that I could live better with my own....One or two people suggested that perhaps it was time for me to forgive and forget....The majority of people who hand out advice about forgiveness have not gone through the sort of experience I had; I was not inclined to forgive, not yet, and probably never.[19]

Lomax learned that Nagase had published a short book, which had been translated into English in 1990, entitled *Crosses and Tigers*, describing his experiences during and after the war. He obtained a copy of it, hoping it would provide him with details about the events of 1943 with which he was obsessed. Indeed, he read about the events leading up to his interrogation and torture: "Suddenly it's as though he [Nagase] steps out from behind a screen and I am looking at a scene familiar to me distanced as though in a dream."[20]

In his book Nagase described in some detail the interrogation of a British prisoner who had been suspected of spying because prison officials had found in his belongings a sketch of the Thai-Burma Railway with names of its stations. The owner of the map claimed he was a railway fanatic and intended to take it home as a souvenir. The

Japanese authorities were not convinced, because the railway and its bridge over the River Kwai were secret matters, and so they charged him with spying. The prisoner stubbornly denied the charge. Had he confessed he would have been executed. Nagase wrote,

> The fierce questioning continued from morning till night for over a week, which exhausted me as well. The military policeman sometimes shouted at me because he got too excited to differentiate between the prisoner and me. The suspect looked weak and good natured, but he repeated his stubborn denials.... The MP beat him with a stick. I could not bear the sight, so I advised him to confess to avoid further mental and physical pain. He just smiled at me. Finally, the policemen applied the usual torture. First they took him to the bathtub.... Then his broken right arm was placed in front and his left arm behind his back, tied with a cord. They laid him on his back with a towel loosely covering his mouth and nose. They poured water over his face. The soaking cloth blocked his nose and mouth. He struggled to breathe and opened his mouth to inhale air. They poured water into his mouth. I saw his stomach swelling up. Watching the prisoner in great torture, I almost lost my presence of mind. I was desperate to control my shaking body. I feared that he would be killed in my presence. I took him by the broken wrist and felt the pulse. I still remember that I was relieved to feel an unexpected normal pulse.
>
> With the prisoner screaming and crying, "Mother! Mother!" I muttered to myself, "Mother, do you know what is happening to your son now!" I still cannot stop my shuddering every time I recall that horrible scene.[21]

Lomax realized with revulsion that it was he whom Nagase was describing being tortured.

Eighteen years after the war, Nagase visited an Allied war cemetery in Thailand and laid a wreath at the base of the white cross in the centre. He wrote,

> The moment I joined my hands in prayer...I felt my body emitting yellow beams of light in every direction and turning transparent. At that moment I thought, "This is it. You have been pardoned." I believed this feeling plainly... the sense of guilt had lain in my mind for a long time. The moment I visited the graves, I felt the sense of guilt vanish.[22]

The experience of forgiveness did not result in Nagase's forgetting the war and the suffering that resulted from it. He continued to support surviving Asian slave labourers who, "unable to return to their native lands, lived out their miserable lives in Thai villages along the rail lines. He opened a temple of peace and courageously criticized militarism."[23]

Lomax's response to Nagase's autobiography was complex. "It all seemed admirable ... but I felt empty. And I wondered at this feeling that he had been forgiven. God may have forgiven him, but I had not; mere human forgiveness is another matter."[24]

Lomax's wife Patti also read the book, and Nagase's description of his experience of receiving forgiveness while laying a wreath at the cross in the cemetery made her even angrier than her husband. "She wanted to know how Nagase could feel pardoned. How could his sense of guilt simply 'vanish' if no-one, and me in particular, had pardoned him?"[25]

Patti wrote to Nagase telling him that one of the prisoners who had been tortured was her husband, who would like to correspond with him to receive more information. She included a picture of Lomax. She wrote,

Dear Mr Nagase

I have just finished reading your book *Crosses and Tigers*. This is of particular interest to me because my husband is the Royal Signals Officer who had been arrested, along with six others, in connection with the operation of a radio in the railway workshop camp near Kanchanaburi in August 1943. My husband also had with him a map of the railway. He is the man you describe on page 15 of your book, being tortured so terribly....

My husband has lived all these years with the after effects of the cruel experiences he suffered and I hope that contact between you could be a healing experience for both of you. How can you feel "forgiven," Mr. Nagase, if this particular Far Eastern prisoner-of-war has not yet forgiven you? My husband does understand the cultural pressures you were under during the war but whether he can totally forgive your own involvement remains to be seen and it is not for me, who was not there, to judge.[26]

Nagase wrote back:

Dear Mrs. Patricia M. Lomax

I am now quite at a loss after reading your unexpected letter.... The words you wrote to me "If this particular Far Eastern Prisoner of War has not forgiven you" has beaten me down wholely, reminding me of my dirty old days. I think having received such a letter from you is my destiny… Please tell your husband that if I am a bit useful for him to answer any questions that he has had in mind, I am willing to answer them. Anyhow, I am beginning to think I should see him again. Looking at the picture, he looks healthy and tender gentleman, though I am not able to see inside of his mind. Please tell him to live long until I can see him…. The dagger of your letter thrusted me into my heart to the bottom.[27]

Lomax described Patti's and his own reaction to Nagase's letter:

Patti thought this was an extraordinarily beautiful letter. Anger drained away; in its place came a welling of compassion for both Nagase and for me, coupled with a deep sense of sadness and regret. In that moment I lost whatever hard armour I had wrapped around me and began to think the unthinkable: that I could meet Nagase face to face in simple good will. Forgiveness became more than an abstract idea: it was now a real possibility.

As the days went by it seemed that Nagase's sincerity might be utterly genuine. I began to appreciate more fully how damaged he must be by what he had done, however unwillingly; an interrogator suffering in retrospect with his victims. Nor was his concern to make reparation some occasional thing; it was truly almost a way of life… He had also become a devout Buddhist.[28]

Lomax and Nagase arranged to meet, together with their wives, in Kanburi, Thailand, where Lomax had been imprisoned. At the pre-arranged site, Lomax saw Nagase approaching him, and, as he came closer,

I remembered him saying to me again and again, "Lomax, you will tell us," and other phrases he had recited in the voice I hated so much….

He began a formal bow, his face…agitated, … I stepped forward, took his hand and said "Ohayo gozaimasu, Nagase san, ogenki desu ka?" "Good morning, Mr. Nagase, how are you?"

He looked up at me; he was trembling, in tears, saying over and over "I am very, very sorry…" I somehow took command, led him out of the terrible heat to a bench in the shade; I was comforting him, for he was really overcome. At that moment my capacity for reserve and self-control helped me to help him, murmuring reassurances as we sat down. It was as though I was protecting him from the force of the emotions shaking his frail-seeming body. I think I said something like "That's very kind of you to say so" to his repeated expressions of sorrow.

He said to me "Fifty years is a long time, but for me it is a time of suffering. I never forgot you. I remember your face, especially your eyes." He looked deep into my eyes when he said this...

He asked if he could touch my hand. My former interrogator held my arm, which was so much larger than his, stroking it quite unself-consciously. I didn't find it embarrassing. He gripped my wrist with both of his hands and told me that when I was being tortured – he used the word – he measured my pulse... He was kind enough to say that compared to my suffering his was nothing; and yet it was so obvious that he had suffered too, "Various sufferings, various suf-ferings in my heart and mind."[29]

Lomax spent several days with Nagase in Thailand. He realized by now he had forgiven Nagase for his involvement in his torture. But Nagase needed to receive from him a formal expression of that forgiveness.

I still needed to consider the matter of forgiveness, since it so con-cerned him. Assuming that our meeting, in itself, constituted forgive-ness, or that the passage of time had made it irrelevant, seemed too easy; once someone raises forgiveness to such a pitch of importance you become judicial. I felt I had to respond to Nagase's sense of the binding or loosening force of my decision.

A kind Thai woman who we met that week tried to explain the importance of forgiveness in Buddhism to me; I understood that whatever you do you get back in this life and if what you have done is tainted with evil and you have not made atonement for it, evil is returned to you in the next life with interest. Nagase dreaded hell. ...Even if I could not grasp the theology fully, I could no longer see the point of punishing Nagase by a refusal to reach out and forgive him. What mattered was our relation in the here and now, his obvi-ous regret for what he had done and our mutual need to give our encounter some meaning beyond that of the emptiness of cruelty. It was surely worth salvaging as much as we could from the damage to both our lives. The question was now one of choosing the right moment to say the words to him with the formality that the situation seemed to demand.[30]

They decided that after their meeting in Thailand, Nagase would accompany the Lomaxes on a trip to Japan. During his stay in Japan,

Lomax "never felt a flash of the anger I had harboured against Nagase all those years, no backwash of that surge of murderous intent I had felt on finding out that one of them was still alive."[31]

As the time approached for their return to Britain, Lomax decided the time to formally forgive could not be deferred. He asked to meet Nagase privately in the hotel room in Tokyo where Nagase was staying:

> There in that quiet room…I gave Mr. Nagase the forgiveness he desired.
>
> I read my short letter out to him, stopping and checking that he understood each paragraph. I felt he deserved this careful formality. In the letter I said that the war had been over for almost fifty years; that I had suffered much; and that I knew that although he too had suffered throughout this time, he had been most courageous and brave in arguing against militarism and working for reconciliation. I told him that while I could not forget what happened in Kanburi in 1943, I assured him of my total forgiveness.
>
> He was overcome with emotion again, and we spent some time in his room talking quietly and without haste.[32]

The next day Nagase and his wife accompanied Lomax and his wife to the airport.

> As the plane tilted us over the bay of Osaka, I held my wife's hand. I felt that I had accomplished more than I could ever have dreamed of. Meeting Nagase has turned him from a hated enemy, with whom friendship would have been unthinkable, into a blood-brother. If I'd never been able to put a name to the face of one of the men who had harmed me, and never discovered that behind that face there was also a damaged life, the nightmares would have always come from a past without meaning. And I had proved for myself that remembering is not enough, if it simply hardens hate…. Sometimes the hating has to stop.[33]

"Sometimes the hating has to stop" is the way Eric Lomax ended his book. A fundamental motive for forgiveness is the repentance of the one who has caused the injury. If forgiveness is significant in the Buddhist beliefs held by Nagase, it is even more central to Judaism and Christianity, which base their notion of forgiveness on the model of God's forgiveness.

Biblical indications

Early in the Hebrew Bible we find that human beings had become corrupt. The world was "filled with violence" and God "regrets that He made man on earth" (Genesis 6:5-6). He brings on a flood and only Noah, his family and some chosen animals survive.

After the flood, God made a covenant with all children of Noah – and, in fact, with all living creatures – not to destroy the world again, no matter how disappointed God might become. This is forgiveness as a pure act of unconditional grace, a unilateral decision on the part of God. There is no apology, no remorse, and no repentance.

"The rainbow covenant is a declaration of pre-emptive forgiveness. God binds himself in advance to associate mercy with justice."[34] In a similar way, Christ dying on the cross asked God to forgive those who had put him there "because they did not know what they were doing" (Luke 23:34). These are models of divine forgiveness.

The minority report on forgiveness would insist that, to the extent it is possible, we should take this divinely unconditioned forgiveness as our model. But the majority report would stress that, between human beings, forgiveness often happens only when the sinner sincerely makes amends, as we see in Nagase's transformation as validated by his former victim Eric Lomax. Inner contrition in this paradigm of forgiveness must be followed by outward acts of ceasing to do evil and beginning to do good.

We see this developed in the Joseph story. Eleventh son of the patriarch Jacob, Joseph as a youngster observed a reconciling meeting between his father and his uncle Esau (Genesis 33). Later, Joseph was the envy of his ten older brothers.[35] They resented his dreams, and especially they resented that their common father, Jacob, seemed to love Joseph more than them (Genesis 37). They plotted to kill him and later sold him into slavery.

After many adventures, Joseph became viceroy of Egypt; he eventually met his brothers when they came to Egypt during a famine. He finally disclosed to them who he was and, when they were silenced in shock and fear, he told them: "Do not be distressed or feel guilty because you sold me. Look! God has sent me ahead of you to save lives" (Genesis 45:4-5).

This is a singular biblical instance of forgiveness. When Jacob died, Joseph repeated his forgiveness, this time with greater force. "Don't be afraid. Am I in the place of God? You intended to harm me, but God intended it for good" (Genesis 50:20).

Forgiving means overcoming anger and the desire for vengeance. This is certainly the case with the God of the Hebrew Bible: "Compassionately, however, he forgave their guilt instead of killing them, repeatedly repressing his anger instead of rousing his full wrath" (Psalm 78:38).

But overcoming anger and bitterness can take place even without forgiveness. Jacob wronged his brother Esau, cheating him of his father Isaac's blessing as the eldest son. As a result, Esau nursed ill will against Jacob and planned to harm him after the death of their father.

When Rebecca, their mother, heard about this, she warned her beloved Jacob to stay away, "until your brother's anger cools. When it has subsided and he forgets what you have done to him, I will send and fetch you back" (Genesis 27:44-45).

In other words, the way Rebecca believes Esau will overcome his desire for revenge is not by an act of forgiveness but simply by forgetting what has happened. Memory, or the lack of it, is a crucial factor in his healing process. By contrast, forgiveness is a deliberate decision to change one's attitude and to overcome one's anger and desire for revenge.

The Joseph story is about this change of consciousness. But it sets up a precondition for forgiveness. Between the brothers' initial reunion in Egypt and Joseph's eventual disclosure of his identity, a seemingly unrelated incident happens. Joseph accuses his brothers of being spies and demands they bring their youngest brother Benjamin the next time they visit Egypt.

Later he plants money and his silver chalice in their saddlebags, allowing him to accuse Benjamin of theft and threatening to imprison him. What this means is that Joseph wants to see if his brothers are capable of repentance and remorse. They are.

After the first allegation they say, unaware that Joseph is listening to them, "We deserve to be punished because of what we did to our brother." At the second encounter, as Benjamin is about to receive his sentence for attempted theft, Judah begs to be imprisoned in his place. "This is significant," Michael Dobkowski points out, "because it was Judah who, years earlier, had proposed selling Joseph into slavery. Now he is willing to suffer his fate rather than see a brother be made a slave."[36]

Dobkowski argues that one paradigm of divine forgiveness for both Judaism and Christianity is the love of a parent for a child. A parent knows quite well that a child will make mistakes. True parenthood is the willingness to empower the child to make mistakes because without that, no child can become mature and responsible.

Forgiveness is that empowerment, because it means that a child is safe in the knowledge that no error is final. The root meaning of the word "forgiveness" is suggestive of this parental paradigm. The Hebrew word for the capacity to forgive is *rachamim*, which "comes from the root *rechem*, meaning a womb."[37]

"A judge, charged with administering the law, cannot forgive, but a parent can. The concept of forgiveness comes into full sight when God is envisaged as both judge and parent, when law and mercy join hands."[38] The psalmist wrote, "Fortunate is one whose transgression is forgiven, whose sin is covered…. Fortunate is the person whom the Lord does not hold guilty, in whose spirit there is no deceit" (Psalm 32:1-2).

The teaching on forgiveness in the New Testament builds on the tradition found in the Hebrew Bible. It has an inner logic that can be discovered in the writings of St. Paul and in the Synoptic Gospels of Mark, Matthew and Luke. "Forgiveness is part of the larger context of salvation."[39]

First, there is the universality of sin discussed earlier. Paul writes about this in the first chapters of his Letter to the Romans. Both Jews and Gentiles labour under the power of sin. Jews have violated the Law of God given to them through Moses; Gentiles have desecrated the Law of God written in their consciences.

The consequences of sin are also universal. Beginning with the original sin of Adam and Eve in the Garden of Eden, the authors of Genesis follow the progressive decline of relationships between human beings, starting for the Jews with the murder of Abel by his brother Cain, and for the Gentiles in the futility of their thinking and a darkening of their minds, leading to all kinds of idolatry, lust, impurity and degrading of their bodies.

The crucial point for Paul and for the later Christian tradition is the impossibility for human beings by themselves to reverse the consequences of the original turning away from God by their first parents, Adam and Eve. One consequence of this turning away from God is a moral impotence.

Under the power of sin, humans can see the good and even long for it, but they consistently choose a lesser good that is only apparently good but lacks some crucial factor found in the ideal good. This is the paradox of the enslaved or servile will.

God's response to this moral impotence is the gift of grace that enables the will to embrace the ideal good and not the apparent good, which is deprived of some central element. This grace comes through Christ and his gift of the Holy Spirit.

Discouraged by his incarcerated will, Paul cried out, "Wretched man that I am! Who will rescue me from this body of death?" (Rom. 7:24), and immediately answers his own question: "Thanks be to God through Jesus Christ our Lord!" (Rom. 7.25).

The challenge for Christians according to St. Paul is to accept in faith the gracious initiative of God in their direction, as did their ancestor Abraham who believed that God's promises of fruitfulness would be fulfilled, though that seemed impossible according to nature.

The challenge for Christians who have survived torture is the need to pass on to those who have tortured them the gift of forgiveness and reconciliation first received in the Christian's conversion to God. On this point, the Synoptics are clear and unequivocal.

When Jesus responded to his disciples' request that he teach them how to pray, he told them they should express the desire that God's name be held holy, express their longing for the coming of God's kingdom, and ask for their daily bread. They then should ask for forgiveness of their trespasses. But the forgiveness is conditional, as Sister Diana knew so well: "Forgive us our debts as we also have forgiven our debtors" (Matt 6:12).

Another powerful teaching of Jesus about the reciprocity of forgiveness is the parable in Matthew 18, which represents an answer to Peter's question about how many times he should forgive. "As many as seven times?" asks Peter. Jesus responds with a Semitic expression, "Not seven times, but I tell you seventy-seven times" (Matt 18:21-2).

Then Matthew relates Jesus' parable of the king who listened to the pleading of his slave and forgave him a huge debt only to discover that the same slave refused to forgive an insignificant debt owed to him by a fellow slave. When the king heard about it he was angry and turned the unforgiving slave over to the torturer until he paid the entire debt, an ambiguous outcome for this discussion of the possibility of forgiveness by torture survivors.

Notwithstanding this troublesome aspect of the parable, the overall message is clear: Jesus seems to ask his followers to think of themselves as people who have been forgiven a great debt and to behave in the opposite way of the unforgiving slave.

Two central collections of Jesus' teachings to his followers can be found in the Sermon on the Plain in Luke and the Sermon on the Mount in Matthew. Both include the teaching on forgiveness within the larger context of a universal love that reaches out to enemies as well as to friends. In relating this material both Luke and Matthew tell us not only what we must do to be saved, but also what sort of persons we must be.

Within the context of forgiveness the teaching represents inverted logic because it turns upside down our normal expectations reflected in the majority report on forgiveness. "But I say to you that listen, love your enemies, do good to those who hate you, bless those who curse you, pray for those who abuse you" (Luke 6:27-8).

Luke has Jesus announce the reward for such behaviour: "Your reward will be great, and you will be children of the Most High: for he is kind to the ungrateful and the wicked. Be merciful just as your Father is merciful" (Luke 6:35b-6).[40]

Theologian Peter Ely speaks of a salvific triad in Christianity consisting in a renunciation, spoken of in this parable and in the Sermons on the Mount and on the Plain, the Law of the Cross, and forgiveness.[41] The three are related.

When the rich man asks Jesus what he needs to do to inherit eternal life, Jesus counsels him to keep the commandments, and then, when the man confesses he has done that from his youth, Jesus recommends he sell whatever he has, give the money to the poor, and follow him (Mark 10:21; Matthew 19:21). This is renunciation.

When Jesus asks his disciples who they say he is, Peter answers that Jesus is the Messiah. Jesus congratulates him and then goes on to talk about his upcoming torture and violent death: Jesus "began to teach them that the Son of Man must undergo great suffering, and be rejected by the elders, the chief priests, and the scribes, and be killed, and after three days rise again" (Mark 8:31). This is the Law of the Cross. God's way of reversing evil is not to take it away but to accept it voluntarily and thus transform it into good. Renunciation and the Law of the Cross lead to forgiveness because forgiveness is a form of renunciation and follows the Law of the Cross. Within Christianity we can detect two patterns of forgiveness, ordinary and extraordinary, which we have been calling the majority and minority reports. Ordinary forgiveness follows the pattern of injury, followed by repentance by the guilty party, followed by forgiveness. Forgiveness is extraordinary when the middle step is missing and there is no repentance. It is based on the triad and presumes a highly developed spiritual maturity and openness to divine grace.

Some might say such forgiveness can lead to passivity in the face of evil and to injustice. This would be a perversion of Christ's teaching since the New Testament stresses Christians should resist evil. In fact, renunciation, the Law of the Cross and forgiveness are precisely conditions for the possibility of resisting evil by transforming it into good. "Violating the logic of these three imperatives magnifies evil and sets in motion an escalating series of evils each meant to overcome evil, but each in fact deepening it."[42]

It is important to understand that evil in the present context does not have an independent existence and is not, therefore, an abstract reality. Rather it represents something missing in goodness. The good is fundamentally real and is related to the source of all good, whom we call God.

Forgiveness has two aspects, one private and the other public. If a survivor of torture follows the ordinary path of forgiveness, but does not achieve the assurance that their persecutors have repented, what can he or she do? Eric Lomax was freed from 50 years of hatred when he forgave Nagase, but his case is unusual.

How can the ordinary survivor come to forgiveness within his or her own person when their tormentors show no contrition and achieve immunity from prosecution from the World Court or other judicial bodies?

Sister Diana Ortiz's efforts to obtain full disclosure from her own government about its part in her ordeal were ultimately unsuccessful; in fact, key officials continued to deny she had been abducted, tortured and raped preferring to believe the Guatemalan position that she had engaged in a self-kidnapping to disguise a lesbian love affair in which she had willingly participated.

At the time of writing, it is unclear if Canadian Maher Arar will obtain enough information from the inquiry into his torture in Syria to enable him to move toward forgiveness and acceptance. Though it is rare to establish interpersonal forgiveness for state-sponsored torture, it is possible for survivors to do so through the transformation and healing of their memory of the interpersonal violation they suffered.

Augus ine on memory

This possibility offers us hope. "Hope has two beautiful daughters. Their names are anger and courage; anger at the way things are, and courage to see they do not remain the way they are." This anonymous aphorism, wrongly attributed to St. Augustine, is germane to the ongoing struggle of survivors of torture. While we cannot credit Augustine for this thought about the two lovely daughters of hope, we can say his rethinking of the meaning of the past in terms of the present can be of help for the healing of memories of torture.

His fourth- and fifth-century CE reflections on memory suggest to us today that the transformative power of our recollection can overcome the past horror of torture so that it need not continue to oppress us in the present.

Before his conversion to Christianity, the young Augustine thought the past was fixed, unchangeable, and immovably real. A metaphor represented time for him and most other philosophers of his epoch. But he wrote a book during this period entitled *On Music* in which he showed our memory of a musical note played early in a performance is transformed later by the association of this note within the context of other notes.[43] This thought contained *in nuce* his later position on the past and its relationship with the present.

As a Christian seeking to express his sincere repentance for his sins and his sense that he had been forgiven by God in Christ, Augustine wrote his autobiography *Confessions*. Because he needed to make right his past, he developed his earlier thinking on the "pastness" of the past to say that it exists in the present through our memory, and does not have an independent, nor abstract reality apart from what we remember about it. Augustine says the following in the *Confessions*:

> What now is clear and plain is, that neither things to come nor past are. Nor is it properly said, "there be three times, past, present, and to come;" yet perchance it might be properly said, "there be three times; a present of things past, a present of things present, and a present of things future." For these three do exist in some sort, in the soul, but otherwise do I not see them; present of things past, memory; present of things present, sight; present of things future, expectation.[44]

Time is inseparable from memory for the mature Augustine. The past only occurs through the trace it leaves in the future and this trace is found especially in our psyche. According to Augustine, the past only exists through memory; there cannot be any entirely independent past event unaffected by what comes later. A musical note is only situated and defined by its place in a sequence, "such that the end of a musical composition still to be heard can change the nature of what we have already heard."[45]

Augustine realized that implementing Christ's teaching on forgiveness required a temporal rather than a spatial framework. He sought forgiveness for his past life and reconciliation with God. The Christian commitment to forgiveness in time required a drastic revision of the theory with which philosophers had previously worked.

Sister Diana Ortiz

What does this have to do with the aftermath of torture? In the case of Sister Diana Ortiz, the realization that she might have unknowingly associated herself with guerrillas in the Guatemalan village of San Miguel Acatán where she had done her missionary work helped her understand how it could have happened that her police abductors had mistaken her for a guerrilla, or at best one of their sympathizers.

It eventually became clear to her that the military authorities had perceived her as a threat to their national security. This changed her memory of what had happened. Their incorrect perspective was a defective good leading to the evil of her torture, which they believed was in aid of their national security.[46] Later, the bitterness she initially felt that her suffering was the result of a case of mistaken identity by her kidnappers was transformed by her realization that the very fact she was a nun and therefore represented the Church which opposed the military regime in Guatemala was reason enough for her to have been abducted and tortured.[47] The reinterpreted past for Sister Ortiz changed in the present through a transformation of her memory.

In the epilogue of her book, Sister Ortiz summarizes how she has integrated the terrible experience she went through in the first week of November 1989 with her present life in the 21st century.

> I have forgiven God for not working some dramatic miracle. I've learned that God was working a quiet miracle all along, healing me through other people. I still have the horrible past with me – I carry it in my memory and in my skin and I always will – but laid over

it, like new skin over a wound, is a newer past, a past of caring and love.... As I improve, I have faith and hope and trust again, on my good days. But even on my good days, the smell of cigarette smoke reminds me of the burns the torturers inflicted on me. The sight of a man in uniform reminds me of the Policeman. I jump if someone runs up behind me, and if someone stands too close or stares at me, I back away. I sleep with the light on. I ask people not to smoke, not to stare, not to talk about torture tactics in front of me, and not to invite me to movies that are violent.... On my bad days I still say I should have died back in that prison, before I had to be used to inflict pain, before I had to make a choice about another person's life or death. I still wished I had died.[48]

The Gestapo who tortured Jean Améry, the Japanese who tortured Eric Lomax, the US Marines who allegedly tortured John Walker Lindh, Hisséne Habré and his DDS who tortured Souleymane Guengueng, the American CIA agents who may have tortured Omar al-Faruq, the Syrians with their Canadian and American collaborators who may have tortured Maher Arar, the French paratroopers who tortured Henri Alleg, the Spanish inquisitors who tortured Elvira de Campos, the officials of the Royal Government of Bhutan who apparently tortured Tek Nath Rizal and Rongthong Kuenley Dorji, and the Gestapo who tortured Peter Moen: all pursued what they thought was the good in their interrogative efforts to find out the truth, but it was a defective good inasmuch as it violated human rights and the sanctity of the persons involved, both victims and torturers. This is because the end, which one may pursue as a good thing, does not justify the means used, especially when they constitute a personal violation of the human right of physical, psychological and moral integrity immune from violation through torture.

According to Amnesty International's statistics for 2001, more than 150 governments engage in torture or ill treatment. The number in 1999 was 114. The War on Terror makes it all the more important that all people of good will, and especially Catholics, will continue to speak out against torture and defend human rights.

Conclusion

In her seminal study of torture, *The Body in Pain*, Elaine Scarry has shown us that in essence torture is a story or a discourse in which the victim is being taught the futility of acting like a subject, of aspiring to anything beyond abject victimhood and objectification. Persons who have attempted to behave in a lofty and selfless manner, who are prisoners of conscience, suffer the subversion of their souls through the vulnerability of their bodies when they undergo torture. The hopes and ideals they have constructed until that point are effaced by the new story being told to them by their torturers, that they are absolutely alone and in total solitude, and that this solitude of the torture chamber is a prelude to their death.[1]

While in basic agreement with Scarry's analysis, the present analysis is an attempt to break through that solitude of the many anonymous victims of torture in order to present a contrasting story about torture, a story that is being constructed by some in the Catholic community and many others who are committed to human rights. The victims are not alone; some Catholics and others choose to stand in solidarity with them.

The history and contemporary information about state-sponsored torture supplied by my book deserve attention. Its narrow focus speaks to the mixed success of the effort of the Catholic Church in Chile and Argentina to deal with the problem. Torture is a worldwide crisis, especially in our present context of the war on terrorism. Other institutions have shared in the effort to combat it, notably the courts of Spain, Chile, Mexico, Belgium, Senegal and Argentina, not to mention the United Nations Organization with its conventions and protocols. Non-governmental organizations such as the International Red Cross and Red Crescent, Amnesty International and Human Rights Watch have taken leadership positions in the struggle at various points in the past.

But it is the Catholic story that has arrested my attention and given rise to this book. There are several reasons for this. First, thanks to the candor and humility of the late Pope John Paul, some Catholics have acknowledged their Church's past failures in this area, and proclaimed to all that they have changed their story on torture. Catholics' public commitment to eradicate torture made before and after its twentieth-century watershed of Vatican II represents a strong moral voice against the ongoing institutionalization of torture as a system of investigation and coercion. Second, official and unofficial Catholic opinion on torture has persuasive power throughout the world. A major argument of the book has been that this position needs to be more strongly and widely communicated and be made more consistent through changes in universal church law and moral teaching at the level of military chaplains and laity in armed security forces.

In this concluding chapter, some further analysis will be offered as to why the work of combating torture and abuse of prisoners constitutes an unfinished task and a constant challenge for the Church. The first reason is political in the wide sense of the word. Ideological and cultural consensus in some quarters has allowed torture to become a legitimate response to a perceived national emergency. The prophetic voice of those Catholics who are committed to the contemporary vision of their Church as a defender of human rights and who have condemned the use of torture as a method of interrogation and of political intimidation has not been strong enough to overcome this majority perspective in some countries. Furthermore, there is the serious issue of the penchant of Catholic theology to divide the human spirit from matter.

Chilean poet Ronaldo Muñoz pointed to this topic of the split between the inner self and one's concrete substance when he dedicated an "anti-Creed" to the parishioners of a wealthy parish who, after receiving Holy Communion at their Christmas Eve Mass, turned over to police a group of religious peacefully protesting torture outside their church.

> And by all means the public denunciation
> of social sin
> is not Christian nor evangelical,
> because the Christian is to be a sign
> of reconciliation
> and *not* of conflict
> and because consensus
> and *not* the truth
> will set us free.
>
> And so,
> Merry Christmas!

For oppressors and oppressed,
For torturers and tortured.
Because Christmas is a great mystery,
much above such material things
as economic oppression
and the torture of the body.[2]

One version of Catholic thinking represented by the parishioners described by Muñoz would say that the role the Church was called to play in society was one of conflict resolution and peace-making between opposed political communities. By speaking out clearly and forcefully to condemn the use of torture, Catholic leaders would have to be even-handed and careful lest such a position be taken in an unspiritual manner.

The stated goal of some state-initiated torture is to find out the truth. The torturer believes that his victim knows something that is vital for the security of the state or at least that this person holds ideas and thoughts that contradict the ruling ideology. Hence the torturer inflicts pain and coercion on the tortured. He thereby implicitly privileges spirit over matter and splits them apart. The human rights advocate would defend their intrinsic unity and claim that the violation of one is at the same time a violation of the other.

The 2004 decision of officials in the Vatican to open the archival records of the Inquisition to scholars has laid to rest many anti-Catholic calumnies on the one hand, but on the other hand, has confirmed that Church-approved torture did take place in the past "in the service of the truth" as the late Pope put it in his millennial confession of the sins of the Church. As evident as this documentary evidence from history might unfortunately be, the contemporary position taken by the Church's teaching office rejecting state-sponsored torture as a method of interrogation or, what is even worse, as a means of intimidation is equally clear and noteworthy. Any discussion of Catholic perspectives on torture must start there and not in the Inquisition.

The present study has made extensive use of first-person narratives of survivors of torture, despite the fact that some readers might find this material disturbing, even prurient. I have done this in order to avoid the split between torture as a concept and its terrible and substantial reality. It is important that we understand how horribly evil torture really is. Given the continuing risk of dividing the spirit from the flesh in this most physical of matters, I deemed it important to be as clear and as graphic as possible. Furthermore, such narratives offer torture survivors another opportunity to tell their story and, in doing so, to gesture in the direction of closure and healing of their many wounds. Publishing one's testimony and having it heard by a larger readership gives rise to the hope that something positive might emerge from the terror.

Another reason to include first-person narratives of torture is that the Catholic community is constructing a new story based on what it has learned from its past about torture, what it has heard from such accounts as these, and on its hope for a future free from torture.[3] Through their intention to become stalwart defenders of human rights, some Catholics are in the process of a cultural re-construction that is especially relevant today.

We began the book within the context of newfound fear about national security in Western democracies after the tragic events known as 9/11. One theme throughout the book is that Central and South America went through a similar terrorist threat to their national sovereignty after the Second World War, reaching its height in the 1970s and '80s, and they described their struggle as a battle between Marxism and Christianity. Because their governments had reason to believe that they were under siege by left-wing guerrillas, they allowed their military and paramilitary forces to indulge in human rights abuses, including the widespread use of torture, in order to preserve their traditional way of life, which many described as a Catholic civilization. Based on first-person evidence of survivors describing their experience under national security detention, we argued that, even within the context of war, torture was different and especially egregious. The point in this was not only to comment on the Dirty War in Argentina and other such events in the past, but also to offer a warning about the present situation in the so-called War on Terror.

The theological grounds for condemning torture are that it violates the human person and community in a particularly immoral way. The capacity to establish community based on mutual trust and respect is one way that human persons share in the "image and likeness of God," and in many ways torturers willfully destroy this even as they violate their victims' will and personal integrity.

In some ways the book could have ended at this point, since there is little to add to this argument in favour of human rights. But the fact that judicial torture has played such a significant part in Western cultural history suggests that it will not be easy for the Catholic Church and other institutions such as the United Nations to construct an alternative storyline about it. And so it was necessary to present the case for torture and to underline the deleterious role played by ancient Roman law and the ecclesiastical version of it the thirteenth-century return to the use of torture to extract confessions from those accused of serious crimes when partial evidence suggested they were guilty. In that chapter, the contemporary discussion of the use of torture to solve the "ticking-bomb" scenario was presented for the readers' consideration.

If we had to ask why one could choose to torture someone else, it was also incumbent to present an even stronger case against using torture. The slow development of Catholic theological teaching against torture found its way into this section where the preferential option of law prevailed over the moral and pastoral instincts of Jesuit theologians like Adam Tanner, Friedrich Spee, and Paul Laymann, who were faced with the hysterical depredations of the seventeenth-century witch and sorcerer trials in Germany and elsewhere.

Two types of arguments were presented. The deontological argument invokes the inviolability of the human person, which makes torture everywhere and always wrong. The utilitarian argument appeals to the fact that, as an interrogational tool, torture often elicits false or misleading information. Within our present historical context, the existence of a universal convention against torture, with the novel legal provision of universal jurisdiction attached to it, adds legal jeopardy to other reasons against involvement in torture. Other prudential reasons against a government engaging in torture include the difficulty in controlling abuses of it when it is officially sanctioned and the phenomenon of contagion. The Gestapo in the Second World War used torture against the French Resistance and then newly free France resorted to its use against popular insurgencies in Vietnam and Algeria. The Shangri-La of Bhutan learned from its neighbours how to suppress anti-national rebellions by the judicious use of this method.

The chapter dedicated to the study of torturers is not intended to deny their personal responsibility for their brutality. But it makes the illiberal argument that there is possible mitigation in torturers' moral accountability due to their military education and especially as a result of the fog created by a pervasive ideology. Theologically, the universality of sin and of redemption grounds the hope for salvation even within the most vicious regime using torture against their opponents.

The perception of the torturer as himself a victim of systematic evil suggested the order of the material presented in the book. As to the ideas themselves, we have stressed not only the physical pain inflicted on the torture victim, but the spiritual and psychological damage as well. While the physical hurt done by torture to its victims is momentous, its spiritual harm was stressed as well in an effort to avoid the division discussed earlier between the soul and the body.

Narratives about torture and its long-term effects are replete with religious ethics. In his compelling testimony to the consequences involved even with the threat of torture, entitled "I Gave the Names," Adrian Leftwich described how as a young man he had sold out his political comrades and personal friends when faced with the prospect of torture by the apartheid regime of South Africa. He lived with his guilt and continued to deny personal responsibility for what he had done until sixteen years later in Great Britain. Two friends ended their discussion with him about the events that led up to his betrayal of his friends when one of them said, "No. It was not okay at all. Whatever the pressures were, it was not okay to behave like that." Leftwich goes immediately on to say, "I know it seems unbelievable, but I had never previously allowed myself to admit this simple truth."[4] For the survivor of torture situations, the harm done is extensive, the road to recovery is a long one and, unlike Leftwich, many never arrive anywhere near their destination.

The chapter entitled "The Church and Torture" dealt with only three countries: Argentina, Chile and Canada. We could have discussed many others in light of the Church's struggle to make the teaching on fundamental human rights their own. An institution as old as the Catholic Church finds its history to be a palimpsest or a parchment from which one piece of writing has been erased to make room for another, leaving the first still visible. After the takeover of the Argentinean government by the military in 1976, priests sympathetic to the regime, some of them Spaniards, scoured the texts of St. Thomas Aquinas and his successors for justification for the use of torture by the state.[5] If most of the discussion of Church and torture had to do with bishops and priests, especially military and police chaplains, this was not intended to deny the fact that the main group charged with the challenge and moral duty to defend human rights and prevent torture are the laity, without whose involvement this defense can and will never happen.

The poignant account of how divine forgiveness for torture slowly came to fruition in the lives of Eric Lomax and Diana Ortiz necessitated allowing them to talk with us, their readers, at length and in their own voices. Their eventual liberation from the desire for vengeance involved many others and was a protracted process. The approach taken to recovery from torture here is that it is not primarily a medical or psychological process, but a spiritual one.[6]

The deliberate infliction of physical pain and cruelty on someone in order to extract information from them represents the ultimate violation of human dignity. A human being is special, inviolable and worthy of ultimate respect as a result of our reverence for God, our Creator and Lord. Despite the many arguments that might be advanced for torture in certain situations, no one should authorize or perform it. To ask someone to degrade and deface the image of God in a man or woman is to exact a double violation of both the tortured and the torturer. A modern liberal democracy that permits or encourages this practice, even as a strategy for survival, betrays its ultimate reality and meaning which has been connected with the absolute prohibition of torture.[7]

Endnotes

Introduction

1   Presiding at a Eucharistic celebration in St. Peter's Basilica on March 12, 2000, the First Sunday of Lent, the Pope led a "Confession of Sins Committed in the Service of the Church." Then-Cardinal Josef Ratzinger, the head of the Congregation for the Doctrine of the Faith, the successor organization to the Holy Office which had had Church responsibility for the work of the inquisitions, was given the task of confessing "the use of force in the service of truth"; cf. International Theological Commission, "Memory and Reconciliation: The Church and the Faults of the Past," December 1999, #5.3; John Paul II, "Inquisition Requires Calm, Objective Analysis," *L'Osservatore Romano*, November 11, 1998.

2   The position of the Catholic Church on human rights is analogous to that of contemporary Germany. Consider this dramatic confrontation in 1987 between General Augusto Pinochet of Chile and Nolbert Bluem, at that time West German Minister of Labour, captured by a writer of *Der Spiegel*. "I accept the principle of non-intervention in the internal affairs of other states," said Bluem to Pinochet, "but that principle has one exception: human rights. Here interference is an obligation. Therefore, Mister President, stop torturing." Pinochet, according to the writer, was caught off guard. He threw back the Nazi experience in the face of the German diplomat. Bluem responded that his own country's terrible history gave him not only the right to give his opinion but an obligation to defend human rights wherever they were violated. Pinochet was stymied by this, but retorted, "And what did you do at Stammheim?" a reference to the prison where the Baader-Meinhof gang died. Bluem then proposed an exchange: Pinochet would get free rein to investigate prisons in Germany if Bluem were allowed the same privilege in Chile. Pinochet ended the exchange in this way: "These [accusations] are lies invented by the communists. I am a committed Christian and I pray every day. We must combat communism." Cited in William T. Cavanaugh, *Torture and Eucharist* (Oxford: Blackwell, 1998), 72–73. "The German legal position outlawing the use of torture to obtain evidence includes not only its use by German authorities but its use in any other jurisdiction as well. The only person convicted of involvement in the 09.11.2001 tragedy, Moroccan Mounir El Motassadeq, having been convicted in 2003 of aiding and abetting several thousand murders and sentenced to 15 years in prison, was freed by a German appeals court and now faces a new trial. His defence attorney, Josef Graessle-Muenscher, said that he intends to have the charges dropped against his client as soon as the new trial begins on the basis of the fact that key evidence against him was obtained by US authorities by the use of torture." Reuters, *National Post*, August 5, 2004, A8.

3   *Nunca Más. The Report of the Argentine National Commission on the Disappeared*. Introductions by Ronald Dworkin. (New York: Farrar Straus Giroux, 1986), 1.

4   John Macquarrie, *Principles of Christian Theology* (New York: Charles Scribner, 1966), 30–32.

5   This was only the first Convention on Torture sponsored by the United Nations Organization. In 1984, a second was passed. Not yet adopted, but currently in the last stages of finalization, is an addendum to the 1984 agreement known as the

"Optional Protocol" permitting signatories to undertake unannounced inspections of prisons and detention centres of other signatories. These conventions were reframed into more legal form in 1998 in the "Statutes of Rome" that have been ratified by 66 countries at the time of writing. As well, the European Commission has produced a draft regulation that would ban member states trading in "equipment and products which could be used for capital punishment, torture or other cruel, inhuman or degrading treatment or punishment," cf. Steve Wright, "Putting Restraints on the Torture Trade," *Guardian Weekly*, March 27–April 2, 2003, 25.

6   Dan Gardner, "After 9/11, the Gloves Came Off," *Ottawa Citizen*, February 3, 2004, A7.

7   Article 1, Convention Against Torture and Other Cruel, Inhuman or Degrading Treatment or Punishment, http://www.hrweb.org/legal/cat.html (accessed June 2, 2003).

8   John Simpson and Jana Bennett, *The Disappeared and the Mothers of the Plaza: The Story of the 11,000 Argentinians Who Vanished* (New York: St. Martin's Press, 1985), 92–103.

9   Dan Gardner, "Agony Inc.," *Ottawa Citizen*, February 1, 2004, C3.

10   Ibid.

11   E.g. Tacitus, *The Annals of Imperial Rome*, III, 21, trans. Michael Grant, revised edition (London : Penguin, 1956), 130.

12   Edward Peters, *Torture* (New York: Basil Blackwell, 1985), 1.

13   Susan Neiman, *Evil in Modern Thought: An Alternative History of Philosophy* (Princeton, NJ: Princeton University Press, 2002), 256.

14   Ibid., 34.

15   For example, judicial torture was condemned by Tertullian in De corona 11, and De idolatria 17, by St. Augustine in Civitas Dei 11, by Pope Nicholas I with respect to the Bulgarians in 866; cf. P.K. Meagher, "Torture," *New Catholic Encyclopedia*, V. 14 (Washington, DC: Catholic University of America, 1967), 208.

16   Martin Robertson and Amnesty International, *Torture in the Eighties* (Oxford: Amnesty International Publications, 1984), 4.

17   Peter Maass, "Torture, Tough or Lite," *The New York Times*, March 9, 2003, Week in Review, 4.

18   W.G. Sebald, *On the Natural History of Destruction*. Translated from the German by Anthea Bell. In Charles Simic, "Conspiracy of Silence," *The New York Review of Books*, February 27, 2003, 8. Améry was the nom de guerre of Hans Meyer, an Austrian-born Jew who became the pioneer of Holocaust survival literature. Irene Heidelberger-Leonard, *Jean Améry Revolte in der Resignation* (Stuttgart: Klett-Cotta, 2004).

19   Find a Grave Cemetery Records, Jean Améry. http://www.findagrave.com/cgi-bin/fg.cgi?page=gr&GRID=94908pt=Jean%20Amery.

20   "The U.N. High Commissioner for Human Rights, the authoritative interpreter of the international Convention Against Torture, has ruled that lengthy interrogation

may incidentally and legitimately cost a prisoner sleep. But when employed for the purpose of breaking a prisoner's will, sleep deprivation 'may in some cases constitute torture.'" Dana Priest and Barton Gellman, "CIA's Dirty Little Secrets Exposed," *The Washington Post*, In *Guardian Weekly*, January 2–8, 2003, 29.

21 John Conroy, *Unspeakable Acts, Ordinary People* (New York: Alfred A. Knopf, 2000), 6.

22 Ibid., 34.

23 This is "an extremely heavy chair, whose seat is a sheet of corrugated iron; on the back part there is a protuberance where one of the wires of the shock machine can be inserted [and] in addition to this, the chair had a wooden bar that pushed your legs backwards, so that with each spasm produced by the electrical discharge your legs would hit against the wooden bar, causing deep gashes"; Lawrence Weschler, *A Miracle, A Universe* (New York: Pantheon, 1990), 41.

24 *Torture in Brazil: A Report by the Archdiocese of Sao Paulo*, Translated by Jaime Wright, Edited by Joan Dassin. (NewYork: Vintage Books, 1986), 19.

25 Priest and Gellman, "CIA's Dirty Little Secrets Exposed," 29.

26 Edwin Dobb, "Should John Walker Lindh Go Free?" *Harper's Magazine*, May 2002, 33.

27 Raymond Bonner, Don Van Natta, Jr., and Amy Waldman, "Questioning Terror Suspects in a Dark and Surreal World," *The New York Times*, Sunday, March 9, 2003, 1, 14.

28 Nunca Más , 52; Gardner, "Torture Inc.," *Ottawa Citizen*, February 1, 2004, C4.

29 For Whom the Liberty Bell Tolls: Special Report on Civil Liberties," *The Economist*, August 31, 2002, 18. "Dr. Suzan Fayad, a psychiatrist who works with Nadeem, an Egyptian organization which rehabilitates victims of violence," argues that "torturing radical Islamists makes them more violent…. Islamists don't believe too much in psychiatry and rehabilitation. They believe God will help them…. It's torture that makes them angry and take up terrorism." A possible example of this would be Dr. Ayman al-Zawahiri, a surgeon who became Osama bin Laden's deputy. Dr. Zawahiri was imprisoned in Egypt and, according to friends, "beaten frequently after the assassination of President Anwar Sadat in 1981. The humiliations – including, reportedly, the betrayal under torture of a fellow Islamist – marked him for life. He left prison with renewed commitment to the Islamist cause, and made regular trips to Afghanistan to support the anti-Soviet mojahedin." Owen Bowcott, "September 11 Blamed on Trail of State Torture," *Guardian Weekly*, January 30–February 5, 2003, 3.

30 Bonner, Van Natta, Jr., Waldman, "Questioning Terror Suspects, " *The New York Times*, Sunday, March 9, 2003, 14.

31 Ibid.

32 Ibid.

33 Marina Warner, "Who's Sorry Now? Edited Version of the Amnesty Lecture in

Human Rights Delivered in Oxford University in 2002," *Times Literary Supplement*, August 1, 2003, 10.

34   Astiz belonged to a small group of officers commanding an anti-terrorist task force, GT 3.3/2, based at the Naval Mechanics School in Buenos Aires, ESMA. Known as "grey wolves," they were permitted to act autonomously and were not required to report their day-to-day activities to higher authorities in the Argentine Navy. Astiz and the others in his unit were responsible for the disappearances of hundreds, and perhaps as many as 2000 people, almost none of whom survived. They, but not Astiz, also looted the personal belongings of those he arrested, and made money from the sale of orphaned children to childless couples. John Simpson and Jana Bennett, *The Disappeared and the Mothers of the Plaza: The Story of the 11, 000 Argentinians Who Vanished* (New York: St. Martin's Press, 1985), 346.

35   Carlos Escudé, "Natural Law at War," *Times Literary Supplement*, May 31, 2002, 27.

36   Peters, *Torture*, 177.

37   Ibid. In a book by Alec Mellor entitled *Je dénonce la torture*, a French document from the counter-insurgency campaign in Algiers is cited which sets up the regulations for ethical torture: (1) It is necessary that torture be properly conducted; (2) It must not take place in front of children; (3) It must not be performed by sadists; (4) It must be done by an officer or another responsible person; (5) It must be humane, that is, it should cease immediately when the type [sic] confesses. And above all, it must leave no marks; 178; cf. Paul Aussaresses, *The Battle of the Casbah: Terrorism and Counter-terrorism in Algeria, 1955–1957.* Robert L. Miller, trans. (New York: Enigma, 2002).

38   Richard Cohen, "Torture Is a Beast with a Rapacious Appetite." *Guardian Weekly*, March 13–19, 2003, 28; Michael Ignatieff, "Lesser Evils: What It Will Cost Us to Succeed in the War on Terror," *New York Times Magazine*, May 2, 2004, 51.

39   Ian Parker, "Obedience" in *Granta* Vol. 71 (London: Granta Publications, 2000), 99–126.

40   "Argentine Armed Forces Past Crimes," *The Economist*, July 12, 2003, 33.

Chapter 1

1   Quoted in Frantz Fanon, *The Wretched of the Earth*, trans. Constance Farrington (New York: Grove Press, 1963), 268.

2   CBC News, Maher Arar: Timeline, November 6, 2003 http://www.cbc.ca/news.background/arar

3   Arar's experience is consistent with that described in the Report on September 11 Detainees' Allegations of Abuse at the Metropolitan Detention Center in Brooklyn, New York, which details allegations of "slamming, bouncing, and ramming detainees against walls"; "bending detainees' arms, hands, wrists, and fingers"; "lifting detainees, pulling arms, and pulling handcuffs"; "rough or inappropriate handling of detainees"; and "verbal abuse"; cf. "Patriot Acts," *Harper's Magazine*, April 2004, 26.

4   Maher Arar, Press Statement, November 4, 2003.

5   http://www.cbc.ca/news/background/arar/arar_statement.html.

6   Ibid.

7   James Rusk, "Another Canadian Describes His Torture," *The Globe and Mail*, February 26, 2004, A5.

8   Maher Arar, Press Statement.

9   "Daily life in that place was hell: Arar," CBC News, November 5, 2003. http://www.cbc.ca/stories/2003/11/04/arar031104

10 Ibid.

11 DaNeen L. Brown and Dana Priest, "Deported terror suspect details torture in Syria. Canadian's case called typical of CIA," *Washington Post*, November 5, 2003, P. A01.

12 Maher Arar, Press Statement.

13 Ibid.

14 DaNeen L. Brown and Dana Priest, "Deported Terror Suspect Details Torture in Syria: Canadian's Case Called Typical of CIA," Washington Post, November 5, 2003, A01; Keith Jones, "The Maher Arar Case: Washington's Practice of Torture by Proxy," World Socialist Website,http:www.wses.org/articles/2003/nov2003/arar- n 18.shtml, accessed November 18, 2003.

15 Jones, "The Maher Arar Case."

16 Stewart Bell, "Detainee's Tale Offers Clues to Arar Case," *National Post*, February 24, 2004, A1, A8.

17 Ibid.; Colin Freeze, "Arar Anxious to Begin Battle of Clearing Name," *The Globe and Mail*, April 30, 2004, A6.

18 Kenneth Roth, "The Law of War in the War on Terror," *Foreign Affairs* 83: No. 1 (January/February 2004): 2.

19 Ibid.

20 The deaths of three prisoners in custody are under review. Two died at Bagram in December 2002. Major Elizabeth Rouse, a US Army pathologist, signed a death certificate for Dilawar, age 22, from Yakubi in eastern Afghanistan and stated that the cause of death was "blunt-force injuries to lower extremities complicating coronary artery disease." Another prisoner, Mullah Habibullah, brother of a former Taliban commander, died the same month. The third suspicious death is that of Abdul Wali, a former commander, who died four days after he presented himself for questioning at the request of the governor of Kunar. He died after allegedly undergoing inter-rogation by a private contract employee of the CIA. Suzanne Goldenberg, "America's Afghan Gulag," *Guardian Weekly*, July 2–8, 2004, 17.

21 Michael Ignatieff, "Lesser Evils: What It Will Cost Us to Succeed in the War on Terror." *New York Times Magazine*, May 2, 2004, 51; "Out of Mind," Harper's Magazine, May 2004, 22; Duncan Campbell, "America's Afghan Gulag," *Guardian Weekly*, July 2–6, 2004, 15.

22   Nick Ut, "Vietnamese Girl Fleeing in Terror After a Napalm Attack," Associated Press, 1972.

23   Eddie Adams, "Murder of a Vietcong by Saigon Police Chief," Associated Press, 1968. Albert Bandura, "Moral Disengagement in the Perpetration of Inhumanities," Personality and Social Psychology Review 3 (1999), No. 3, 199.

24   Susan Sontag, "Regarding the Torture of Others," New York Times Magazine, May 23, 2004, 27.

25   "Harper's Index," Harper's Magazine, May 2004, 13.

26   Ibid., 25.

27   Adam Hochschild, "What's in a Word? Torture," The New York Times Op-Ed, Sunday, May 23, 2004, WK11.

28   Edward Peters, Torture, 1.

29   Ibid.

30   Ibid.

31   Ibid., 2

32   Ibid., 1–2.

33   Universal Declaration of Human Rights, http://www.un.org/overview/rights.html.

34   UN Convention Against Torture, http://www.hrweb.org/legal/cat.html; Mark Bowden, "The Dark Art of Interrogation," Atlantic Monthly, October 2003, 72.

35   Julian Borger, "'Dirty' War for Profit Evades Reach of Law," Guardian Weekly, May 6–12, 2004, 6; Seymour M. Hersh, "Torture at Abu Ghraib. American Soldiers Brutalized Iraqis. How Far Does the Responsibility Go?" The New Yorker, May 10, 2004, 42–47; "Chain of Command. How the Department of Defense Mishandled the Disaster at Abu Ghraib," The New Yorker, May 17, 2004, 38-43.

36   Even though an interrogation technique is non-invasive and without pain or other physical side effects it may still be torture. Preliminary research of Dr. Scott H. Faro, director of Temple University's Functional Brain Imaging Center on functional magnetic resonance imaging or fMRI promises to become a much more accurate polygraph device than is now available. With this brain-imaging technology scientists can see how a lie sparks activity deep in our limbic system, the centre of emotion and self-preservation. The lie gathers, as it were, support from the memory banks in the left and right temporal lobes and then makes a dash to the frontal cortex, where a decision is made to suppress what the brain knows to be true. Ronald Kotulak, "Lips Can Lie, but Your Brain Will Spill the Beans: New MRI Study Finds Your Mind Is an Open Book," Chicago Tribune, November 30, 2004, 1.

37   Mark Danner, "The Logic of Torture", The New York Review of Books, June 24, 2004, 71.

38   Ibid.

39   Ibid.

40   KUBARK Counterintelligence Interrogation – July 1963, archived at "Prisoner
      Abuse: Patterns from the Past," National Security Archive Electronic Briefing Book
      No. 122, p. 83; www.gwu.edu/nsarchiv/NSAEBB/NSA-EBB1222. 'KUBARK' is a CIA
      codename. Human Resource Exploitation Training Manual – 1983, National Security
      Archive Electronic Briefing Book No. 122, "Non-coercive Techniques"; www.gwu.
      edu/ nsarchiv/NSA-EBB/NSAEBB122; Mark Danner, "The Logic of Torture," *The New
      York Review*, June 24, 2004, 71.

41   Ibid.

42   *Harper's Magazine*, October 2004, 18.

43   Howard Temperley, "Societies with slaves," *Times Literary Supplement*, January 9, 2004,
      6.

44   Gitta Sereny, *Albert Speer: His Battle with Truth* (New York: Alfred A. Knopf, 1995),
      311.

45   Bowden, "Dark Art," 74.

46   Bowden, "Dark Art," 74; Dan Gardner, "A Choice of Evils: If the Stakes Are High
      Enough, Is Torture Permissible?" *Ottawa Citizen*, February 6, 2004, A7; John Conroy,
      Unspeakable Acts, Ordinary People (New York: Alfred A. Knopf, 2000), 212–13.

47   Ignatieff, "Lesser Evils," 86.

48   Gitta Sereny, Albert Speer, 247. Sereny makes these comments within her discussion
      of the March 30, 1941 speech by Hitler to the Wermacht General Staff outlining
      the policy of extermination of Soviet commissars, the educated classes of Eastern
      Europe, and the Jews during the then upcoming invasion of Russia. She said that
      this lesson taught to us by Hitler was relearned in Vietnam. I would argue that it
      was relearned yet again with the widespread use of state-sponsored torture during
      the Second World War and after.

49   Slavoj Zizek, "Between Two Deaths," *London Review of Books*, 3 June 2004, 19.

50   Ibid.

51   Conroy, *Unspeakable Acts*, 203.

52   Dum Dum refers to the place near Calcutta, India where these bullets were first used.
      They are described in the Declaration as "expanding bullets," and the Convention
      considering them to be in violation of the laws and customs of war demands the
      following: "The Contracting Parties agree to abstain from the use of bullets which
      expand or flatten easily in the human body, such as bullets with a hard envelope
      which does not entirely cover the core, or is pierced with incisions."

53   The Fourth Geneva Convention (U.N.T.S. No. 973, vol. 75, p.287; August 12, 1949)
      was "Relative to the Protection of Civilian Persons in Time of War."

54   Karl Rahner, "On Bad Arguments in Moral Theology," Theological Investigations
      18 (New York: Crossroads, 1983), 74–85; "The Problem of Genetic Manipulation,"

Theological Investigations 9, Trans. Graham Harrison (London: Darton, Longman & Todd, 1972), 238-43.

[55] J. Mahoney, *The Making of Moral Theology: A Study of the Roman Catholic Tradition* (Oxford: Oxford University Press, 1987), 207–10; "The Spirit and Moral Discernment in Aquinas," in *Seeking the Spirit: Essays in Moral and Pastoral Theology* (London, 1981), 63–80.

[56] The question of whether France belongs on this list is complicated by the fact that many are no longer Catholic in the country, but especially because the ongoing disclosure of the systematic torture used as a counter-terrorism tactic in the 1950s has met with widespread dismay and even incredulity; cf. Paul Aussaresses, *The Battle of the Casbah. Terrorism and Counter-terrorism in Algeria, 1955–57*, trans. Robert L. Miller (New York: Enigma, 2002), and the original published admission of torture by a military officer, Jacques Massu, *La Vraie Bataille D'Alger* (Paris: Plon, 1971), 167–70.

[57] A more complete list can be found in Martin Robertson and Amnesty International, *Torture in the Eighties* (London: Amnesty International Publications, 1984).

[58] This occurred at a Eucharist celebrated by the Pope on the First Sunday of Lent, March 12, 2000 and was called "Confession of Sins Committed in the Service of the Church"; *Origins* Vol. 29, No. 40, 647, March 23, 2000. The Pope bundled up "2000 years of Church injustice into one comprehensive plea for forgiveness and purification of crimes against the Jews, women, minorities in general, and some historical episodes in particular, such as the Crusades and the Inquisition. After invoking each category, what he actually said was, 'We forgive and ask forgiveness....'" Marina Warner, "Who's Sorry Now?" *Times Literary Supplement*, August 1, 2003, 10. In the theological background paper published by the International Theological Commission of the Vatican, torture and the Inquisition are discussed in Part 5, entitled "Ethical Discernment" and is called "The Use of Force in the Service of the Truth," 'Memory and Reconciliation: The Church and the Faults of the Past," December 1999, http://www.vatican.va/roman_curia/congregations/cfaith/cti-docum

[59] Pope John Paul II, "Inquisition Requires Calm, Objective Analysis: Address by the Holy Father of October 31, 1998 to the International Symposium on the Inquisition held at the Vatican," *L'Osservatore Romano*, November 11, 1998; http://www.petersnet.net/browse/695.htm

[60] Pastoral Constitution on the Church in the Modern World, *Gaudium et Spes*, 27; Pope John Paul II, Encyclical Letter *Veritatis Splendor*, 80.

[61] Diarmaid MacCulloch, "A holy excuse for boredom," *Guardian Weekly*, April 15–21, 2004, 19.

[62] Vatican II, *Gaudium et spes*, 80.

[63] Drew Christiansen, "Whither the 'Just War'?" *America* 188 (March 24, 2003), 8.

[64] Kenneth R. Himes, "Intervention, Just War, and U.S. National Security," *Theological Studies* 65:1 (March 2004), 157.

[65] Jack Mahoney, SJ "Christian Doctrines, Ethical Issues, and Human Genetics," *Theological Studies* 64: 719-49.

66   Paul Ricoeur, Symbolism of Evil (Boston: Beacon Press, 1967), 52.

67   Henri Alleg, The Question, Trans. John Calder, Pref. Jean-Paul Sartre (London: John Calder, 1958), 42–44.

68   "Missing the Mark," Forerunner Commentary, http://www.bibletools.org; Thomas Ryan, Four Steps to Spiritual Freedom (Mahwah, NJ: Paulist Press, 2003), 25.

69   Constitution on the Church in the Modern World, Gaudium et spes, Part I, Chapter 1, "The Dignity of the Human Person," and Chapter 2, "The Community of Man-kind," #12–32, in The Teachings of the Second Vatican Council, Complete Texts of the Constitutions, Decrees, and Declarations, Introduction by Gregory Baum (Westminster, MD: The Newman Press, 1966).

70   Rape is often part of the torture experience: cf. Sister Diana Ortiz, The Blindfold's Eyes: My Journey from Torture to Truth (Maryknoll, NY: Orbis, 2002), 63–64.

71   Ariel Dorfman, "His Eye is on the Sparrow," in Last Waltz in Santiago, trans. Edith Grossman (New York: Viking Press, 1988), 11; in William T. Cavanaugh, Torture and Eucharist. Theology, Politics, and the Body of Christ (Malden, MA: Blackwell, 1998), 1.

Chapter 2

1   Mark Bowden, "The Dark Art of Interrogation," The Atlantic Monthly, December 2003, 70.

2   Elaine Scarry, The Body in Pain: The Making and Unmaking of the World (New York: Oxford University Press, 1985), 16. In suggesting here that the etymology of pain implies a judgment on its meaning I am making use of the "cognitional structure" of experience, understanding and judgment developed by the late Bernard J.F. Lonergan, SJ, cf. his Method in Theology (New York: Herder, 1972).

3   Maher Arar: statement, November 4, 2003, CBC News, INDEPTH: Maher Arar, http://www.cbc.ca/news/background/arar_statement.html

4   The information from the unnamed source in the Canadian intelligence community was originally published by The National Post; http://www.ctv.ca/servlet/ArticleNews/story/CTVNews/107278922.

5   John Milbank, Being Reconciled: Ontology and Pardon. Radical Orthodoxy Series (New York: Routledge, 2003).

6   In July 2003, Spain's first new mosque in 511 years opened its doors in Granada. "This is a moving day for Muslims all over the world," said Hassan Seddadi, a 25-year-old Morrocan who now lives in Granada; Charleston.Net: http://www.charleston.net/stories/071103/wor 11mosque.shtml. At the same time, the Vatican will not al-low Muslims to pray in the former mosque that is now the cathedral of Córdoba in southern Spain, saying that they must "accept history," Guardian Weekly, May 6–12, 2004, 2.

7   Karen Armstrong, The Battle for God (New York: Alfred A. Knopf, 2000), 3–4.

8   Stephen Sedley, "Wringing out the Fault," London Review of Books, 7 March 2002, 27–31.

9   Ibid., 31.

10 Henry Kamen, *The Spanish Inquisition: A Historical Revision* (New Haven, CT: Yale University Press, 1998), 188–90.

11 The other two were terrible as well. The garrucha, or pulley, "involved being hung by the wrists from a pulley on the ceiling, with heavy weights attached to the feet. The accused was raised slowly, then suddenly allowed to fall with a jerk. The effect was to stretch and dislocate the arms and legs. The toca or water torture ... [involved] [t]he accused [being] tied down on a rack, his mouth [being] kept open and a toca or linen cloth [being] put down his throat to conduct water slowly from a jar. The severity of the torture varied with the number of jars of water used," Kamen, *The Spanish Inquisition*, 190.

12 In a similar way, meticulous records kept by the Supreme Court of Brazil during the military dictatorship there from 1964 to 1985 were the basis of the influential account Brasil: Nunca Mais published through the good offices of the Archbishop of Sao Paulo, Cardinal Arns. The author of A Miracle, A Universe asked observers why the judges had allowed the denunciations of torture to be entered into the record and then allowed these records to be preserved. "What do you mean?" they would answer. "It was the law – they had to." Another explained: "Record keeping like that is a part of a long Iberian tradition of thoroughly recording acts of state, which, as acts of state, could not by definition be viewed as suspect or illegal"; Lawrence Weschler, *A Miracle, A Universe* (New York: Pantheon, 1990), 47–8.

13 Henry Charles Lea, *A History of the Inquisition of Spain*, 4 volumes (New York: Macmillan, 1906–08), Vol. III, 233.

14 It is still the case that a devout Jew will change into clean clothes on the Sabbath.

15 Lea, *A History*, 25, cited in Henry Kamen, *The Spanish Inquisition*, 191.

16 Lea, *A History*, Vol. III, 233-4.

17 Henry Shue, "Torture," *Philosophy and Public Affairs* 7: 2:131.

18 Kamen, 187–92. Methods of torture were categorized by degrees based on the strength of judicial suspicion, and from this custom comes the expression "undergoing the third degree," cf. Stuart Turner, Sahika Uksel and Derrick Silove, "Survivors of Mass Violence and Torture" in *Trauma Interventions in War and Peace: Prevention, Practice and Policy. International and Cultural Psychology.* Ed. Bonnie L. Green, Matthew J. Friedman, Joop T.V.M. de Jony, Susan D. Solomon, Terence M. Keane, John A. Fairbank et al. (New York: Kluwer, 2003), 188.

19 Ibid., 135–6.

20 Michael Slackman, "What's Wrong with Torturing a Qaeda Higher-Up? A Dangerous Calculus," *The New York Times*, Sunday, May 16, 2004, WK4.

21 Dershowitz, "Torture could be justified." CNN Access, March 3, 2003; http://edition.cnn.com/2003/LAW/03/03/cnna.Dershowitz.

22 Slavoj Zizek, "Are We in a War? Do We Have an Enemy?" *London Review of Books*, 23 May 2002, 3.

23 Jonathan Alter, "Time to Think About Torture," *Newsweek*, November 5, 2001.

24 "Is Torture Ever Justified?" *The Economist*, January 11, 2003, 9.

25 Bruce Hoffman, "The Case for Torture," *National Post*, January 26, 2002, B2.

26 Dan Gardner, "A Choice of Evils: If the Stakes Are High Enough, Is Torture Permissible?" *Ottawa Citizen*, February 6, 2004, A.6.

27 Slavoj Zizek, "Are We in a War? Do We Have an Enemy?", 3.

28 John Conroy, *Unspeakable Acts, Ordinary People* (New York: Alfred A. Knopf, 2000), 28.

29 Ibid., 18.

30 Ibid., 34.

31 Alec Mellor, *La Torture. Son Histoire – Son Abolition – Sa Réapparition au XXe Siècle* (Paris: Les Horizons Littéraires, 1949), 66–68.

32 Ibid., 68.

33 Peters, *Torture*, 42.

34 Ibid., 43.

35 Ibid., 51.

36 Conroy, p. 28.

37 Ibid., 50.

38 Casuistry is an effort to determine ethics on a case-by-case basis. Using indications found in sacred scripture and in the writings of respected ecclesiastical authorities from the past, a casuist will attempt to explain whether a particular action is right or wrong according to specific circumstances. Casuists differed from other theologians because their effort was not to defend or to explain the content of Catholic faith but to answer a specific moral question. For instance, if a husband and wife were inadvertently locked inside a church in which the Blessed Sacrament was reserved in the tabernacle, how long should they refrain from marital intimacy inside the church in deference to the sacred presence? Various answers were given by different casuists to this case, but most would allow them their marital rights after 48 hours if they continued to be forced to remain inside the church.

39 Antonio Diana, *Omnium Resolutionum Moralium*, Tomus Primus, Liber 5, (Venice: Apud Nicolaum Pezzana, 1728), Resolutionem 1.

40 Ibid., Resolutionem II – "cum hoc non sit torquere." Twentieth-century jurisprudence on torture makes it clear that "there does not need to be a bloody act to be torture. Indeed, there doesn't have to be any physical contact at all. A landmark case from more than two decades ago involved the concert pianist Miguel Estrella. Kidnapped by Uruguayan officers in Montevideo, Estrella was repeatedly shown a saw and told he would have his hands cut off. The threat was never carried out but the UN Human Rights Committee still declared it to be torture," Dan Gardner, "Agony Inc.," *Ottawa Citizen*, February 1, 2004, C5.

41   Ibid., Resolutionem II, #5 "eumque elevatum," "suspensumque interrogare."

42   Ibid., Res. XXIX, #1, 7.

43   Ibid, #2.

44   This would not be acceptable today, either in Church thinking on ethics or in that of the wider public. In discussing the fact that between 1997 and 2000 Amnesty International received reports of torture in 150 countries, Alex Neve, secretary-general of Amnesty International Canada, said, "And perhaps most shocking of all [is the fact that] we discovered that in 50 states, that's over one-quarter of the nations on this planet, children were being tortured. Children!" Gardner, "Torture Inc.," C3.

45   Juan de Lugo, *Disputationes Scholasticae et Morales*, Editio Nova, Tomus Septimus (Paris: Apud Ludovicum Vivès, MDCCCCIII), D. XXXVII, Sectio XIII, 885.

46   Ibid., 883.

47   St. Alphonus de Liguorio, *Theologia Moralis*, 9th ed., Ed. Leonard Gaudé, C.SS.R. (Roma: Typographia Vaticana, 1907, reprint, 1953), Lib. IV, Cap. III, Art. III, 630.

48   *New Catholic Encyclopedia*, Vol. XIV (London: Macmillan, 1967), s.v. "Torture."

49   This was first done by Field Marshal Keitel in his Nacht und Nebel decree and then by Himmler, head of the Gestapo, in a circular dated June 12, 1942, officially authorizing its use in certain cases; Alec Mellor, *Je Dénonce la Torture* (Paris: Mame, 1972), 12.

Chapter 3

1   Jean Améry, *At the Mind's Limits: Contemplations by a Survivor on Auschwitz and Its Realities*, trans. Sidney Rosenfeld and Stella P. Rosenfeld (Bloomington, IN: Indiana University Press, 1980), 22.

2   Dave Broadfoot, *Old Enough to Say What I Want: An Autobiography with Barbara Sears*. (Toronto: McClelland & Stewart, 2002), 258–9.

3   Stephen Macedo defines "universal jurisdiction" as based "entirely on the nature of the crime," while Luc Reydam points out that universal jurisdiction authorizes a state to punish conduct "irrespective of the place where it occurs, the nationality of the perpetrator, and the nationality of the victim"; ed. Stephen Macedo, *Universal Jurisdiction: National Courts and the Prosecution of Serious Crimes Under International Law* (Philadelphia: University of Pennsylvania Press, 2003); Luc Reydams, *Universal Jurisdiction: International and Municipal Perspectives* (Oxford: Oxford University Press, 2004), 227.

4   Albert R. Jonsen and Stephen Toulmin, *The Abuse of Casuistry: A History of Moral Reasoning* (Berkeley, CA: University of California Press, 1988), 178.

5   Herbert Radtke, "Torture as an Illegal Means of Control," in Franz Böckle and Jacques Pohier, *The Death Penalty and Torture. Concilium. Religion in the Seventies* (New York: A Crossroad Book, 1979), 4.

6   Tertullian, De Corona, Ch. 11; De Idololatria, Ch. 17, cited in Radtke, "Torture," 40.

7   Lactantius, *Divinae Institutiones*, V.20; VI, 10.

8   Augustine, *City of God*. Book XIX, No. VI, Trans. W.C. Greene, The Loeb Classical Library, Vol. VI (London: Heinemann, 1960), 145–57.

9   Ibid.

10   Ibid.

11   Resp. ad Consult. Bulgar, Denzinger 648, cf. Henry Denzinger, *Enchiridion Symbolorum, defniitionum et declarationum de rebus fidei et morum*, 30th Edition, ed. K. Rahner.

12   Francesco Compagnoni, "Capital Punishment and Torture in the Tradition of the Roman Catholic Church," in Böckle and Pohier, *The Death Penalty and Torture*. 41–2.

13   Ibid.

14   Alec Mellor, *La Torture – Son Histoire, Son Abolition, Sa Réapparition au XXe Siècle* (Paris: Les Horizons Littéraires, 1949), 124–5.

15   The authors of Malleus Maleficarum, Jacob Sprenger and Heinrich Kramer, both Dominican friars, claimed that their book was a practical commentary on the 1584 papal bull of Pope Innocent VIII (Summis desiderantes affectibus) in which the Pope expressed alarm at the reports that certain persons in Germany were entering into relations with the devil and practicing black magic. Ronald Modras, "A Jesuit in the Crucible: Friedrich Spee and the Witchcraft Hysteria in Seventeenth-Century Germany," *Studies in the Spirituality of Jesuits* 35 (September 2003), 14–15.

16   Mellor, *La Torture*. 129–30; Modras, "A Jesuit in the Crucible," 34.

17   J. Wicks, "Adam Tanner." *New Catholic Encyclopedia*, Vol. XIII (New York: McGraw-Hill, 1967), 932–3.

18   Friedrich von Spee, Advis aux criminalistes sur les abus qui se glissent dans le process de sorcelerie (originally published in 1631 as Cautio criminalis, Lyon: 1660). Ronald Modras argues that von Spee's motive in this was not temerity but the fact that he had not obtained permission to publish the book from his Superiors in the Society of Jesus. Modras, "A Jesuit in the Crucible," 24–5.

19   Adam Tanner, *Theologicae Scholasticae*, 4 Volumes, Ingolstadt, 1626-7, Disputatio IV, De Iustitia, Questio V, Dubium 1, #5.

20   Peter Binsfeld, *Enchiridian theologiae, pastoralis et doctrinae necessariae sacerdotibus curam animarum administratibus*, Augustae Trevirorum: Henrici Bock, 1612, Caput XXIX, De Expositione Octavi praecepti, 'De iustitia et iniustitiae Iugiceis, 442–43.

21   Tanner, Quest. IV, Dubium I, #8.

22   Tanner, Quest. V, Dub. 1V, #130-1, 133.

23   Tanner, Quest. V, Dub. 14, #123-6.

24   Tanner, Quest. V, Dubium 1, #10-11, 15-16.

25   Mellor, *La Torture*, 130.

26   Paul Laymann, SJ, *Theologia Moralis in Quinque libros*, Editio Tertia, Nichola Henrici, 1630, Libr. III, De Iustitia, Tractatus VI, Cap. V. #6-12.

27   Laymann, #48 & 50.

28   Ibid, #53.

29   Edward Peters, *Torture* (New York: Basil Blackwell, 1985), 149.

30   V.S. Naipaul, *The Return of Eva Perón* (Harmondsworth, Middlesex, UK: Penguin, 1974), 110.

31   Ibid.

32   Martha K. Huggins, Mika Haritos-Fatouros and Philip G. Zimbardo, *Violence Workers: Police Torturers and Murderers Reconstruct Brazilian Atrocities* (Berkeley, CA: University of California Press, 2002), 23–4.

33   Heinz Holzhauer, *Rechtsgeschichte der Folter: Amnesty International, Foter-Stellungnahmen, Analysen, Vorschläge zur Abschaffung* (Baden-Baden, 1976) in Radke, "Torture as Illegal Means of Control," 10.

34   Richard Cohen, "Torture Is a Beast with a Rapacious Appetite," *Guardian Weekly*, March 13–19, 2003, 28.

35   Dan Gardner, "A Choice of Evils: If the Stakes Are High Enough, Is Torture Permissible?" *Ottawa Citizen*, February 4, 2004, A6.

36   Marcus Gee, "The Face of Evil," *The Globe and Mail*, June 8, 2002, F5. (The quote is from Guengueng, not Habré.)

37   Ibid.

38   Reed Brody, "The Case against Hissène Habré," *International Civil Liberties Report*. http://www.hrw.org/justice/habre.

39   Gee, "Face of Evil, " F4–5.

40   Stephen J. Pope, "The Convergence of Forgiveness and Justice: Lessons from El Salvador," *Theological Studies 64* (December 2003), 818, 821.

41   *The Economist*, July 12, 2003, 33. Prior to President Kirchner's judicial reform, human rights advocates had been forced to make use of a loophole in the existing Argentine amnesty laws which had failed to include those involved in kidnapping the children of women who had been tortured while pregnant, given birth to a child, and then killed. These children are known as the "living disappeared" and some have agreed to co-operate in the p,rosecution of the perpetrators. Lucy Ash, "The Living Disappeared," http://news.bbc.co.uk/1/hi/programmes/crossing_continents/150425.stm.

42   Virginie Ladisch, "Argentine Military Officer Extradited to Spain on Genocide Charges," in Crimes of War, http://www.crimesofwar.org/onnews/news-argenina.html.

43   Mar Roman, "Accused Argentine Tormentor Finally Facing Justice," *Winnipeg Free Press*, July 20, 2003, B3.

44   Ibid.

45   Ibid.

46   If living standards can be determined by GDP per head, Chad is ranked the tenth
     lowest in the world with $180, Bhutan the seventeenth with $230. Chad and Bhutan
     are also similar in area with Chad comprising 1,284 square kilometres, Bhutan 1,440
     and in median age with the average Chadian being 16.7 years old and the average
     Bhutanese being 18.4. *The Economist Pocket World in Figures*, 2003 Edition (London:
     Profile Books, 2003), 26, 232.

47   John Scofield, "Bhutan Crowns a New Dragon King," *National Geographic*, Vol. 146,
     no. 4, October 1974, 570.

48   There are two versions of Mahayana Buddhism practised in Bhutan: Nyingmapa in
     the East of the Kingdom, and Kyagjukpa in the West.

49   Horacio Verbitsky, *The Flight: Confessions of an Argentine Dirty Warrior*. Esther Allen,
     trans. (New York: The New Press, 1996), 12–14, 24–37, 52–3, 77–8, 84–5, 101–16,
     145–6.

50   "Your place or mine? Special Report on Kashmir," *The Economist*, February 14, 2004,
     24. India has the greatest number of torture and custodial deaths in the world. Ac-
     cording to government documents, there were 1,307 deaths in judicial custody in
     2002 alone; Pankaj Mishra, "Bombay: The Lower Depths," *New York Review of Books*,
     November 18, 2004, 17; Rama Lakshmi. "In India, Torture by Police Is Frequent and
     Often Deadly," *The Washington Post*, August 5, 2004.

51   Xinhua News Agency, February 23, 2004; "8,000 Police Officers Punished for Cor-
     ruption, Torture," reprinted in *National Post*, February 24, 2004, A12.

52   The head of a monastery could torture his monks as a punishment and a warning.
     The "Trimpon," or district judge, was permitted the use of torture to obtain evidence
     and to extract judicial confessions and to obtain the names of accomplices.

53   The office of the United Nations High Commissioner for Refugess (UNHCR) com-
     missioned a study by sociologist and social worker Cindy Dubble to evaluate the
     claims made by Bhutanese refugees in Nepal. Ms. Dubble took in-depth interviews
     from alleged victims, considered corroborating evidence such as medical records,
     cross-checking for consistency between interviews, and she verified torture in 95
     out of 100 reported cases. "Victims universally suffered severe beatings and most
     were kept tied or in handcuffs. All report horrible conditions of confinement in small
     or crowded spaces with inadequate sanitation facilities, and minimal, or purposely
     adulterated food. Common forms of torture in Bhutan include the wearing of shackles
     welded onto the victims' legs, solitary confinement, and exposure to severe cold
     weather. A frequent interrogation technique involves placing thick boards above
     and below the victim's thigh, tied at one end. During questioning a guard stands
     on the top board, putting unbearable pressure on the leg. Many methods of torture
     involve degrading behaviours, such as being paraded naked or being made to imitate
     animals and combat each other in mock 'bull-fights' for the guards' entertainment."
     http://www.bhootan.org/thronson/thronson_protest.htm.

54   "Bhutan: Fear of Torture/Ill-treatment." Amnesty International Urgent Action Bulletin, AI Index ASA 14/02/97, 12 August 1997.

55   D.N.S. Dhakal, Christopher Strawn. *Bhutan: A Movement in Exile* (Jaipur: Nirala, 1994), 194–5; Michael Hutt, *Unbecoming Citizens: Culture, Nationhood, and the Flight of Refugees from Bhutan* (New York: Oxford University Press, 2003); Tek Nath Rizal, *Ethnic Cleansing and Political Repression in Bhutan: The Other Side of the Shangri-La – An Account of a Prisoner of Conscience* (Kathmandu, Nepal: Human Rights Council of Bhutan, 2004).

56   Dhakal, Strawn, *Bhutan*, 195.

57   Ibid, 195–6.

58   Amnesty International. "Bhutan Crack-down on 'Anti-nationals' in the East." AI Index: ASA 14/01/98.

59   "Nepal/Bhutan: Bilateral Talks Fail to Solve Refugee Crisis – International Community Should Take Concerted Action," Amnesty International Press Release, AI Index: ASA 31/060/2003, 28 October 2003. http://web.amnesty.org/library/Index/ENGASA310602003?

60   I am using this word in the same sense as René Girard uses it for the connection between mimetic desire and violence, cf. René Girard, *Things Hidden Since the Foundation of the World* (Stanford: Stanford University Press, 1987), 11–12.

61   Leon R. Kass, "'Making Babies' Revisited," in *Bioethics*, Thomas A. Shannon, ed. (Ramsay, NJ: Paulist Press, 1976), rev. ed., 460–1.

62   Amnesty International, *Bhutan: Fear of torture/ill-treatment*, AI Index: ASA 14/02/97, 12 August 1997.

63   AI Index: NWS 22/006/1997, 4 November 1997.

Chapter 4

1   Anonymous torturer in Jean-Pierre Vittori, *Confessions d'un professionnel de la torture*, 14–15.

2   In 1999, Amnesty International published the alarming finding that people "disappeared" (or remained "disappeared" from previous years) in 37 countries, Annual Report (London: Amnesty International Publications).

3   Ibid.

4   Giorgio Agamben, *Homo Sacer: Sovereign Power and Bare Life* (Stanford, CA: Stanford University Press, 1998), 8, 71–2; John Milbank, *Being Reconciled: Ontology and Pardon* (London: Routledge, 2003), 90–1.

5   *Nunca Más*, xvi.

6   Cited in Tina Rosenberg, *Children of Cain: Violence and the Violent in Latin America* (New York: William Morrow, 1991), 83.

7   Peters, *Torture*, 187.

8   Archdiocese of São Paulo, *Torture in Brazil* (New York: Vintage, 1998), xxvii.

9   James F. Keenan, "Can a Wrong Action Be Good? The Development of Theologi-
    cal Opinion on Erroneous Conscience," *Église et Théologie*, 24 (1993):211; Thomas
    Aquinas, *Scriptum super libros Sententiarum Ivm* 38. 2. 4. q.a 3; see also IV. 27.1.2. q.a. 4
    ad 3; IV.27.2, expositio.Ibid.

10 Ibid.

11 Keenan, "Can a Wrong Action Be Good?" 212.

12 For instance, according to Catholic sacramental theology a person can be a torturer
    right up to the last minute of his life, but on his deathbed repent, receive sacramental
    absolution through confession of his sins and be forgiven.

13 Richard B. Hays, "Relations Natural and Unnatural: A Response to John Boswell's
    Exegesis of Romans 1," *Journal of Religious Ethics* 14 (1986): 186–95.

14 Stanley Milgram, "Behavioral Study of Obedience," *Journal of Abnormal Social Psychology*
    67 (1963): 277–85; "Some Conditions of Obedience and Disobedience to Authority,"
    Human Relations 18:1 (1965): 55–57 ; *Obedience to Authority* (New York: Harper & Row,
    1974); Ian Parker, "Obedience," *Granta* 71 (Autumn 2000), ed. Ian Jack (London:
    Granta Publications, 2000), 101–25.

15 C. Haney, C. Banks and P. Zimbardo, "Interpersonal Dynamics in a Simulated Prison,"
    International Journal of Criminology and Penology 1 (1973), 69–97.

16 Arendt, Eichmann, 252.

17 Al Kennedy, "Torture, the British Way," *Guardian Weekly*, November 5–11, 2004, 5.

18 D. Mantell. "The Potential for Violence in Germany," *Journal of Social Issues*. 27.4
    (1971): 101–12; W. Kilham & L. Mann, "Level of Instructional Obedience as a Func-
    tion of Transmitter and Executant Roles in the Milgram Paradigm," *Journal of Personality
    and Social Psychology* 29 (1974): 696–702; M. Shanab and K. Yahya, "A Behavioural
    Study of Obedience in Children," *Journal of Personality and Social Psychology* 35 (1977):
    530–36.

19 Janice T. Gibson, "Training People to Inflict Pain: State Terror and Social Learning,"
    Journal of Humanistic Psychology 31.2 (1991): 75.

20 The first trial "began on 7 August 1975, when 14 officers and 18 soldiers of non-
    commissioned rank were brought before the Athens Permanent Court Martial on
    charges arising from torture during interrogation. Although all Greek Constitutions
    since the first in 1822 (including those of 1968 and 1973 promulgated by the Junta)
    contain general prohibitions against torture, there is no specific prohibition in the
    Greek Penal Code, which would have to provide the precise implementing law.
    Therefore, only indirect charges could be preferred against the 32 ESA defendents.
    These charges were repeated abuse of authority, violence against a superior officer,
    unconstitutional detention, ordinary and serious physical injury, repeated insults to
    a superior, and recurrent moral responsibility for ordinary or serious physical injury."
    Torture in Greece: The First Torturers' Trial 1975. Amnesty International Publications, 1977,
    12.

21 Janice T. Gibson and Mika Haritos-Fatouros, "The Education of a Torturer," *Psychology
    Today*, November 1986, 52.

22   Mika Haritos-Fatouros, "The Official Torturer: A Learning Model for Obedience to the Authority of Violence," *Journal of Applied Social Psychology* 18 (1988): 1114.

23   Gibson and Haritos-Fatouros, "The Education of a Torturer," 56.

24   Haritos-Fatouros, "The Official Torturer," 1117.

25   Ibid.

26   Janice Gibson, "Training People to Inflict Pain: State Terror and Social Learning," *Journal of Humanistic Psychology* 31 (Spring 1991):81.

27   Haritos-Fatouros, "The Official Torturer," 1117.

28   Amnesty International, *Evidence of Torture* (London: Amnesty International Publications, 1977).

29   Haritos-Fatouros, "The Official Torturer," 1116.

30   Martha K. Huggins, Mika Haritos-Fatouros and Philip G. Zimbardo, *Violence Workers: Police Torturers and Murderers Reconstruct Brazilian Atrocities* (Berkeley, CA: University of California Press, 2002).

31   Ibid., 11.

32   Ibid.

33   Robert Jay Lifton, "Doubling: The Faustian Bargain," in *The Web of Violence*, eds. Jennifer Turpin and Lester R. Kurtz (Chicago: University of Chicago Press, 1997), 30.

34   Ibid.

35   Huggins, *Violence Workers*, 59.

36   Ibid.

37   Ibid. 144.

38   Ibid., 188.

39   Ibid., 181.

40   Ibid., 198.

41   Ibid., 199.

42   Ibid.

43   Ibid., 188.

44   Frantz Fanon, *The Wretched of the Earth*, trans. Constance Farrington (New York: Grove Press, 1963), 267–70.

45   Jean-Pierre Vittori, *Confessions d'un professionnel de la torture : La guerre d'Algérie* (Paris: Ramsay Image), 13–14.

46   Ibid., 205.

47   Keenan, "Can a Wrong Action Be Good?" 206. Theologians who agree with this

moral distinction would include: Klaus Demmer, "La competenza normative del magistero ecclesiatico in morale," in K. Demmer and B. Schüller, eds., *Fede cristiana e agire morale* (Assisi: Cittadella Editrice, 1980), 144–69; Josef Fuchs, *Christian Ethics in a Secular Arena* (Washington, DC: Georgetown University Press, 1984); Louis Janssens, "Norms and Priorities in a Love Ethics," in *Louvain Studies*, 6 (1977), 207–38; "Ontic Good and Ontic Evil," in *Louvain Studies* 12 (1987), 62–82; Richard McCormick, *Notes on Moral Theology* (Lanham, MD: University Press of America, 1981); B. Schüller, "The Double Effect in Catholic Thought: A Re-evaluation," in *Doing Evil to Achieve Good*, eds. R. McCormick and P. Ramsey, (Chicago: Loyola University Press, 1978), 165–92.

48 Keenan, "Can a Wrong Action Be Good?" 207.

49 Tina Rosenberg, *Children of Cain: Violence and the Violent in Latin America* (New York: William Morrow, 1991), 96.

50 Mark J. Osiel, *Mass Atrocity, Ordinary Evil, and Hannah Arendt: Criminal Consciousness in Argentina's Dirty War* (New Haven, CT: Yale University Press, 2001), 16.

51 Ibid., 4.

52 Rosenberg, *Children of Cain*, 96.

53 Ibid., 5.

54 Ibid., 40.

55 Ibid., 40–1.

56 Ibid.

57 Ibid., 41.

58 Ibid., 102.

59 "'Blond Angel of Death' indicted for nuns' murders," Reuters, *National Post*, May 21, 2004, A13.

60 Herbert Butterfield, *The Whig Interpretation of History* (London: G. Bell, 1950), 112.

Chapter 5

1 Marguerite Feitlowitz, *A Lexicon of Terror*, 10.

2 "The third degree" is a term used in the United States to refer to police interrogations that include torture.

3 Edward Peters, *Torture* (Oxford: Basil Blackwell, 1985), 124–25.

4 Jean Améry, *At the Mind's Limits: Contemplations by a Survivor on Auschwitz and its Realities*, trans. Sidney Rosenfeld and Stella P. Rosenfeld (Bloomington, IN: Indiana University Press, 1980), 34.

5 Ibid.

6 Ibid, 22.

7   Ibid., 25.

8   Ibid., 27.

9   Ibid., 28.

10   Charles Darwin. The Descent of Man, in *Darwin: A Critical Norton Collection*, ed. P. Appleman, (New York: Norton, 1979), 202.

11   B. Inhelder and J. Piaget, *The Growth of Logical Thinking from Childhood to Adolescence: An Essay on the Construction of Formal Operational Structures* (New York: Basic Books, 1958); J. Piaget and B. Inhelder, *The Psychology of the Child* (New York: Basic Books, 1969).

12   S. Freud, *Three Essays on the Theory of Sexuality*. The Standard Edition (London: Hogarth Press, 1953), Vol. 7, 125–245; E.H. Erikson, *Childhood and Society*, Second Edition (New York: W.W. Norton, 1963).

13   André Guindon, *Moral Development, Ethics and Faith*, trans. Kenneth C. Russell, Novalis Theological Series (Ottawa: Novalis, 1992), 34.

14   World Health Organisation, *The ICD-10 Classification of Mental and Behavioural Disorders: Diagnostic Criteria for Research* (Geneva: WHO, 1993). José Aldunate, SJ, "Reflexión sobre tortura en Chile," Mensaje, Edicíon N. 535, Diciembre 2004.

15   P. Davis, "Medical Problems of Detainees: A Review of 21 Ex-detainees Seen in the Past Two Years in Johannesburg," in *Towards Health Care for All: NAMDA Conference 1985*, eds. A.B. Zwi & L.D. Saunders, Johannesburg, South Africa: National Medical and Dental Association, 15–18. Cited in Michael A. Simpson, "Traumatic Stress and the Bruising of the Soul: The Effects of Torture and Coercive Interrogation," in *International Handbook of Traumatic Stress Syndromes*, eds. John P. Wilson and Beverley Raphael (London: Plenum Press, 1993), 669.

16   P. Watzlawick, J.H. Beavin, and D.D. Jackson, *Pragmatics of Human Communication* (London: Faber & Faber, 1968), cited in Simpson, "Traumatic Stress," 678.

17   J. Barudy, "A Programme of Mental Health for Political Refugees: Dealing with the Invisible Pain of Political Exile," *Social Science Medicine* 28 (1989): 715–27, cited in Stuart Turner, Sahika Yuksel and Derrick Silove, "Survivors of Mass Violence and Torture," in *Trauma Interventions in War and Peace: Prevention, Practice and Policy*, eds. Bonnie L. Green et al, International and Cultural Psychology. Series Editor: Anthony J. Marsella (New York: Kluwer, 2003), 185.

18   Turner, Yuksel and Silove, "Survivors of Mass Violence," 193.

19   Ibid.

20   David Stafford, *Ten Days to D-Day* (London: Little Brown, 2003), 1–2, 326. Peter Moen, *Peter Moen's Diary*, trans. Bjorn Koefoed, (New York: Creative Age Press, 1951), 1.

21   *Peter Moen's Diary*, 7.

22   Simpson, "Traumatic Stress and the Bruising of the Soul," 671.

23   *Peter Moen's Diary*, 3.

24   Ibid., 4.

25   Ibid., 6–7.

26   Simpson, "Traumatic Stress," 671; Ole Vedel Rasmussen, "Medical Aspects of Torture," *Danish Medical Bulletin*, January, 1990, cited in John Conroy, *Unspeakable Acts, Ordinary People* (New York: Alfred A. Knopf, 2000), 172.

27   *Peter Moen's Diary*, 7

28   Ibid., 7.

29   Ibid., 29.

30   Ibid. 30–1.

31   Ibid., 38.

32   H. Gollwitzer, *Dying We Live: The Final Messages and Records of the Resistance* (New York: Pantheon, 1956), cited in Simpson, "Traumatic Stress," 678.

33   *Peter Moen's Diary*, 47–9.

34   Stafford, *Ten Days*, 238.

35   *Peter Moen's Diary*, 50.

36   Ibid., 57–8.

37   Ibid., 69.

38   Ibid., 71.

39   Ibid., 81.

40   Scarry, *The Body in Pain*, 13.

41   Ortiz, *The Blindfold's Eyes*.

42   Ibid., 37–8.

43   Scarry, *The Body in Pain*, 9.

44   Améry, *At the Mind's Limits*, 34–5; Georges Bataille, "L'Homme souverain de Sade, Étude II des Études diverses sur l'éroticism," *Oeuvres completes*, Vol. 2 (Paris: Gallimard, 1987), 164–75.

45   Ortiz, *The Blindfold's Eyes*, ix–x.

46   Confirmation of this comes from the success of the child soldier reconciliation programs in Liberia and Sierra Leone.

Chapter 6

1   For instance on October 9, 1973, shortly after the military coup in Chile, Cardinal Silva was instrumental in establishing the influential organization COPACHI (Committee of Co-operation for Peace in Chile) to co-ordinate assistance efforts and to document allegations of disappearances and other human rights abuses. Much of this information assembled by COPACHI was confirmed in 2004 by the publica-

tion of the results of a government commission set up by President Lagos. Cf. "El Informe de la Comíson sobre prison politica y tortura," *Mensaje*, Edicícion No. 535, Diciembre 2004.

2   Larry Rohter, "Back in Argentina, Priest Faces 'Dirty War' Charges," *New York Times*, April 26, 2004, A3.

3   Ronald Dworkin, Introduction, *Nunca Más*, xi.

4   Ibid., 248.

5   Ibid., 249–50.

6   Ibid., 248–49.

7   Cindy Wooden, "Torture Harms All Humanity: John Paul II," *Prairie Messenger*, June 2, 2004, 1.

8   Catholic News Service, *Prairie Messenger*, July 14, 2004, 4. Among the matters that need to be clarified in view of this teaching is the apparent contradiction between this strong condemnation of state-sponsored torture by Pope John Paul II and the public support offered to General Pinochet by two Vatican officials during his "house arrest" and judicial process regarding his extradition from Great Britain to Spain to face an indictment of crimes against humanity including torture made by Judge Baltasar Garzon in 1998. Chilean Jorge Cardinal Medina Estevez, 77, has led the Congregation for Divine Worship and the Discipline of the Sacraments since 1996. In late December 1998 Cardinal Medina told a Chilean newspaper, La Cuarta de Santiago, that the Catholic Church has taken "discreet steps" in an attempt to free the former dictator. "There had been discussions at every level on this affair, and we're hoping that they will have a positive outcome," His Eminence said. "I've prayed and prayed for Senator Pinochet as I pray for all people who have suffered." The Cardinal called Pinochet's October 16, 1998, arrest in England on Garzon's warrant a "humiliation" to Chilean sovereignty that the church "deplored." The day before Medina's comments, the Papal Nuncio to Chile, Archbishop Piero Biggio, told reporters that he concurred with the government's argument that Pinochet's arrest was a violation of diplomatic immunity. John L. Allen, Jr., "Chilean Cardinal: Church Attempting to Help Free Dictator," *National Catholic Reporter*, January 15, 1999.

9   Wooden, "Torture Harms All Humanity," 1.

10   Among the statements by Pope Paul VI defending human rights is "Human Rights and Reconciliation" of October 23, 1974, a message issued in union with the other bishops assembled in synod: "We call attention here to certain rights most threatened today. The right to life: This right is basic and inalienable. It is grievously violated in our day by contraception, abortion and euthanasia, by widespread torture, by acts of violence against innocent parties, and by the scourge of war, genocide, mass campaigns against the right to life...."

11   Paragraph 531 of the Puebla document, which was approved by John Paul II, states: "Condemnation is always the proper judgment on physical and psychological torture.... If these crimes are committed by the authorities entrusted with the

task of safeguarding the common good, then they defile those who practice them, notwithstanding any reasons offered."

12 Ascanio Cavallo Castro, Manuel Salazar Salvo, and Oscar Sepúlvedo Pacheco, *La ː storía occulta del regimen militar* (Santiago: Editorial Antártica, 1990), 95, 102.

13 Hrvoje Hranjski, "Rwandan Court Clears Bishop of 1994 Genocide Charges," Associated Press, June 15, 2000; "Rwandan Bishop Cleared of Genocide," BBC News, June 15, 2000. A Rwandan court found Bishop Augustin Misago not guilty of charges that he had actively participated in meetings when the former Hutu extremist government officials discussed plans to kill minority Tutsis. Presiding Judge Juliere Ruaremara dismissed each of the seven genocide charges against him. Misago was bishop of the southern Rwandan diocese of Gikongoro where tens of thousands died at the hands of Hutu soldiers, militiamen and ordinary civilians during the 100-day genocide. Defence lawyers argued that Misago had no choice but to attend the security meetings where the killings were discussed. "If he had refused to go, he would've been killed himself," said Alfred Pognon, one of Misago's lawyers. Misago was the highest-ranking Roman Catholic cleric of more than 20 nuns and priests accused of participating in the genocide. Two priests have already been convicted and sentenced to death, and the first trial of a priest has begun in Arusha, Tanzania, under the jurisdiction of the International Criminal Court.

14 In early November 2004, the head of the Chilean armed forces, General Juan Emilio Cheyre, published a statement in a leading Chilean newspaper, *La Tercera*, that rejected the military's traditional defence that Cold War realities could have justified their abuse of human rights and participation in torture. "Does the context of a global conflict excuse the human rights abuses that occurred in Chile? I have one, unequivocal response. No. Human rights violations can never be justified," General Cheyne wrote. He went on to say that this position is "irreversible": "The Chilean army has taken the tough, but irreversible, decision to assume responsibilities as an institution for all of the punishable and morally unacceptable acts of the past." La Tercera, 5 de noviembre de 2004; "Chile Army Admits Rights Abuses," BBC News, 5 November 2004, http://news.bbc.co.uk/1/hi/world/americas/3987341.stm.

15 Mons. Carlos González, Mons. Alejandro Jiménez, and Mons. Carlos Camus, "Excomunión a torturadores," *Mensaje* 296 (January–February 1981), 68; Cavanaugh, *Torture*, 116.

16 Marguerite Feitklowtiz, *A Lexicon of Terror: Argentina and the Legacies of Torture* (New York: Oxford University Press, 1998), 125.

17 Ibid., 126.

18 Ibid., 126.

19 Ibid., 221.

20 Ibid., 221–2.

21 Ibid., 222.

22 It is difficult to know how the Archbishop could legally take this retroactive action against Fr. von Wernich concerning the allegations about his past involvement

with torture, given the present law of the Church promulgated in 1983. This is because the various tables of excommunications imposed universally in the Church on its clergy do not include participation with torture. Homicide, abduction and mutilation are mentioned in Canon 1397 as offences that could suffer the penalty of excommunication "ferendae sententiae." Canon 285.1 urges clerics to "shun anything unbecoming to the clerical state in accordance with particular law"; C 287 directs clerics to "do their utmost to foster peace and harmony based on justice," and C 289 states that "military service ill befits the clerical state"; cf. *The Code of Canon Law: A Text and Commentary*, commissioned by the Canon Law Society of America, eds. James A. Coriden, Thomas J. Green, Donald E. Heintschel (New York/Mahwah: Paulist Press, 1985), 932–9.

[23]   Feitklowtiz, *A Lexicon of Terror*, 222.

[24]   Página 12, April 15, 1995, 11.

[25]   Feitklowtiz, *A Lexicon of Terror*, 222.

[26]   On August 21, 2003, President Kirchner legally abolished the punto final or full stop law (1986) and the obediencia debida, or "due obedience" law, which excused soldiers who were obeying orders. This has led to the prosecutions against Alfredo Astiz, Miguel Cavallo and Father von Wernich, among others. Because the Argentine constitution does not seem to allow for Kirchner's actions, the whole debate has now ended up in the Supreme Court; cf. "A Full Stop Removed: Argentina's Courts May Now Be Able to Try Soldiers Properly Again," *The Economist*, September 6, 2003, 33.

[27]   Ibid., 193–5.

[28]   The details of the motivation behind the service of Cavallo at the ESMA are not public knowledge.

[29]   Ibid., 195.

[30]   Ibid.

[31]   Ibid. 195–6.

[32]   Ibid, 196.

[33]   Ibid., 196.

[34]   Ibid.

[35]   Ibid., 196.

[36]   Ibid.

[37]   Ibid., 197.

[38]   Ibid.

[39]   Ibid., 196–7.

[40]   Horacio Verbitsky, *The Flight: Confessions of an Argentine Dirty Warrior*, trans. Esther Allen (New York: The New Press, 1996), 30.

[41]   Ibid.

[42]   *Nunca Más*, File No. 4952, 251.

[43]   Emilio F. Mignone, *Witness to the Truth* (Maryknoll, NY: Orbis, 1988), 8.

[44]   Ibid., 9.

[45]   Nunca Más, 251–2.

[46]   Feitlowitz, *A Lexicon of Terror*, 197.

[47]   Ibid., 197.

[48]   Ibid., 222.

[49]   Ibid.

[50]   Ibid., 222–3. On April 20, 2005, Alfredo Scilingo was convicted in Spain of crimes against humanity and sentenced to 640 years in prison.

[51]   Chaplains played this role on both the "right wing" of the national security crisis in Central and South America and on the "left wing." James "Guadelupe" Carney, an American and former Jesuit priest, returned to Honduras from exile in Nicaragua in September 1983 as the chaplain of a band of 96 Cuban-trained rebels. According to the self-confessed Honduran army torturer in the Battalion 3-16 death squad, Florencia Caballero, Father Carney and nearly 70 of these guerrillas were captured and then executed. Dr. Leo Valladares Lanza and Susan C. Peacock, *En Busqueda de la Verdad que se nos Oculta. Un informe preliminar del Comionado Nacional de los Dececbos Humanos sobre el Proceso de Desclasificación*, Honduras, C.A., 31–32; James Le Moyne, "Testifying to Torture," *New York Times Magazine*, June 5, 1988, 47.

[52]   Sherene H. Razack, *Dark Threats and White Knights: The Somalia Affair, Peacekeeping, and the New Imperialism* (Toronto: University of Toronto Press, 2004), 5.

[53]   Ibid., 5.

[54]   Peter Worthington, "Chaplain Left in DND Chill," *Toronto Sun*, July 9, 1996, 11; Allan Thompson and Sonia Verma, "Investigator Linked in Somalia Furor," *Toronto Star*, August 29, 1999, A1, A6; Allan Thompson, "Chaplain in Somalia Affair Keeps Job," *Toronto Star*, August 30, 1999, A1; *National Post*, August 28, 1999, A1; *Ottawa Citizen*, August 30, 1999, A3; *National Post*, August 30, 1999, A5.

[55]   Emilio Mignone, *Witness to the Truth: The Complicity of Church and Dictatorship in Argentina, 1976–1983*, trans. Phillip Berryman (Maryknoll, NY: Orbis Books, 1988), 16–18.

[56]   The term "ordinary" is used in canon law to designate a cleric or prelate who has ordinary and day-to-day ecclesiastical jurisdiction according to the legal provisions of his office.

[57]   Dominique Le Tourneau, "La nouvelle organisation de l'Ordinariat aux Armées," *Studia Canonica* 21 (1987), 37–66.

[58]   *The Code of Canon Law*, Canon 295 and 569.

[59]   Article IV, 3° of the Constitution discusses this as "cumulative" jurisdiction; cf Le Tourneau, 47–8.

60   Mignone, *Witness to the Truth*,17.

61   Ibid.

62   This would mean a return to and expansion of D 86.c.25 of the 1140 Decretum, a collection of laws by the Bolognese scholar, Gratian, which had decreed that clerics could not apply torture.

63   Steven H. Miles, "Abu Ghraib: Its Legacy for Military Medicine," *The Lancet* 364 (Number 9435), 21 August 2004.

64   *Guardian Weekly*, Dec. 10-16, 2004, 3.

65   Islamic chaplains face special challenges to exercise their role authentically in the present war on terror as evidenced by the unproven allegations made against Captain James J. Yee of the US Army; cf. Tim Golden, "Fevered Spy Hunt at Guantánamo Collapsed as Evidence Dissolved," *New York Times*, Sunday, December 19, 2004, 1, 16.

Chapter 7

1   Archbishop Desmond Tutu, Foreword, Vern Neufeld Redekop, *From Violence to Blessing: How an Understanding of Deep-rooted Conflict Can open Paths to Reconciliation* (Ottawa: Novalis, 2002), 9.

2   Solomon Schimmel, *Wounds Not Healed by Time: The Power of Repentance and Forgiveness* (Oxford: Oxford University Press, 2002), 43.

3   Ortiz, *The Blindfold's Eyes*, 189.

4   Ibid., 189.

5   Ibid., 212–13.

6   Ibid., 287.

7   Ibid., 189.

8   Ibid., 219.

9   Ibid., 368.

10   Michael Dobkowski, "Forgiveness and Repentance in Judaism after the Shoa," *Ultimate Reality and Meaning: Interdisciplinary Studies in the Philosophy of Human Understanding* 27 (June 2004): 94.

11   Ibid., 96.

12   Eric Lomax, *The Railway Man* (London: Jonathan Cape, 1995), 210.

13   Ibid., 220.

14   Ibid., 225–26.

15   Ibid., 239.

16   Ibid.

17 Ibid.

18 Ibid., 239–41.

19 Ibid.

20 Ibid., 247.

21 Ibid., 247–49.

22 Ibid., 251.

23 Schimmel, *Wounds Not Healed*, 116.

24 Lomax, *Railway Man*, 252.

25 Ibid.

26 Ibid., 252–3.

27 Ibid., 254–5.

28 Ibid., 255.

29 Ibid. 264–6.

30 Ibid., 269.

31 Ibid., 274.

32 Ibid., 274–5.

33 Ibid., 276.

34 Dobkowski, "Forgiveness and Repentance, " 97.

35 René Girard calls this jealousy "mimesis."

36 Dobkowski, 98.

37 Ibid., 97.

38 Ibid.

39 Peter Ely, SJ, "Forgiveness in Christianity," Ultimate Reality and Meaning 27 (June 2004): 110. Much of the analysis of forgiveness in this section comes from Father Ely's insightful article.

40 Ibid, 112.

41 Ibid., 115–17.

42 Ibid., 117.

43 Saint Augustine, On Music, trans. Robert Catesby Taliaferro, in *The Fathers of the Church: A New Translation*, Vol. 4 (New York: Fathers of the Church, Inc., 1947), 164; Book Six, Chapter 4, 329–30.

44 Saint Augustine, *Confessions*, Universal Library (New York: Grosset & Dunlap), 272, Book XI, No. 26 [XX].

[45]   John Milbank, *Being Reconciled: Ontology and Pardon* (London: Routledge, 2003), 53.

[46]   By "partial good" I do not intend to condone torture, whether used as a method of
       interrogation or as a means of oppression through terror. Thomistic epistemology
       insists that our moral lives are essentially teleological in the sense that we cannot
       choose a course of action unless we have decided it is "good" for us to perform it. A
       defective or partial good is a choice or action that is missing some essential elements.
       Evil in this framework is an imperfect good.

[47]   Ortiz, *The Blindfold's Eyes*, 253.

[48]   Ibid., 475.

Conclusion

[1]   Lawrence Weschler, *A Miracle, A Universe: Settling Accounts with Torturers* (New York:
      Pantheon, 1990), 237–8.

[2]   Fr. Ronaldo Muñoz, DD.VV., El antievangelio de algunos cristianos. In: Hernán Vidal,
      *El movimiento contra la tortura "Sebasián Acevedo," derechos humanos y la producción de símbolos
      nacionales bajo el fascismo chileno* (Minneapolis: Institute for the Study of Ideologies
      and Literature, 1986), 146–8 as cited in William T. Cavanaugh, *Torture and Eucharist*
      (Maldon, MA: Blackwell, 1998), 261–2.

[3]   Jessica Senehi, "Constructive Storytelling in Intercommunal Conflicts: Building
      Community, Building Peace," in *Reconcilable Differences: Turning Points in Ethnopolitical
      Conflict*, eds. Sean Byrne and Cynthia Irving (West Hartford, CT, 2000), 96–114;
      "Language, Culture, and Conflict: Storytelling as a Matter of Life and Death," *Mind
      and Human Interaction* 7 (August 1996): 151–64; "Constructive Story Telling: A Peace
      Process," *Peace and Conflict Studies* 9 (December 2002): 41–62.

[4]   Adrian Leftwich, "I Gave the Names," *Granta* 78 (Summer 2002), 29.

[5]   David Rock, *Authoritarian Argentina: The Nationalist Movement, Its History and Its Impact*
      (Berkeley, CA: University of California Press, 1993), 227.

[6]   Weschler, *A Miracle*, 240.

[7]   Michael Ignatieff, *The Lesser Evil: Political Ethics in an Age of Terror* (Toronto: Penguin,
      2004), 136–44. By "ultimate reality and meaning" here is meant an axiom that people
      in the West cannot reduce or relate to anything else and constitutes the horizon in
      the light of which they understand whatever else they understand. It represents for
      them a supreme value for which they would sacrifice everything and which they
      would not lose for any reason whatever.